INDEX

Essays, Fragments, and Liberal Arts Homework

Jeff Pike

ISBN: 0692629580
ISBN 13: 9780692629581
Library of Congress Control Number: 2016902272
Pike Editorial, Olympia, WA

This is for all the lonely people

ACKNOWLEDGMENTS

I've been fortunate and am grateful that circumstances have enabled me the time and opportunity for this project. Writing is a lonely chore, not to say eccentric, but I have felt the support of friends and loved ones all the way.

Phil Dellio and Jack Thompson gave up large portions of their summers to read large portions of the manuscript. They kept me honest, caught mistakes, and cleaned up my some of my run-ons. Scott Woods and Steven Rubio also read parts and offered valuable insights at critical times.

Jeremy Engdahl-Johnson has kept me going in more ways than one.

Mary Maurer designed my first book and I was delighted to find her available to do my second.

My father passed away in 2009, but he provided key support to me in getting my first book done. I still remember. This one is for him too. Thanks again, Dad.

I want to say a word in defense of Wikipedia, which has a ways to go but makes a great backstop and starting point. It is packed with information vetted by those who care most about it, though not without agendas. It's not perfect, but it's getting there, and I went to it whenever I felt the need to double-check anything and/or start somewhere. It's a valuable resource and for now only getting better.

Friends, family, blog commenters, and random social media allies have chipped in too, in all kinds of ways. I can't begin to list them. You know who you are, and thank you.

"I have travelled a good deal in Concord."

—Henry David Thoreau

INTRODUCTION

Count me as a student in the Bob Uecker school of what do you call it, cultural criticism, by which I mean his advice on how to catch the knuckleball: "Wait until the ball stops rolling and then pick it up." In many ways my blog, *Can't Explain*, which is the source of most of the pieces in this book, has been an ongoing and still going attempt to synthesize two competing impulses: the critic's business of sorting through music, movies, books, and whatnot for relative values, and the fan's business of unconditional mother-bear love. I want to explain, like critics do, but I also want to "can't explain," as fans do, to honor the ineffable joy that I (we) have found. Fans call for more mystifying and less demystifying when it comes to the objects of their (our) adoration. It's the mystifications that are the pleasures of the fan.

But I still have some natural instinct for skepticism and quick dismissals—the critic's stance, trying to avoid the term "contrarian"— though I've consciously attempted to dial it back for some time now. Call it muzzy-headed utopianism, but I prefer to live in a world with a minimum of irrational lashing out, which is found in abundance wherever people are sharing opinions about music, movies, books, and whatnot. I'm perhaps not often enough interested in rationalizing and explaining, because it doesn't necessarily work that way for me. I identify more with Roy Neary in *Close Encounters of the Third*

Kind, when he bursts out: "This means something. This is important."
I also want to belong to the Roy Neary school of criticism.

But I have to be honest. I'm not even as hip as either Bob
Uecker or Roy Neary. Even as I embarked on my so-called professional turn at criticism—a meager resume extending from approximately 1982 to 1995 as I count it, most of it at the level of city
alternative newsweeklies—one of the things I found hardest was
being on the front lines and actually making the calls. This came
as a surprise to me. I hadn't realized how much I looked to others
for cues (namely, in my case, critics), nor how long it took me to
understand how I felt about some things—a lifetime, I'm certain,
in many cases. In fact, this is a problem that I suspect is shared
by most pros, who evidently struggle with it—the prevailing herd
mentality, I mean, objectively observed from without, which not
only dictates opinions along social axes of professional relations,
but further attempts to define the broad centers of attention, in
a chicken-and-egg paradox of which came first, the trend or the
trendsetters. After the golden adolescent years, as leisure gradually mutates into the baseline requirement employment, charting
the zeitgeist is notably hard work, not to mention ill-paying.

An early assignment I was given to do a roundup of capsule album reviews in the style of Robert Christgau's *Village Voice* Consumer
Guide yielded an interesting view of the problems. This was in 1982.
A slush pile of 20 or 30 albums was handed off to me, and I needed
to rate and write up at least a dozen of them. Of course, I was in hog
heaven, but a deadline put some taint on that, and certainly making
the assessments did. My three favorites under this unnatural close
scrutiny were *Kissing to Be Clever* by Culture Club, *Sports* by Huey Lewis
& the News, and *Sundown* by Rank and File. In the crucible of the editorial process, I believe I was brave and right on Culture Club, which
looked perilously close to an uncommercial novelty act. I was brave
and wrong on Rank and File, which probably is as derivative as others
scoffed. And I was an abject coward on Huey Lewis, finding excuses
to downgrade the star rating. Somehow I understood that Lewis was

a suspect outlier for reasons beyond the music itself, it was communicated to me as a kind of social pressure—I'm not even sure how exactly—that Huey Lewis & the News was a too-happy too-easygoing lightweight in the already lightweight division of white pop blues. He did not rate.

But "right" and "wrong"—what do I mean by that anyway? I suppose I am talking about the critical judgment of history—the many knuckleballs still rolling around out there, even as we recede into the future. On comparative commercial terms, Huey Lewis lingers at least as much as Culture Club, probably more so. (Rank and File have long since fallen into the empty maw of pop culture. You say you've never heard of them? You should check out their first album, *Sundown*.) I loved that album *Sports* (and all its hits) and still like it, and I was touched when I read years later that Huey Lewis had won a place among the greatest rock stars of all time for the developmentally disabled audience. I wondered if that was actually a demographic. And I also wondered, all those years later, if that demographic wasn't perhaps more sanguine than me about the social pressures mitigating against Huey Lewis—and what that meant about my honesty as a critic.

I admit I'm a little exasperated by the critical enterprise such as it is, at this point, especially in the writing I see about music and movies. The beats are narrow and jealously guarded, starting with rock critic, movie critic, book critic, and branching beyond by publications and other affinities orbiting variously monied centers of gravity (for example, *Rolling Stone*, Pitchfork, and what's left of *Spin* and the *Village Voice*). The vigilant focus on latest product releases—more than anything it starts to feel like a fascination with the eternal now. If it will be gone in a minute, why bother with it? Rejecting the eternal now in pop culture is the first sign you're doing it wrong, I know that, but I can't keep up anymore, it comes so fast today.

At the same time, I like to read criticism—in some moods, I gorge on it. My favorite critics evoke a feeling of shared discovery, and often enrich my sense of what they discuss, pointing out things and making connections I hadn't seen. I especially like the discursive encyclopedic approach of Robert Christgau, Roger Ebert, or David Thomson, alighting on and connecting with impressive numbers of songs, albums, books, movies, and stories. Or writers such as Francine Prose, Stephen King, or Anne Fadiman, who can be infectious discussing their reading habits.

The critical focus on product releases seems to me too often to miss the point, which is where I start to find myself shading over into identifications with fans, who rave their ecstasies to dawn, figuratively speaking. The music and stories and books that shaped and affected me in such profound and surprising ways, and continue to work on me, long past their eligibility for best of the year—I want to write about that too. The objects, and my experience of them, the way they live with me. It's the most important way I know to connect with these artifacts, blending into the fabric of my life. On his radio show, Bob Dylan once said that he has nothing against new music, it's just that there's so much more old music to listen to. Put me down for that excuse too—especially with regard to ye olde books I insist on reading.

It's more problematic with critics when it comes to disagreements anyway, I have to admit. I understand this is one of the main reasons why people don't like them. It's one of the reasons I don't either. They are so opinionated. It's probably why I dislike the critics I do—Pauline Kael, likely my most egregious blind spot, judging by the depth and universality of her regard. In fact, not liking Pauline Kael is one reason I'm tempted to feel like a pretender. What bothers me about her is what I think bothers most people about any critic (including myself, I'm sure), which is essentially the use of a belittling wit, or snark as we call it now (and often very funny too, which is one of the worst parts), as shorthand for a complete dismissal of something. Sometimes, something *important*, in my opinion. They high-handedly have no interest in engaging. It is infuriating. I know they have busy lives.

∼𝒮

Here's another possibly interesting dividing line between critics and fans: the necessity for minimal sorting information, such as year of release, names of artists, directors, performers, songs, especially before (or while) encountering them, assembling a certain baseline of information for later analysis, a sort of ongoing cataloging process. For many people I know, often myself included, this is essential—they don't see the point of listening to music, especially, without this information. Indeed, the primary seduction of iTunes for me for as long as it lasted, almost 10 years, was, in fact, its approximation of a database, where each song could be labeled and made instantly sortable by an array of beguiling and irreducible data points: song title, artist, songwriter, album, year, genre, time, and more. There was even a place for notes on individual tracks. Of course, there was some work to do filling in the gaps in the tagging. And then there was always still *more* work to do—it went on for years. It took me a little while to catch on to that.

Yet at one point in my life, maybe 20 years ago, I had a phase in which I experimented with letting go of that need for data—somewhat uneasily, it's true, and I was never *entirely* comfortable with it. It happened when I started listening to a station in Seattle, C89.5, which was broadcast from a high school and played good electronic dance pop music. This infatuation lasted intensely from 1994 to 1998, lingering into the 2000s. It was perhaps the last time I was so happy to turn to the radio and indiscriminately let it play for hours at a time. The station was actually some kind of formal vocational project for the students, who maintained its bare-bones rudimentary broadcasts of endless music, which was rarely if ever announced. The announcers doing the station ID at the top of the hour were obviously high school kids and not always that articulate on a microphone anyway. I realized the extent to which the station did not announce anything on the morning of September 11, 2001, driving to work. The music played and they didn't say a word. I only caught on something was going on because I happened to stop for gas and the people at the station were behaving weirdly, blaring their radios on news stations.

Years later, of course, I suffered the pains of my ignorance from those years of listening to anonymous music, when I realized some of my favorite songs in the world were not really known to me by title or artist. So much of that music, which I loved so intensely, virtually gone. I've since rectified that somewhat, incompletely, as songs continue to turn up in strange places—I have quite a collection of 1996 dance anthologies now, for example. Just this year, I had occasion to track down "DJ Girl" by Katalina, from circa 1997. I still feel like that period of time in my music listening is somewhat shrouded in mystery now.

But I found there was a certain freedom in it too, the fan's freedom let's call it, with songs reduced even further to free-floating, recurring hooks, which were great, or which didn't quite work, but kept coming and moving along—so exciting when the good ones came around again. I got to know the songs by their hooks, sometimes a vocal on the chorus, but more often some synthesizer figure that played perfectly off the beat or the momentum of the song. I was usually working on other things at the time, so my head would come up on these hooks, soar with them, and then move along with them. It also mimicked the way music is heard in clubs, the unfamiliar interspersed in with hits and standards—many wonderful moments and lost gems there too.

𝔔

Ironically, just at the time I was beginning to write for money, I went to the sidelines in terms of my tastes and interests, more toward hipsterish marginalized realms of postpunk, underground and foreign films, Black Lizard crime novels, etc. Or I looked back—I started looking back a lot in the '80s, that is obvious to me now. In 1980, Ronald Reagan's landslide election came as a great shock to me— that he won at all, and that he won so overwhelmingly. The world I grew up in and knew changed radically after Reagan's election, per- haps most fundamentally in the widespread fealty, where once there had been skepticism, toward the omniscient, omnipotent market and our corporate overlords, and there has been no going back since. It's not a better place—the economic, lifestyle, and health numbers bear that out as well as, on the most obvious level, the simmering gridlocked government, the total inability in the political realm to do anything without approval of the overlords. The rest of us eke out livings in an overpriced system with crumbling infrastructure, with jobs hemorrhaging overseas and financial freefall as close as auto ac- cidents. You know all this.

It was a time and I was at an age for historical perspective in 1980. Record guides from *Rolling Stone* and Robert Christgau helped illu- minate obscure corners of pop music's history, and rolling programs of classic double features at numerous cheap repertory theaters did much the same for film. The lion's share of my reading has always been out of the library stacks. It might have been a matter of growing up to some degree, but also, perhaps unconsciously, it became harder for me to embrace popular culture after 1980. Fruit of the poison tree, or something like that. I mostly lost interest in contemporary radio and TV programming, and I didn't like the general direction of the movies either, with the coming of ever more calculated sum- mer blockbusters alternating every six months with Oscar showcases, a Reaganistic style that is worse than ever today.

So in a way this collection of pieces I've written over the past 25 years is pretty much what it appears to be: by turns eccentric con- sumer guide, English major reports, and sentimental indulgences, stocked up with specific cultural products that mean something to me one way or another, some of which are more than quite well known and obvious for my demographic, and others perhaps more suitably gnomic—vicissitudes of taste, and browsability, you can never have enough of either, or both, I always say. I like to think my sensibility is keyed more toward the weird than the predictable, though I also fear I'm too often predictable.

I was seduced early by the '70s rock critic milieu, which makes that the narrow place I'm starting from, and from there I went on to become an American Studies major in college and in life. All these things show, and give me away at every turn I'm sure, but somehow, perhaps inevitably, I still keep retreating to talking about myself. It's a bad habit, in a way, I know. And so, perhaps inevitably, I have also pilfered an autobiography into these assessments, outlining main events and themes of my life and how they came to intermesh and decorate the public objects under consideration. And vice versa, to be sure.

For simplicity, and probably because I'm lazy, I just alphabetized it all. There are many recurring themes, such as obvious attempt to engage with canons, as well as with the idea itself of canons, my cultural inheritance, such as it is. File those under "liberal arts homework." Various personal themes round it out, such as the place of sentiment and mass popularity, a number of familiar socio-psychological factors, a personally momentous move from Minneapolis to Seattle in the mid-'80s, fortunes of employment, adventures with drugs and love, even the story of a few pets—well, you'll see. This is part of how I got here—which brings me back to Bob Uecker. Everything else should be self-explanatory, I hope.

—Olympia, Washington, 2015

A

oming first in the alphabet, the letter A is overly familiar and taken for granted, abused for its position as often as it is offered as a mark of excellence. Hence all the Aarons of the world who take their first rankings as a given—and why shouldn't they?—simply expecting all the A qualities of life. And by "A qualities" you know immediately that I am talking about excellence, because, in the end, in many ways, it is everything the letter A is about—or, more exactly, people's unseemly grasping after it. Consider the worst abuses of the letter A, the human psychology for which is found in ancient documents now known as yellow pages telephone directories, where a column or more could occur of names beginning with at least three of them, often more, e.g., AAAA House & Key. There's a reflexive state of mind for you, isn't it? Locked out of the house. Panicked. Worried. Look up a locksmith. There they are. Yes. Better get AAAA. These charlatans don't even pretend to stand for anything. I think they just add another A every generation or so. At least Alcoholics Anonymous, the Automobile Association of America, and the American Association of Retired Persons go to the fig leaf of real names. But alas the telephone directory mentality presides as well over sporting organizations, financial instruments, even meat regulations. It's not good enough to get a Grade A cut of meat. Oh no, it has to be Grade AAA. There appears to be no such thing as B in many of these places—on the rare occasion when it does appear, as with the unwieldy exercises of financial instrument ratings agencies (AAa and Bb, and all that … speaking of charlatans), even then there is never a C. It is a tiny alphabet indeed in these worlds. And what is the meaning of all the As? They most often attempt to signal an increase in excellence, as with minor league baseball teams. But you see the problem, the classic one of psychological inflationary forces. It's rather like deciding that "excellent," with its crashing crescendo at the back of the throat on the "ex" and the satisfying many syllables, just didn't say enough in conversation any longer, and from now on one needed to say "excellent excellent" to mean the same thing. "Excellent excellent pie, Mrs. Cleaver." It is ridiculous on its face. Thank you, grasping world of commerce. And knowing people as we do, I think it's not unlikely that by the time of the 22nd century or so people will indeed be thanking hosts for excellent excellent excellent evenings. These are just a few of the problems familiar to the letter A, which otherwise does such valuable and important work for the language, as a vowel and in many other ways. (2013)

A.I. Artificial Intelligence (Steven Spielberg, 2001)

An interesting project: go through *A.I.* and catalog all uses of the word "real"—and its counterpart, "artificial," which already is in the title two or three ways (because it's also artificial to use an acronym). The boy-robot David, played brilliantly in an unsettling performance by Haley Joel Osment, is constantly reminded by others that he is "not real." When he is abandoned in the woods by Monica Swinton (Frances O'Connor), in one of the most wrenching scenes in a picture that is full of them, he shamelessly pleads and grovels, drawing on his understanding of the Pinocchio story to ask if he can come home again if he is a real boy. "That's just a story," Monica says. "But a story tells what happens," David responds. "Stories are not real," she says. "You're not real."

The story of this film is a real interesting one, involving a collaboration that seemed unlikely at the time between Stanley Kubrick and
Steven Spielberg. Starting in 1984 they traded notes, design ideas,
and suggestions back and forth, riffing on a Brian Aldiss story,
"Supertoys Last All Summer Long." But as with so many movie projects it never came to be. After Kubrick's death Spielberg took it up
again. The result is a formal collaboration that feels at once like both
of them—and a little strange and disorienting at that, because directors with such distinctive visions so rarely collaborate. In the end it
feels more like a Spielberg project (with some admixture of Gene
Roddenberry's optimism in there as well), concerned with families
and impossible love lost and found, and unafraid of the heartwarming gesture, though it has no answers about the human (or inhuman)
condition. The ghost of Kubrick hovers over it in the visual schemat-
ics, in the ways it so freely philosophizes and addresses its largest issues, and in its many fine precisions.

A.I. is practically a clinic in how to put together a science fiction
film, with fully developed set pieces that sound the themes and advance the story and entertain hugely all at once. An early sequence
in which visionary robot inventor Professor Allen Hobby (William
Hurt) holds court with his students in a musty library setting is a
great example. "I propose that we build a robot who can love," he
declares in suitably stentorian tones. "But can we find human beings
to love it back?" one of his students asks. Yes, it turns out, that is the
question.

The picture breaks down into three parts, each between 30 minutes and an hour. The family drama of the Swintons is first. Like all
other families of this unspecified future time, they are required to
obtain a license to bear children, and now their only son, Martin, is
hospitalized in a cryogenic coma because of a debilitating condition.
That is the situation into which David steps. When Martin unexpectedly recovers and comes home again, sibling rivalry between David

and Martin erupts and quickly grows toxic. Spielberg, who not only directed but wrote the screenplay, is clearly in his element here, moving naturally in and around family dynamics and staging scenes that feel utterly natural to anyone living in America in the last century.

In the second section, David is left to fend for himself in a world where humans and machines are very nearly coequal, and the humans revile the machines. This is the long dystopic passage of the picture, the nightmare carnival ride, all jarring noise, glaring light, special effects, and sudden, swift violence. David teams with lover-robot Gigolo Joe (Jude Law) and travels to the hallucinatory Rouge City, a kind of Pleasure Island (a transparent swipe from the original Disney *Pinocchio*) cum New Orleans French Quarter—and a bit of another 2019 Los Angeles too.

From there, for the third section, it's across the sea to the underwater city at the end of the world, Man-hattan, pronounced with emphasis on the first syllable, because "robots that go there don't come back." This section takes place far in the future. It's the shortest of the three and also the most controversial, with its critics arguing against it as a massive self-indulgence on Spielberg's part.

Osment is a preternatural presence, staying within himself and yet obviously capable of taking direction. One distracting detail is that he never blinks on-camera. I can thus become conscious of my own blinking when he is in the frame—it takes some effort not to, and yet there is 12-year-old Osment managing it in performance. The trajectory of his development from herky-jerk robotic tics to more natural boyishness is so subtle you never notice it until the early scenes are seen again. David is also, even at his most winning, always slightly creepy—that sense of him never goes away.

Osment's performance, Spielberg's script, and the conceptual underpinnings worked out so painstakingly between Kubrick and

Spielberg altogether produce such a powerful sense of situation that there are any number of paths it could have gone down. Interestingly, Spielberg chooses a fairy-tale place of infinite sadness. This truly is one of the saddest movies I know. Its sadness is there every step of the way once David has attached himself so fiercely to the Pinocchio story—which is set up perfectly, growing out of the sibling rivalry with Martin—and it just becomes more and more heartbreaking. Even when David is in the most outrageous danger, all he thinks about is his plan: find the Blue Fairy and she will make him a real boy, and then he can go home again.

And look, about the third section, obviously I must have unresolved mother issues if I can find so many ways to connect with it. But to me it is way beyond cheap sentiment and into some other realm entirely, and not an easy feel-good one by any means. (Also, for that matter, who among us does not have unresolved mother issues? Isn't that part of the human condition?) It's often when the best directors are overreaching themselves—I think of Hitchcock with *Vertigo*, for example—that the strangest good things happen, and that's how I read the end of *A.I.* It's the center of gravity of the whole thing for me, taking its position in the philosopher-like 19th-century structure of the picture, as *synthesis*. If it also happens to be a major KO punch to the head and heart, I'm not sure that's a bad thing. I think the ability to do that, in fact, might have been the very quality Kubrick most admired in Spielberg, and the reason he sought him out as collaborator. (2012)

Steve Almond, *Candyfreak* (2004)
I picked up on this when it was still new, hearing about it on an NPR story, with aptly named author Steve Almond carrying on infectiously about a candy factory he had toured as part of putting this book together. He was talking about coconut coming down from up above like snowflakes, settling into the softening chocolate of a candy bar whose name I didn't get, or can't remember—maybe the Idaho Spud?

It's a great book, actually, as much fun to read as it was to hear him that day, part candy bar history, part new journalism as he tours obscure Mom 'n' Pop candy bar factories (candy still a regionalized industry but rapidly fading), and part memoir, getting his personal life mixed up in it like the candy that melts on your hand before you get it into your mouth. I found myself looking at candy displays in a way that I hadn't since I don't know when, and I tried some of the more localized choices available to me—the Idaho Spud one of them. I remembered how people I knew growing up were kookoo for Nut Goodies, manufactured in St. Paul, Minnesota. Somehow I drifted over into the corporate choices like so many of us—Snickers, Milky Way, M&Ms, and Hershey's and Nestle chocolate (the latter more than the former, but neither is really good chocolate, and there's also the problem of the corporate behavior). From his picture, Almond looks skinny, so I guess he's got the metabolism for an infatuation that brings so many of the rest of us down. I tend to think of candy as a kind of evil nowadays. But Almond's book got me out of that for the time it took to read it. I probably gained five pounds while I was at it too. (2011)

The Amityville Horror (Stuart Rosenberg, 1979)

As it happens, I came to *The Amityville Horror* very late—actually well after the 2005 remake. At a garage sale in 2007 I found a box set with the original and first two sequels, plus a couple of documentary episodes from the History Channel about the house in Amityville, George and Kathy Lutz, Jay Anson, and related matters. The woman at the garage sale told me the TV documentaries were scarier and creepier than any of the movies. Because I am slow about everything, it was another couple years before I actually got around to looking at the flagship production, so let's say 30 years after the fact.

It was about what I expected, except somehow it did get under my skin. On a conscious level, sitting on my couch in the dark of a fall evening, I kept remarking to myself what an extremely annoying movie it was, but when the phone rang and I jumped I realized the movie had done its work on me. Director Stuart Rosenberg (*Cool Hand Luke*, *The Pope of Greenwich Village*) and crew do it the old-fashioned big-money *Exorcist* way, which is very much its model: by dynamics. Slow down the action to a crawl. Then speed it up. Show a tender moment. Interrupt it with mortal peril. Make everything very quiet. Then loud. Mix and match with provocative elements: People standing with their backs to dark windows. Blood. Swinging axes. Insects and vermin. The dog interested in something in the basement. A woo-woo friend trying to be helpful. Children in danger. A kitchen sink. Religious iconography, ceremonies, and belief systems (or fragments thereof) as needed—Roman Catholic, of course.

It thus becomes a straightforward problem of rhythm and pacing, assembling and burnishing the elements, but it's not fair to reduce it to that. It's a straightforward problem, after all, that every movie has to solve, and if *The Amityville Horror* succeeds on terms it sets for itself I think I'd look a little silly complaining about it. So I don't. But I resent it a little, and don't mind looking silly for that. For some reason, I don't even recall how it came into my possession now, I read the original book by Jay Anson some 20 years ago, which also gave me something of a bad scare, but in a slightly different way.

The intent of the book (which one of the History Channel shows pointedly refers to as "a novel") is obviously to make your eyes pop out and your socks roll up and down your ankles as you read. By masquerading as nonfiction, it works a wedge into further anxiety, much as, say, the documentary about *The Exorcist*, which is nearly as insidiously disturbing as the very disturbing *Exorcist*, because the idea that *these are things that actually happened* is enough to rotate the events described into some infinitely more unpleasant place psychologically. There's a clip of Anson himself on a TV talk show masterfully using this technique, talking about how people he'd given the manuscript to review were subsequently involved in auto accidents, mysterious fires, etc. Well played, Mr. Anson, well played—except then we learn, oh ha ha, that Anson himself died within the year at the age of 58 of a heart attack. And he doesn't really look like a heart attack candidate either.

For the record, no, I don't think powerful demonic forces are at work. I think strange things happen, and the Amityville franchise has been able to profit from an oddly generous share of them. All the talk of Indian burial grounds and flies thriving in the dead of winter and a priest barked at in an empty room may (or may not) be pure fiction. But the mysterious mass murder that happened in the house in 1974, little more than a year before the Lutz family acquired it and moved in, is as real as teardrops. The oldest boy in that family got up in the middle of the night (3:15 a.m., to be specific), murdered his parents, murdered his two brothers, and murdered his two sisters. Nobody heard the rifle shots and there was no evidence anyone in the family moved from their beds or attempted to interfere or get away. All of them were lying on their stomachs, face down.

A great backdrop for great evil, of course. No Indian burial grounds need apply. But the movie appears unable to help itself on some level. It is even more ridiculous than the book (and though it scared me the book is very ridiculous), using, for example, the ever-popular idea of a portal to hell in the basement. It is balls to the walls about hitting the extremes. Put Margot Kidder, as Kathy Lutz, in pig-tails so she looks like Mary Ann from *Gilligan's Island*. Make priests the victims of incredible accidents. Raise the sound level high on flies buzzing (incidentally prompting a meditation on how the noun we have made of the lovely verb is actually one of the most repulsive creatures on the planet) (no offense, you-who-will-inherit-the-earth). Cold spots in the house. Unexplainable foul moods. Rocking chairs that rock themselves. What now, Father Delaney in a coma? Kathy Lutz wakes up screaming: "She was shot in the head!"

Hey, I'm really not giving much away. This is just from the first half. In addition to the dynamics ploy (which means you can't brace for a lot of it even forewarned), it is also classic throw-everything-you've-got-at-it filmmaking, Hollywood style. Some of these things inevitably are going to stick to your walls. A favorite scene of mine occurs late, has nothing to do with anything, but somehow raises my anxiety sky high. Once again Kathy Lutz is besieged. Her phone is mysteriously not working, again, and she desperately needs to reach someone. A disheveled man we have never seen appears at the back door, scratching at it. Scratching. "Hello," he says when Kathy opens the door. "Everybody wanted to come over to welcome you to the neighborhood." Then he shows her he is carrying a six-pack of beer. Something distracts her and when she returns to the door he is gone. We never see him again.

It's the inexplicability of much of this, in scenes like that, that makes *The Amityville Horror* work. Who was that guy at the door? Why did Jay Anson die? Why didn't the sound of the rifle fire—six shots!—appear to wake *anyone*? But you see I am talking about elements that belong in the narrative frame, or are associated with the book—background, incidental information. The foreground events in this movie are all too often quite explicable: forces of demonic possession are strong, see? An *exorcism* is likely called for. But foolish modernists and followers of Vatican II won't hear of it. That is a portal to hell in the basement, man. But they are all by-the-numbers fantasy points, which drags things down for me. *The Amityville Horror* is worth seeing once, maybe, because somehow it could well find a way to get you. After that, or in the sequels, there is only more of an all too explicable Hollywood sameness. (2014)

Paul Anka, "(You're) Havin' My Baby" (July 27, 1974, #1, 3 wks.)
No consideration of "Havin' My Baby," no matter how ironic or sincere, can avoid discussion of the song's topic. It's the elephant here. It's really almost sick. What's this line? "Whoa, the seed inside ya /

Baby, do you feel it growin'"? The ownership distinctions are troubling. It's his baby. She's havin' it. Or, technically: (she's) havin' it.
It's not hers, or even theirs, but his. In the first person: "Havin'
MY baby ... What a lovely way of sayin' how much you love ME." No
one sees a problem with this in terms of gender relations? Well of
course they do. That's why you just can't find this song any more,
or at least it's not easy. Not even all the many Paul Anka best-ofs
include it. iTunes doesn't have it. Is it *ever* on the radio? For the
most part, I think its time came and went, the time for such open
displays (key word here being "open"). It got left waiting at the station. Remember that 1974 was at the center of high-flying years for
feminism, and note that the song is marinated in sentiment, sentiment in the first person as a matter of fact, with only some anonymous unidentified babe singing harmony, and what can you say?
It's the social phenomenon, purely social phenomenon, of *backlash*.
It flares in the moment, flares tremendously high—three weeks at
#1!—before disappearing forever into the dustbin of history. That's
my take on this one. Well, maybe not forever. (2005)

Jane Austen, *Emma* (1815)
True confession: In many ways Jane Austen's novels work for me like
genre novels. If I haven't looked at them in a while they are instantly
absorbing, and perfectly charming, and I want to read another right
away. But they resemble one another enough that I don't always
have the energy to actually finish the next one. I love this world of
Jane Austen's that is so single-mindedly focused on achieving happy
unions between consenting adults, and all the daunting complexities
back of them. There is always a deeply practical woman at the center
of it, a few good men and women, and a host of lovable (and one or
two not so lovable) recalcitrants to round it out. *Emma* concludes on
three felicitous—if I may use the vernacular—marriage-weddings, a
typical if hyper Austen climax. Much of the novel is sorting out who
ends up with whom. It does not achieve the dramatic tensions of *Pride
and Prejudice*, but it's a pleasant journey. There is comfort even in

the characters one does not like, partly because they resemble people we've known so well and are thus reassuring of our judgments.
Austen was an alert observer of people, so even when her plotting
begins to go flat or wayward it remains enjoyable to follow along with
her scenes and characters. It works at levels that are at once gossipy
and vital, and enormously complicated, with fractured families and
webs of relations across them, laid against an ever-shifting timeline
of seasons and holidays, across events both pedestrian and momentous occurring in regular rhythm. The language seems to me unusually lucid by 19th-century standards, and the society, while plainly
antiquated, nonetheless recognizable. It's people just getting on with
their lives, respecting their fundamental needs for human congress,
to love and to be loved, and to be accorded respect and dignity too,
in a world where both are so very easy to lose. (2014)

B

The bulbous B pretends to be more important than it is by way of its position as the second letter of the alphabet. In fact, it is just the 20th most frequently used letter, ahead of only V, K, J, X, Q, and Z. But consider the word "alphabet," derived from the Greek for "alpha" and "beta," the first two letters of the alphabet. Thus the bumptious B even horns in on the word itself we use for the enterprise at hand. Yet isn't this the way after all that people think? One, two, many. Alpha, beta, I'm tired of letters now. And therein lies the rub. The letter B pays a heavy penalty for its presumption, its jolly persistent appearances in the ABCs of things and all its bubbly baby talky buh buh buh. If the letter A is the alpha top of the top best of all, the letter B necessarily becomes the fall guy for everything else, winding up with a sleazy extra coat of "loser" for its troubles. B movies, B girls, B team, B squad, 2 hip 2 B square, the graduate school F, baby. For people, behaving for all the world as if there is no C, D, or E (let alone P, Q, or R), it's either A—which as we've seen tends to endorse its own indignity of inflations in the echo chamber of AA, AAA, AAAA, AAAAA, and so on, but which remains always at least *kind of* terrific, good, and acceptable—or it's our friend we are suddenly not so sure about ourselves, the letter B, which suddenly seems to stink of something rather unpleasant. But come now. The letter B does have some things going for it. Unlike the vowels and many of the consonants we will see, a B is always a B. It has no multiple duties and is not approximated elsewise. And that is integrity, people, an element in short supply in this English alphabet. The sound it represents is always the same moderately complex consonant noise involving coordination with the voice and lips—by name a "voiced bilabial stop" (the term itself gaudy with Bs). Who can say what the logic was of putting that particular and distinct mouth noise second in the alphabet. We're stuck with it now (but then, we also seem to be stuck with the silent "gh" in "night" and "tight" too). Puns: "be" is a very important word, let's not forget, and "bee" can combine with either or both quite harmoniously, e.g., "don't worry, bee happy" (accompanied by illustration of bumblebee). And say, here's a thought. Could the prominent position of the letter B actually reflect some primal instinct? Remember, babies are important to the species, and they get two of the darn things in a simple four-letter word: *baby*, which also, for what it's worth, happens to be what many of us call our sex partners at one time or another. And then all that baby talk. Granted, the letter G has some stake in this too with the classic "goo-goo gah-gah," and of course "mama" and "papa," but after that isn't it all boo boo buh buh bub bub bub bub bub, etc. Crying out loud, look at the word we have for it: babbling. (2013)

Angelo Badalamenti, "Twin Peaks Theme" (1990)
On a winter night many years after the hubbub of *Twin Peaks*, in those bad Bush years, I stepped into a late-night bookstore insomniac and bleary that had just started playing the *Twin Peaks* soundtrack album. I could not figure out what it was. It was the most beautiful feeling, a prolonged extended déjà vu. I became acutely aware that it was raining outside and very dark, but the lights of the storefronts across the street were visible, bars and a pharmacy and a pizza takeout. And of things like how the rain streaked against the window and what that did to the lights and what it sounded like when cars or now and then a truck drove by. It changed the whole scene and mood and I surreptitiously watched the other patrons, who sometimes seemed to be

moving and swaying to the music. I skulked around the bookstore some 20 minutes and finally gave up and had to ask the clerk what it was. The answer was not surprising. (2013)

Joan Baez, "Diamonds and Rust" (Nov. 8, 1975, #35)
I've spent most of a lifetime undervaluing Joan Baez. But even back then, when it barely crested the charts to qualify as a hit, I could hear this for what it is: gorgeous, sweetly bruised song of rue, the bittersweet affirmation of love past. One more piece that emerged out of Bob Dylan's wildly acclaimed (and, I have always thought, somewhat overstated) mid-'70s divorce album *Blood on the Tracks*. The great return to form—another one of those. Six months later, Joan Baez stepped up to offer this memoir, etched in her soul. It starts with a phone call and a voice from long ago heard once again, and then drifts back into memory and nostalgia denied: "Now I see you standing with brown leaves falling all around / And snow in your hair / Now you're smiling out the window of that crummy hotel / Over Washington Square / Our breath comes out white clouds / Mingles and hangs in the air / Speaking strictly for me / We both could have died then and there." The words are wrought carefully, with concrete images of seasons in change and a steadfast tacking away from sloppy confession. The melody is haunting, the musical setting a lush '70s production, helmed by a clarion voice of great power, told without self-pity. (2010)

Beach Boys, "Wouldn't It Be Nice" (Aug. 20, 1966, #8)
Once again emerging from inside the confines of his head, Brian Wilson here offers perhaps the most audacious, naïve, heartfelt, genuine, wrongheaded, thrilling, foolish fantasy of love and marriage ever committed to recording media. Perhaps no hit on the radio ever captured the seductive simplicity of the fantasy quite so completely. It is never, not for a second, the least bit embarrassed about its addleheadedness, and that is its everlasting charm. Used to great effect as the kickoff to the great album *Pet Sounds*, it starts with deceptively

gentle guitar goofing, a snare drum hit, and then the shimmering wall of vocals and melody and words. It can penetrate like the rush from a drug, that moment when you suddenly realize *everything is different now*. Listen to them putting it down: "Wouldn't it be nice if we were older / Then we wouldn't have to wait so long / And wouldn't it be nice to live together / In the kind of world where we belong," they sing, and the sincerity sparkles through. They are evidently as high as we are now, and they continue, "Wouldn't it be nice if we could wake up / In the morning when the day is new / And after having spent the day together / Hold each other close the whole night through." Then they clinch the deal: "Maybe if we think and wish and hope and pray it might come true / Baby then there wouldn't be a single thing we couldn't do." The genius of Wilson & crew here is that they accomplish all this with such basic elements: words, sounds, melody, harmony. This thing is just about perfect the way it is. It doesn't need any help. It's all there all at once. (2010)

Beatles, "Happiness Is a Warm Gun" (1968)
This is mostly a John Lennon song but I've heard rumors that Paul McCartney called it his favorite on the White Album. That alone arguably makes it as good an example as any of a "Lennon/McCartney" composition, so many written by one and tweaked by the other and hashed into their wonderful final forms in the studio (in many ways the real instrument they played over the arc of their career, one reason apropos of nothing I am satisfied to call George Martin the one and only fifth Beatle). I admit I'm a bit of a Beatles crank when it comes to the White Album; I think it somehow manages the feat of being a good deal less than the sum of its parts. But the parts I think are good (this, "Back in the U.S.S.R.," "Good Night," a few others) are very, very good. Lennon later denied "Warm Gun" was the drug song so many assumed it was (i.e., gun = syringe), saying that his period of heroin addiction did not involve injections. Well, maybe. He claimed rather that he got it off a headline in a gun lovers' magazine. He did acknowledge the sexual innuendo, maintaining that side of

it emerged as part of the early courting with Yoko Ono. But trying to "explain" this song falls short of the complexity and piercing harshness so compacted into its less than three minutes: the altogether oppressive vibe, a quasi-rape scene rendered in classic Lennon streams of language, the squawls and menacing lines of guitar, "I need a fix 'cos I'm going down," a mother superior (what?) who "jumped the gun," and a vocal performance that flits in and out of something dredged from the bottom of a soul, with a good deal of dynamics. Plus "bang bang shoot shoot" going on in the background on the chorus—for the comic relief, I suppose. (2011)

Beatles, *Rubber Soul* (1965)
Another way to divide my narrow little world: those who believe *Rubber Soul* properly kicks off with "Drive My Car," as found on the UK version, and those who believe it starts with "I've Just Seen a Face," on the US. Neither song appears on the other version, which is part of what makes me so stubborn on it. Each song frames what follows differently, and even though the great majority of what follows is nearly identical, only shuffled about a bit and with a few additions or deletions, it seems to make a difference. Suffice to say: the lean studied exuberance of "Face" leads off an album I like quite a bit more than the one that starts with a honking shambolic limo fantasy.

Recently, the collective marketing geniuses behind 50 years of united Beatles mess finally closed one circle and released some 13 US versions of Beatles albums on CD (with the inevitable box set of all of them), for which I was humbly grateful, welcoming back an old friend. (I learned the hard way that trying to work with the tags and labels of digital music is harder and less rewarding than you would think.) The distinction between the two versions is no small matter to me somehow. *Rubber Soul*—the US version—is one of the first albums I knew and it has always been a good deal more than a collection of songs. For me, for various reasons, it feels like no less than the Beatles *at their absolute best*, inventing a kind of chamber pop music full of moods and shadings, inventive yet simple, charming but never shallow, insinuating itself into the grains of my life, and forever listenable.

My parents gave me *Rubber Soul* for my 11th birthday in 1966, which is the album I had asked for. They were relieved it was the right album because they had not been able to make out the title in the proto-psychedelic lettering of the brown blob in the upper left corner. They also gave me an anthology of horror short stories, which they knew I liked. I have a birthdate that falls early in the month of March, and many years, especially when I was a kid, it cast a kind of glow over the whole month, which is otherwise useless. That year was a notable example as I immediately went to my bedroom in all my leisure hours, playing the album front to back to front to back and reading the stories.

The stories leaned toward established classics with a literary veneer. I don't remember all the titles but there were things by Poe, Henry James, and Ambrose Bierce, along with "The Yellow Wallpaper" by Charlotte Perkins Gilman, "The Open Window" by Saki, "The Most Dangerous Game" by Richard Connell, "The Monkey's Paw" by W.W. Jacobs, perhaps "A Distant Episode" by Paul Bowles. My own preferences happened to be for even more shocking fare, with twist endings, in the mold of *The Twilight Zone*—e.g., Shirley Jackson's "The Lottery," Jerome Bixby's "It's a *Good* Life"—but anything that was weird and macabre would do.

Years later I came to realize how deeply impressed by the album and book both together I was. At some point the track sequencing of the album became so familiar that I could hear the beginnings of the next song in the ends of many—even still felt disembodied stirrings to flip a record after hearing "Michelle" and "Run for Your Life"— and many of the moods of the stories were compressed into the music as well. This is no doubt part of the reason I keep making such a big deal out of the versions. When you expect to hear "Think for

Yourself" following on the ending strains of "You Won't See Me," and what you get is "Nowhere Man"—which does not belong on *Rubber Soul* (though it does, and I understand why)—it's upsetting to a sense of the order of things. The stories and songs began to interpenetrate more and more.

"The Yellow Wallpaper" is one example, first published in 1892 and now considered a milestone of feminist literature. It takes the form of journal entries by a woman who has been confined by her husband, for the sake of some kind of recuperation, to a single bedroom. She is minded during the day by her husband's sister, the windows barred, and she is forbidden to read or write. She has to keep her journal secret. Gradually she goes mad, manifested by an ever more intense fascination with patterns she sees in the wallpaper of the room. I could lay there in my bed idly reading such a fevered narrative and I happened to have some wallpaper of my own I could look at and search for patterns. Then, perhaps, would come John Lennon singing the lovely song he wrote with Paul McCartney about a strange, tentative one-night stand, "Norwegian Wood": "She showed me her room / Isn't it good Norwegian wood." We are all looking at the walls now.

"Norwegian Wood" remains a candidate for most memorable song of *Rubber Soul*, of course. I think it's so good it's somehow even managed to grow in stature over the years. It's famous partly as the place where George Harrison's interests in Indian music and the sitar began to be felt, as a sitar is used—much like a Western instrument but adding a wonderful texture. What I notice most about the song now is how artfully structured it is, poised and balanced almost like Japanese art, with a light but certain hand, words and music fitted together seamlessly. Lennon wrote "Norwegian Wood" in part based on an affair he'd had, though he was at pains to hide that fact from his wife of the time, Cynthia, which accounts for the elliptical way the story proceeds. McCartney finished off the lyrics, making a strange situation even more so by making it sound as if a lover denied sex has burnt the place down in retribution. That is so at odds with the tone of the song to that point as to be positively disorienting. For years I thought the perception must have had more to do with the stories I was reading than with anything objective in the song, but McCartney later owned up to it. "She led him on, then said, 'You'd better sleep in the bath,'" he told one interviewer. "In our world the guy had to have some sort of revenge." It cheapens the song, though the conflagration was actually the perfect note for me back in my room reading my book of stories.

Another story I read: "The Open Window" by Saki (H.H. Munro, a British writer), first published in 1914, a quick piece of stunt work, done in swift sure strokes. Stories by Saki often seem motivated by effect in the same ways as those of O. Henry, and Saki could work his elements cunningly, as the very short "The Open Window" shows. A young girl tells tales and things are not what they appear. The final result is something of a joke, but somehow with a sickening undertow. In my daydreamy hazes, I heard the end of the first side of *Rubber Soul* with this: Harrison's "Think for Yourself," the weirdly discombobulated "The Word" which follows it, and finally the soothing tones, veering off into incomprehension with the French, of "Michelle." They suit the Saki vibe. "Do what you want to do / And go where you're going to," Harrison sings in "Think for Yourself." Then "The Word," a wailing shouter it took Lennon, McCartney, *and* Harrison to concoct, injects a kind of unpleasant anarchy. The most vilified track on *Rubber Soul* has always been McCartney's "Michelle," which along with "Yesterday" is widely taken as McCartney's nadir (with the Beatles) of "silly love songs" and/or ample reason even not to take him seriously at all. I really don't have a problem with "Michelle" and never have—certainly it's a bit on the cloying side, but it is also disorienting and weird with the language shift and I like that. I see links in "Michelle" to concurrent European pop strains just then coalescing,

19

part of a broader confluence of pop music with image, practiced by the Beatles themselves (or director Richard Lester) in *A Hard Day's Night*. Director Jean-Luc Godard put Chantal Goya in *Masculin Feminin*. David Lynch later picked up the mantle and extended it with *Blue Velvet, Twin Peaks, Mulholland Dr.*, and other films. By its very blandness and gorgeousness, there is something in "Michelle" of the unworldly conflation of beauty and horror. Or maybe that's the book I was reading.

My door was closed, and I lay on the bed reading the book, and I would take breaks every 15 or 20 minutes to turn the album. Sometimes I wanted to look at the album jacket instead of the book. The front and back were two different worlds, the front a color shot from a strange angle with a strange lens, a background of thick green foliage in shadow and the browns and blacks of the Beatles and their leather jackets. The back was more of a toss-off, a collection of black and white shots pasted up around the track listing. I was captivated by the image of Paul smoking a cigarette, holding it in his mouth, eyes closed against the smoke which wreathes his face. The cigarette made it seem sophisticated, and hardened. Then I considered the shot of George dressed as a cowboy, in vest and boots and jeans and cowboy hat. It annoyed me somehow. It was too cheeky. I preferred another shot of him with his head tilted, in shadow. And there was Ringo flaunting his rings. John peeking out from a bush.

Another story I read, which as it happens the Zodiac serial killer of the '60s also likely read: "The Most Dangerous Game" by Richard Connell, first published in 1924. I also ran into it later being taught in high school. There's something at once daring and safe about this story—daring in its willingness to embrace the taboo of premeditated murder as sport (and cannibalism and darker regions by implication—something about it appealed to a famous serial killer, after all), and safe in its assumption that the entertainment of such ideas will always be taken as provocative. Today it feels like the world the story was written in had to be safer just by its ability to be so easily shocked. The song I associated with it was the obvious one, that self-consciously very bad song by Lennon, "Run for Your Life"—I mean "very bad" in the transgressive, immoral, juvenile delinquent sense, which thrilled me. But it's also one of the few Beatles songs in their whole catalog that has aged so poorly, with that extremely unpleasant and very direct shot of misogyny at the center. But it was a high point for me at the time, I have to admit. It's got a great fast tempo, and it's real tuff.

I should note that the tones and textures of these songs may arguably be too tight. Many seem almost interchangeable, or maybe that's something about the way I played the album. This was notably the case with "Think for Yourself." I have always been confused about which side of the album it belongs on and I have spoken with others who have the same confusion, and it's always this song—side 1, in case you were wondering. I wonder sometimes if this isn't also related to missing "In My Life" almost entirely. More likely that's a song I needed to grow into. I think now it's almost certainly the most remarkable song on the album, the one the album should be known by if you had to pick one. It is an amazing song to have been written by a 25-year-old and 23-year-old, Lennon and McCartney, though they later disagreed on who did what and how much. No matter. Few songs anywhere so completely capture and define a feeling that lies on the far side of sentiment. Not nostalgia exactly—not nostalgia at all, I would argue—but simply a poignant awareness that time steals all things except memory, and memory finally fades too with the rememberer, and all that's left are artifacts such as these, and mysteries. The simple lines can be searing: "There are places I remember ... Some have gone and some remain ... Some are dead and some are living ... I know I'll often stop and think about them." The Lennon who'll often stop and think about them has been gone for decades but it's the Lennon I knew and loved best: idealistic, inevitably disappointed, wearing cynicism only as a shallow mask, a shield. But holding close—he believed in love as much as any of them, maybe the most. Though it may be all you need is love (an inferior song) in the end all we have is each other. That is the wisdom of "In My Life." I also think of it as one of the best examples of a Beatles collaboration. Lennon may be the primary author but he has entirely absorbed McCartney's affinity for gentle affection, and adapted it to his own pain. Fifth Beatle George Martin kicks in a lovely bridge and it's done. The best Beatles song on this album, one of the best albums they ever made. (2014)

Chuck Berry, *The Great Twenty-Eight* **(1955-1965)**
In a countdown exercise I did of hit songs I found myself chastised like anyone would be for various exclusions, inclusions, and perceived mistakes in emphasis, which did not surprise me. I mean, 100 seems like a pretty big number, but it's finite, and I know I'm a crank. But in retrospect shutting out Chuck Berry seemed weird even to me, so I made a point of revisiting this essential collection of the best of his best. No question, this is the cream: the virtual invention of numerous familiar rock 'n' roll guitar licks, Berry's guitar playing itself, clean and punchy, often underrated or forgotten, and of course his sly and biting wit, the winking, knowing references to staples of teen life (which sadly metastasized in his late visit to the charts, 1972's "My Ding-a-Ling," his biggest hit but thankfully not included here). This wit, in fact, is what I suspect is most underrated—"Brown-Eyed Handsome Man" alone, the deeply coded mid-'50s assessment of racial relations, demonstrates he knew what he was saying, and saying exactly what he meant, e.g., "Arrested on charges of unemployment" (although the song distractingly doesn't appear to understand some of the most basic terminology used in baseball). Some of the tracks I appreciated most are the less worn: "Too Much Monkey Business" and "Come On," almost perfect expressions of exasperation about the hassles of life. "Havana Moon," with a spooky stripped-down sound. "Beautiful Delilah" and its

hilariously brisk piano tinkling in a distant background. "Oh Baby Doll," upbeat and on the attack. And what do you know, some of the hits sound as fresh as ever too, notably, at this moment, "School Days." To make it the complete package, there's even a mystifying omission—1964's "You Never Can Tell." But I would be less than honest if I didn't also mention the ditches of familiarity, where perhaps I need to accept that I have used up my lifetime supply now: "Maybellene," "Roll Over Beethoven," "Rock & Roll Music," and "Johnny B. Goode." Is it possible to do anything about this? Does it even matter? Maybe just hauling out the old shibboleths and saying nothing else is the best idea after all. Rock 'n' roll it will never die! (2011)

Big Star, "Nightime" (1974)
At the time I was getting to know this song, with the mid-'80s vinyl release of the *Third* album by Big Star, the one with the big blue cover and liner notes by Howard Wuelfing, I was pretty busy myself with a life full of "At night time I go out and see the people," and I felt about it much the same way the singer here sounds, dismal and sour and maybe a little studiously bored. I wasn't having much fun. "And dressing so sweet, all the people to see"—such details caught my attention but really it was the mood of it that seemed to swallow me up, even from the first, a sound that runs all through the near-20 great tracks that cluster around versions of this album. I came to focus on this song as I came to recognize the plight of the singer was my own. "I'm walking down the freezing street / Scarf goes out behind," he sings. It sounds so sad. Then suddenly the song swells into its raw climax, a bleating from the bottom of the soul that never plays quietly in the background: "Get me out of here / get me out of here / I hate it here / get me out of here." I connected with what this song was saying and how it felt all at the same time, and in many ways I followed that trebling vocal performance across a couple thousand miles, Pied Piper style, into a new life in a new city. This is really a dark moment that is captured here, but rendered so

purely and so absolutely that it becomes a moment of exaltation and hope too as much as anything. (2012)

The Blair Witch Project (David Myrick / Eduardo Sanchez, 1999)

In its brief moment, *The Blair Witch Project* was such a many-tentacled phenomenon that even up front it requires a little sorting and unpacking. For your consideration: the over-the-top guerrilla marketing campaign, the extraordinary profit generated (nearly $250 million in revenue on a $25,000 production for a staggering return of 1,000,000%), its use of the so-called "found footage" narrative, the specific strategies of the filmmakers to elicit the performances and create a unique look and feel, and last but not least the episodes of vertigo reported by viewers who could not handle the shaky handheld style of shooting. There's also of course the question of whether it's even scary, or worth seeing at all.

That last is an easy one for me. Yes and yes. It's scary not in the manner of outright shock and mayhem, but rather in exploiting an irresistible dread and hopelessness, whether the sources are supernatural or it's just banal old death from exposure. *The Blair Witch Project* is loud, loose, messy, clumsy, aimless, and obvious. It's a stunt, with all manner of low-budget gaffes, no sense of tonal consistency, and numbing repetitions. Yet somehow it never fails to take possession.

The Blair Witch Project is often held responsible for the rash of found-footage films that emerged as a class nearly 10 years later, starting with approximately *[•Rec]*, in 2007. The idea is that the movie is a compendium of footage shot by the principals; we see it well after the fact, effectively with no transitions or gloss (the editing is a bit mysterious in these things), and no explanation other than what we can glean from what we see. *Blair Witch* explains it this way in a nicely ominous opening note: "In October of 1994, three student filmmakers disappeared in the woods near Burkittsville, Maryland while shooting a documentary. A year later their footage was found."

The story: A quick setup establishes a legend, somewhat incoherent but vaguely disturbing, of a witch that lives in the woods outside Burkittsville, Maryland (formerly known as Blair, though we never learn why the name changed). Heather, Josh, and Mike are making a documentary about it. Among other things Burkittsville was the roaming ground in the 1940s for a serial killer who preyed on children. In a portentous (and pretentious) shot for the documentary, Heather claims there are an unusually large number of children's graves in a cemetery that contains stones going back to the 18th century. A woman Heather interviews details one version of the legend. At a critical point in her story the baby she holds in her arms reaches up to cover her mouth, as if to stop her talking. It looks like serendipity, but it's eerie.

Then the three are off on an overnight into the woods, looking for specific sites: an area where a mass murder occurred, an abandoned cemetery. As the group leaves the car the camera pivots back and takes a long look at it. It's the last we'll see of it. Their planned one night in the woods stretches to six, as they become lost, begin to bicker with one another, and experience ever more disturbing events at night.

This is the heart of the film and what we see is basically footage shot by three actors, with no particular camera skills among them. Each was also given a specific direction by co-directors and co-writers Daniel Myrick and Eduardo Sanchez that the others did not know about—lose the map, run into the woods with no explanation, etc. Nor did they know the others had also been given secret directions. That they did not have fun on this shoot is in front of our eyes. It's often raining and it is clearly cold, and at night someone is playing unpleasant jokes on them. There is much to complain about in this long central passage—the repetitions, the harsh tone the characters (and players) take with one another, and the low impact of the shocks. They find creepy and horrifying things, hear terrifying sounds—but it does not necessarily translate to titillation for us, because the technical skills aren't there (and are precluded anyway by the premise). What we experience more often is the misery of watching miserable people and wishing there was something we could do. Also wishing they would hold the camera still more often.

Yet, for me—and in spite of some egregious passages of performance—this is the best and most interesting part of the movie, the only part that does seem to me to improve and grow more interesting. On the third or fourth day, running low on food and optimism, at odds with one another and beginning to break down emotionally, they decide to use their compass to keep themselves walking south, and they walk south all day. At the end of the day they arrive back at the place where they started that morning, and camp again in the same place. This is when the dimensions become apparent. This is no longer rational. Watching them descend into it, understand it, accept it, is truly chilling.

The famous last scene is great, of course, especially the first time seeing this movie. The ghost story that has evolved into a monster story now becomes the worst and most cruel sort of haunted house story, as Heather and Mike (Josh now lost, only his occasional bellowing voice heard from afar remains) find an abandoned cabin in the woods, and enter. From that point on it's a very good bit of horror movie business all the way up to its indelible final image, perfectly set up from early. (2014)

Blondie, "Heart of Glass" (March 17, 1979, #1)
Another heinous sellout of epic proportions, once again producing results that only the most hardened could object to. In this case, it is New York punk-rock scenesters Blondie dabbling in the dread disco, incidentally inventing a neat counterpoint to the Rolling Stones' "Heart of Stone" and Neil Young's "Heart of Gold," since used elsewhere to good effect by the Pet Shop Boys in "West End

Girls." "Heart of Glass" actually started life in 1975 as a reggae number called "Once I Had a Love." As reconfigured a scant few years later, with producer Mike Chapman given his head at the board, it's one of the smoothest, slickest productions to emerge from the heyday of disco, glistening and sleek and cool. The four-on-the-floor is thankfully understated (but there, oh there), the little guitar flicks almost tender, and the backing vocals positively meditative. It's the swirling layers of keyboards and the ethereal vocals by Deborah Harry that do most of the work. The groove is so fine that this is one of those rare dance songs whose mixes can be judged by their length, i.e., longer better—longer longer bet-ter better—longer longer longer better better better. Sometimes I think I might be getting a little tired of it, but often a change in set-ting, hearing it somewhere that surprises me—such as, these days, on an elevator in an office building—can revive all its charms for me in an instant. (2010)

Blur, Seattle, 1996
Blur was a club show for me toward the end of my serious clubbing days, when I saw a remarkable string of bad-vibe shows. Blur, if I recall correctly, was the one that was oversold with lots of people not used to club spaces, plus it was also on a Friday night, which naturally seemed to bring the drunks out. Particularly on a mossy, frigid night in January when there's nothing better to do than pound a few and go "rockin' to the rollin'," as I heard it explained. Blur was not exactly my thing, post-grunge but with a kind of XTC tidy complexity to them, almost a fussiness, plus what I thought was a heavy David Bowie cum Ray Davies posture. The club Moe was approximately one size too small for them. They probably should have been in a small theater, but whatever. We go. Steve, who usu-ally organized these outings, with his friend Norm who often came, and a fourth person I can't remember. The mood was ugly, people hostile and edgy as we navigated the tiny hallway into the music space, jammed to a standstill but moiling with constant pushing and

shoving. Within a week of this show I also saw Pavement at the same venue, another one of the heavy bad-vibe shows, only with Pavement it had more to do with people passing out and falling down amid serious crowding and potential trampling situations. And there was Garbage, again at Moe, where I got creeped out by some guy I didn't know who wanted to talk to me while Steve and Norm had gone off somewhere. And before that, Boss Hog, the bad-vibe show that started the bad-vibe string. Now mind you all of these shows had their blazing fury wonderful moments, but all too quickly you could be dragged down again into a morass of despair by the crowding or brutish behavior or some sudden flash of alienation, as if you were in a place you didn't belong. And where at the same time, in some other way, you felt you belonged more than anywhere. Finally, out came Blur, which can, as it turns out, truly stomp it up, with this show and their fabulous "Song 2" as proof. But I could never settle into it. Across my vision would come sailing some flying object, say. Yes, right, a full cup of beer. Flying across my field of vision. I'd follow its arc and see that it's going to hit, yes, right there, that big ape in the brown corduroy jacket with the faux fur trimming and the stupid beret cap and bushy sideburns and he's not going to like it. Then it strikes him, on the side of the head, the cup and beer spilling back across his shoulder, and no, he doesn't like it. He sure doesn't. And now you have to keep an eye on him awhile in case of trouble before noticing once again: the racket, that noise. It's music. And it's great. And they could play all night like this, it sounds so good, if only this totally distracting bad shit doesn't get out of control. (2002)

Bongwater, *Too Much Sleep* (1989)
Another brief and intense infatuation, revisiting this now after so much time I suppose I have to concede that Bongwater is a bit of an acquired taste. Pairing a wannabe downtown New York City artiste (Kramer, of Shimmy Disc) with a wannabe movie star (Ann Magnuson) produced a strange, messy, oddly alluring, caustic and

often hilarious studio-bound performance art act. It actually worked. Most aficionados seem to prefer the earlier, more ambitious *Double Bummer*, while the last of their four albums, *The Power of Pussy*, may be their best known, such as it is. But this is the one I like. Everything I like about it best sneaked up on me and so, loath as I am to pass along such advice (even more to get it), I suggest listening to this a few times before giving up. What may sound at first disorganized, meandering, sketchy, or pointlessly self-indulgent comes to cohere in impressive, even amazing ways. (2007)

Boston Legal (**ABC TV series, 2004-2008**)
I decided to confront my David E. Kelley problem, and ours, with a systematic review of *Boston Legal*, which seems to me as good a microscosm as any of the things that make his entertainments so dreadful and so compelling. I started on this originally because of the recommendation of a friend combined with my curiosity about William Shatner, who's pretty good here, though the shtick quickly wears thin.

As usual with Kelley productions, the plots are ludicrous, the characters shallow and unlikable, the court scenes products of jarringly wrong-headed fantasy. No court on TV, let alone any court in the land, ever sees the kinds of things that happen here. The style is uniformly flashy and cheap, exemplified in the ubiquitous "pulsing slo-mo" (a term I invented to cope with the style) in which pans and sweeps and zooms and the action itself are slowed and sped up randomly and abruptly to match the impatient, swaggering moods of the moment. The theme music is obnoxious.

Nevertheless, usually at least once per show, somebody gets an inspired monologue and/or giant metaphorical obvious confrontation—with corporate evil, with government complacency, with hidebound convention, like that. I take them as electrifying thunderbolts—so carefully are we manipulated into caring deeply if only momentarily about the stakes, suddenly so vast in those moments. In spite of myself (and with all due self-castigation, I assure you) I want to stand and cheer in those moments.

The word for this remarkable incubator of human emotion appears to be "dramedy," and Kelley, if not the inventor, has certainly been one of its most successful practitioners: *L.A. Law*, *Chicago Hope*, *Ally McBeal*, and *The Practice*, among a great many others, are all directly his fault. The thunderbolts and various issues of the day, with the attempt to humanize them, make up the bulk of the drama part of that ugly word. The comedy, so-called, tends to derive almost exclusively from what was called "jiggle TV" in an earlier time, incidents of tawdry and repulsive sexuality, telegraphed sitcom style in elaborate set pieces of humiliation. The basic idea is a vision of the noble egalitarian society wherein all are equal in their obsessive-compulsive and pathetic need to get laid. The fact that characters in pursuit of this are reduced to buffoonery by the effort is beside the point, although sometimes it appears to be the jovial point itself, complete with grotesque label of inclusiveness.

The effect is enormously depressing, and in the end that is what I brought away from *Boston Legal*. We are evidently intended to feel a great humanizing sympathy, for example, with Shatner's Denny Crain character as he struggles to confront and ameliorate in various ways his encroaching Alzheimer's. That's a nice idea, and one that deserves an honest effort somewhere, sometime. But this is not it. It's not even close. Nor are the famed drinks-and-cigars balcony scenes that finish most of the shows particularly convincing, with Denny Crain and James Spader's Alan Shore smugly demonstrating the various terms of their heartwarming friendship. It's not that it's hard to believe they are friends with affection for one another (though I wouldn't call it easy). The problem rather is why anything in the lives of these overprivileged and uncharming miscreants offers anything to us at all.

No, the one tiny flame that kept bringing this moth back (and in the end my excuse for making a project of the series) was the thunderbolts—usually various courtroom speeches, sometimes conference room confrontations or other scenarios. It is, of course, one of the basest kinds of entertainment that entertainment has to offer, analogous to scenes in *24* and similar TV torture-porn (torture-porn in the movies is another matter entirely) in which an unlikable character is dealt tremendous pain as a comeuppance, with the result that we feel good about it.

This is dangerous territory, I think, the point where the desensitization and the surrender of critical thinking faculties—so widely bewailed and condemned across the width and breadth of modern society—actually occurs: When we stand and cheer against our own values just because, "for once," we get to see our arguments unequivocally win and stand and our opponents demolished all in one fell swoop. Yeah, it feels good. It feels good on *Boston Legal* when Alan Shore & crew stick it to Big Oil, Big Pharma, Big Conservative Government, etc. (and if you're going to watch this, don't miss the Supreme Court appearances).

Boston Legal may not be the right place to take a stand and ask the questions—*24* has more often been the target of choice over the past decade, but I think it poses questions more appropriate to right-wingers. I think a show like *Boston Legal* has the more interesting questions for my side of the divide, but it's unfortunately so resolutely at least 75% contemptible trash TV that it's hardly the best case study. Still, I kept coming back to it for a reason, groaning when the first DVD of a new season arrived and wondering how in the hell I was going to get through another one. But inevitably, once again, the thunderbolts were thrown, and I was riveted, wrung out, exhausted, thrilled, and confused.

Do I recommend this experience to anyone? Absolutely not. That's why I'm writing. By all means, stay the hell away. At the same time, I do think it raises an important issue: What do we enjoy, and why do we enjoy it? (2010)

David Bowie, "V-2 Schneider" (1977)
Not many of the experimental-style soundscapes hatched by David Bowie and Brian Eno on *Low* and *"Heroes"* impressed me much, but this is one. Kicking off the second side of *"Heroes,"* it's pretty much undeniable, even in the thick of the collaborators' incoherent embrace of Berlin and the Cold War as binary moral imperative—highly alluring in its specific historical moment, but also nonsensical. The love of Bowie (more than Eno, I suspect) for Berlin as the existential center of the West extends ever so delicately into ... what? Well, "Schneider" is not just the last name of a Kraftwerk principal, after all, but also a maneuver in sports such as soccer or rugby that is intended to prevent an opponent from scoring a point. The V-2 rocket is what rained down on London. But never mind trying to make sense of it. Washed through in layers of rocket screams and the static found between radio and television stations, this mostly instrumental track (there's various humming and some singing of the title) rides a rhythm section pattern of sure-footed bass and little snare-drum figures, lets its layers pile high on one another, gets soulful with a sax, coalesces on lovely fragments of melody, throbs, aches, swoons, and briefly flares into gray widescreen before tailing away back into oblivion, all of it accomplished once again in just over three minutes. Meet the new pop song. (2012)

Emily Bronte, *Wuthering Heights* (1847)
I can't recommend entirely without reservation this stone classic of British literature—last time I went through was a bit of a slog. But I certainly think it's worth a try. Emily Bronte's monumental first and only novel (she otherwise focused her literary energies on poetry and died at the age of 30, the year after this was published), *Wuthering Heights* came out the same year as her sister Charlotte's *Jane Eyre* and her sister Anne's *Agnes Grey*. *Wuthering Heights* is the

next-best thing to full-on raving ghost / monster story, wild and howling and weird, gothic on overdose, buckled together with leather strapping and paste. Class distinctions are rendered metaphorically as stark lines between humans and beasts, and the great Byronic hero of *Wuthering Heights*, the remarkable Heathcliff, is of course on the wrong side of that line. Heathcliff notably has powers to compel and bend his betters to his desires, after coming to live with them originally as an orphan found on the streets of London by the family patriarch, adopted out of his soft heart. The combination of Heathcliff's ruthlessness in pursuing his ends and the family's sheltered, genteel naivete is the outline of the disaster imminent from the first page. The forbidden passion between Heathcliff and the scion's daughter Catherine provides much of the dramatic tension, as Heathcliff and his will to power rise to great heights. The rest are humiliated and torn to pieces and put into the earth one way or another, against the backdrop of gray skies and lonely barren moors. "Atmospheric" does not begin to describe it; "deranged" is closer in many passages. It can be a wild ride. In many ways it walks and talks and bears the trappings of the standard 19th-century novel of manners, with gentle folk gathering for fine meals and social occasions, and love interests emerging by degree, and marriage the grand occasion of life. But the like of Heathcliff had never appeared in one of these before. His sheer gravitational force distorts everything around him, making a mockery of the refined upper class and their ways and values. It was the first time I read *Wuthering Heights* that I got the most out of it, taken utterly by surprise by the stunts recorded herein. I'm not sure exactly what made the more recent reading so hard. In part it was the language, which is antiquated and made further eccentric with thick dialect. That was toned down somewhat after Emily's death by her sister Charlotte in a later edition—I can only imagine the original. It's also in part because of the sideways manner it crabs in and around its narrative developments. But it bears powerful images and a grand sweeping story. (2013)

Meredith Brooks, "Bitch" (May 10, 1997, #2)
A friend of mine can't stop talking about seeing Ms. Brooks perform in a dive in Eugene, Oregon, in 1981, saying she (Ms. Brooks) sounded about the same then as she does now except less like Alanis Morissette. Then she (my friend) goes into a rage about how the press release says she's 31. Folks, Meredith Brooks is 38 if she's a day. Don't believe the hype. (1997)

Fredric Brown, *Night of the Jabberwock* (1950)
Fredric Brown grew a checkered 20th-century career as both a science fiction and mystery novelist after establishing himself as a story writer in the '40s and '50s pulps (while keeping a day job as a newspaper proofreader in Milwaukee). He was prolific, author of dozens of stories and many novels, whose quality varies widely. He's always good, carefully written—mark of the proofreader—but like so much from the era it feel rushed, attempting to work the hell out of one or two snap twists, and supplementing that with broadside parody when nothing else would do—a Midwestern O. Henry by way of H.L. Mencken wishing he could be Sinclair Lewis, with always a gentle, affable humor. The aliens turn out to be advertising men on the other planet, or the gladiatorial combat actually was about a corporate merger, things like that—'50s man in the gray flannel suit stuff basically, with proto-Rod Serling twists when he could manage them and occasional splendid results (fans included Philip K. Dick, Ayn Rand, and Mickey Spillane, a motley crew if ever there was one).

Nowhere else that I've seen did Brown get it together quite so economically and so brilliantly as in this little gem, whose surprises come regularly as the story becomes stranger and stranger. It doesn't really cheat with anything, which is just the start of what makes it so good. In its setting, it's already one of Brown's most personal novels—a quiet Midwestern town where our narrator, newspaper publisher in his 50s who still longs to break one big story just once, has put the weekly paper to bed and headed off into the night with a bottle. Right on cue, weird stuff starts. First there is someone pretending to be a character out of a Lewis Carroll novel waiting for him at his home with a strange request. Before our narrator can hear him out he gets a call—there's been a serious auto accident involving prominent citizens on the outskirts of town. On the way into the office, he discovers the town bank being robbed. Then gangsters, guns, eventually more Lewis Carroll, a haunted house, and murder.

Things happen fast and the action is rat-a-tat precise in this short novel. Everything happens practically real-time across the space of a single night, and the whole extravagant Alice conceit is delivered on nicely. The reading experience is like the funhouse scene in a cartoon, with trapdoors, sledgehammers, teacup cars, cigar-smoking bad guys, bizarre images in the mirror, all of it coming at you like a freight train down the tracks on top of you. Just delightful from beginning to end. (2010)

James Brown, Minneapolis, 1979

It was 1979 and James Brown was no longer on the sunny side of 50. I was a skeptic. My friend Cindy decided, in her wisdom, that one of our platonic, marijuana-smoking dates would be to see a James Brown show at the Cabooze in Minneapolis, an amiable honky-tonk with a venerable history. She was quite adamant about doing this. I see very well now that I didn't know anything then, but at the time I thought I was well-informed on musical doings and reasonably hip. I thought James Brown was a one-trick pony just this side of a novelty artist. I thought his music was phony, more or less, or maybe that I was in danger of becoming a phony, wannabe-black cliché if I listened to it. So I hadn't, much. Not that it was easy to find the best James Brown. I had a K-Tel double-LP set I'd bought a few years earlier with the hits I knew and some things that were new to me which I thought were amazing, such as "The Payback." I also had *Sex Machine*, which I did not much care for—they played the songs too fast. So when Cindy promised me it would change my life I just made sure she was bringing marijuana. I was not even then much of a veteran of club shows, so I was a little dismayed with the scene when we arrived: lots of people, no sign of anyone coming to the stage. As it happened, I don't think anyone did come to the stage until after 11 (which was quite late in Minneapolis, where bars closed at 1 a.m.). By this time I was jeering Cindy a little and wishing we could leave. She let it slide right off. Finally, the band came on—but minus James Brown. They ran through some funky chops, and it was pretty good. I think they played at least three songs. Part of me was annoyed, it seemed like just so much bullshit. Part of me was seeing how there was an entertainment strategy at work here. Finally James Brown appeared, front and center, moving and screaming—the volume of sound went up a couple of notches too, not to mention the level of electric anticipation. How to describe changing points in life, before and after moments, indelible impressions? For the next 35 minutes or so he took everybody there on a trip. Mostly I knew the songs but that mattered least. Some kind of spell was cast and we were joined in unison mystically, like. I don't mean hippie kind of shit exactly, though obviously there we were on the West Bank of Minneapolis, but something more visceral and felt in the bones and muscles, and remembered forever. The grooves were rock solid. Everything was motion. Just when you thought it couldn't get any better, it got better. All the playing was fresh and pinpoint. And James Brown could not only move like crazy, he controlled the music and used that to control the crowd. He went through his collapsing routine. He approximated the splits. He spun, crouched, pointed, twisted, and always he was in complete control of the music and using that to control the crowd. It was amazingly short but most of all amazing. Nobody could have possibly left the place feeling cheated in any way, despite the relative brevity. I think I have to call it the best show I've ever seen. Cindy was right again. (2005)

Buzz Barker & the Atomic Bums, "Land of the Free" (1979)
Buzz Barker = Curtiss A. The Atomic Bums = the Suicide Commandos plus keyboardist Mark Goldstein, who wrote the song. This Minneapolis one-off was recorded for the Twin/Tone double-LP anthology, *Big Hits of Mid-America Vol. III*, and it's a scorcher. Both Curtiss A and the Commandos were known for their live acts, which only rarely made it to vinyl. But this is one of those times, with a meditation on American values right in front of the Reagan revolution ("1980's just around the corner," Curtiss A broods as an aside at one point, which I recall as a frequent preoccupation of his at the time). In a lot of ways it seems more relevant than ever: "I like money but I hate the rich / They run this place and the rest of us bitch," it carps, going on to rhyme "home of the brave" with "learn to shave," "Jesus saves," "Sam & Dave," "the New Wave," and "we're in our graves." It stretches out all kinds of ways: Chris Osgood gets a tidy guitar solo. Goldstein sends it into ultra dimensions with haunting lovely long notes near the end. And the band absolutely cooks all through. Sometimes I just have to sit back and gape, still. This was a lift-and-drop needle operation on my stereo for most of the summer that it was released, a constant prelude to leaving my studio apartment and going on all my adventures: day job as delivery van driver, summer school classes, and out at night to the Longhorn to see touring and local punk-rock acts. But it's not just the nostalgia talking when I laud this song so ardently, because I don't think you had to be there to grasp its fundamentals. You just need to listen to it. (2011)

C

I t doesn't take long for even the English alphabet to settle into signs of the all too human tendency to do things simply because "that's the way they've always been done." The letter C, while possessed of a boldly simple, beautiful, and primal shape, nonetheless has no purpose, doing nothing that the letters S and K don't already do perfectly well. (Combined with H it only produces a mouth noise that logically deserves a choo choo ch-boogie letter of its own.) It's not the only consonant to engage in such shenanigans. But it is the first. And at #12 overall in terms of usage frequency, C also happens to be the most often used of these variously "squishy" consonants: G, J, and X, with W and Y arriving late as particularly knotty problems. I know, I know, we're never going to get rid of the QWERTY (fun to type!) keyboard either. And truth be told, partly by its alphabetical prominence—supplying one more finish to one more short alphabet, in this case "ABCs," which my dictionary offers as a word with the definition "the rudiments of a subject"—partly by its comely shape, and partly by generations and centuries of simply acclimating to it, the otherwise ludicrous letter C offers a merely benign object now. I don't mind it much. But this multiplication of the sounds produced by a single letter, depending on the circumstances of its immediate neighbors on a case-by-case basis, is bad business. What, for example, do the hard and soft uses even have to do with one another? The first is a staccato noise made at the back of the throat (the "voiceless velar plosive"), the other is the most sibilant of all the sibilants. A better case for hard and soft uses of a single letter could be made with the mouth noises produced by, respectively, P and B, T and D, or F and V. But no. The hard C is a K, the soft C is an S, end of argument. It's not even an argument. It's instruction, and pedantic instruction. It's "the way we do it." Try to follow along. Followed by the vowels E or I (and sometimes Y, as in "cycle"), the C is soft (usually, though consider "soccer" or [some pronunciations of] "Celtic"). Otherwise the C is hard. Except for things like "muscle" or "Caesar." Good luck figuring out what C is doing in words like "luck." To complicate (or komplikate) matters, an odd '60s gesture of defiance that occasionally persists is to spell hard Cs in specific instances (or specifik instances, maybe) with a K, most notably "Amerika." In a way I don't quite understand (perhaps something to do with the author Franz Kafka), this is intended to signify opposition to fascism (and please don't miss the uniquely weird C in that word). Conceivably it is also related to the Ku Klux Klan. Thus, while generally I am inclined toward sensible reklamation projekts in spelling where possible, I regret the unfortunate politikal implications of this one, not that I would necessarily let it stop me. But you see the problem. (2013)

James M. Cain, *The Postman Always Rings Twice* **(1934)**
Newspaperman James M. Cain's first novel is so radically boiled down to the fundamentals, practically inventing the most characteristic aspects of the noir sub-genre as it goes, that it's little more than a long story, easily finished in one blast—which is usually how it goes, especially on first encounter, because the actions and motivations come at you like firecrackers, swift, abrupt, and compelling. "They threw me off the hay truck about noon," it starts. Last chance to catch your breath. The plot is a classic love triangle, set in down-at-the-heels rural Southern California and related by

drifter Frank Chambers, who wanders into the Twin Oaks Tavern shortly after the aforementioned exit from the hay truck. The tavern is run by an older Greek fellow named Nick Papadakis and his young wife, the luscious Cora. It's not too long before Frank has jumped Cora, who until then has found only disappointment in her sojourn from Iowa to the Golden State, which has netted her a position as short-order cook in a roadside joint and a husband almost twice her age. It's not too long after that that Frank and Cora begin plotting Nick's murder, and not much longer still before they rapidly begin losing trust in one another. There are few surprises now in the basic paces though which Cain puts his characters, or in any of the characters either. Instead, as Albert Camus must have picked up on himself, citing this as a primary inspiration for *The Stranger*, there is something eternally compelling about trying to understand the various shades of motivation for these desperate characters—greed, lust, some unconscious fixation that can never be explained. The sexuality is explosive. Papadakis never gets short shrift as the chump fifth wheel, but brings the pathos by the pailful. And the scenery is sweeping and pinpoint, the inky black shadows of California after dark, the greasy stink of diner kitchens, the musk of unmade beds. Before you know it, it's over—but worth going through slowly one more time to savor how much Cain has packed in here, so efficiently, in such brisk and headlong fashion. (2010)

John Cale, "Fear Is a Man's Best Friend" (1974)
John Cale veered all over the place from Europeanized string chamber music to discordant avant-garde thought experiments to, in his own term, dirtyass rock 'n' roll. He was never the main man in the Velvet Underground, Lou Reed saw to that early and often, but he brought something that was sorely missed in his absence, a natural chaos-maker with formal training that helped shape some of their best stuff. (They were also fine without him, as it turned out, just one more amazing point about that band.) I tend to go for the rock

'n' roll, so I like *Fear* and *Slow Dazzle* and the live *Sabotage* albums best. He peaked for me in the mid-/late '70s. Phil Manzanera is playing guitar on this one, and Brian Eno ... is there. "Fear Is a Man's Best Friend" is the first song on the first side of *Fear*, and lets you in on much of what's ahead: the piano miked tight and very bangy, the stentorian, half-drunken, Welsh shout of sing-along vocals, and the slow-build dynamics, starting with open spaces and Cale working out a simple melody. Then gradually it accrues sound to its sides like burrs until the whole thing is a raging behemoth just seconds from a messy explosion of some kind. I'm exaggerating—that description better fits the formidable eight-minute "Gun," taking a page from John Lennon's primal screaming, which opens the second side of the album. But this is a nice warm-up—more palatable, even sweet, by comparison. (2011)

Glen Campbell, "Wichita Lineman" (Nov. 16, 1968, #3)
Written by Jimmy Webb, produced by Al DeLory, sung by Glen Campbell, with a twangy guitar break by James Burton, the much-honored "Wichita Lineman" is still somehow so much more than the sum of its parts. Jimmy Webb wrote "MacArthur Park" and, more importantly for our purposes here, "By the Time I Get to Phoenix" and "Galveston," which were also hits for Campbell. All were produced by DeLory (except "MacArthur Park," produced by Webb). Glen Campbell was underrated for much of his career, perhaps regarded to too commercial—"Wichita Lineman" comes from the album that also yielded the wonderful sad schmaltz of "Dreams of the Everyday Housewife." But consider the larger pattern: Wichita, Phoenix, Galveston, even MacArthur Park. The sense of place is strong with this team, and indeed, it's the specificity of the working man in Kansas that contributes so much to what makes the song work so well. It possesses a clean and bracing sadness, better in every way than self-pity. The singer is working and he is sad and he is working. It describes a universal experience: unrequited love, and the requirement to keep working. The

sadness is thus exponential and infinite. It has strange, affecting lines: "I hear you singing in the wire / I can hear you through the whine," which mimic the effect of hearing songs like this late at night from strange AM radio stations far away. The Wichita lineman is still on the line. The orchestra swoops and soars. James Burton, perhaps most famous as an Elvis Presley sideman (and Ricky Nelson too), enters. Is it possible anything could ever be more beautiful on this God's green Earth? See also "Downbound Train" by Bruce Springsteen. (2014)

Joe Carducci, *Rock and the Pop Narcotic* (2nd ed., 1995)
I'm not going to argue with anyone that Joe Carducci hasn't produced a remarkable and worthwhile rock-critical tome in *Rock and the Pop Narcotic*. I'd say he could have basically slashed away most of the first part, in which he commits all of the sins he uses that space to indict others for, and made the second part, "The Psychozoic Hymnal," the real substance of the book. It's the kind of exercise—a sweeping, opinionated survey of the history of the music—that we should all be required to perform sooner or later.

Before I get to my really picayune complaints about his treatment of rock critics, I would like to briefly bemoan the overall semi-literacy of this project. I know—oh, how I know—that one of the most difficult problems of the whole rock-critical enterprise (such as it is) is the underlying illiteracy of the rock audience itself. If they can't read your words, will they know a tree has fallen in the forest? But Carducci's fight-fire-with-fire strategy, if that's what it is, mars his book. Don't get me wrong. I appreciate a loose, casual, idiosyncratic voice—Lester Bangs, Richard Meltzer, and Byron Coley are masters of it—but all too often Carducci's clumsy language distracts. Maybe I should shut up and give him the benefit of the doubt? That "write/right/rite" problem that surfaces in such constructions as "playwrite" and "right of passage" is just his sly way of rejecting HOMOnyms. Rite? And I suppose even raising the point at all is only more evidence that I'm a four-eyed fag with nothing better to do than criticize the ability of others to use English correctly.

God knows I don't care about rock music proper, as I learned at excruciating length in the bashing that occupies over 100 pages in the center of the book, "Narcorockcritocracy!" I was certainly happy to see Carducci take time from his busy schedule to really give it to me and my kind, those who appreciate New Order more than Uriah Heep. I am talking, of course, about rock critics.

Now the last thing I want is to be put in the position of defending those who have provoked all the varying degrees of scorn (mixed with love too, I admit) I have for them: the bandwagon jumpers who cheer with cultivated ironic lust for last night's college radio permutations (staff of *Spin*), the dweebs who turn the enterprise into a series of idle math problem, e.g., the Sex Pistols + the B-52's = Pussy Galore (Ira Robbins and his merry *Trouser Press* band), the pathetic power-hungry dildoes who'd've preferred to lead a revolution (Dave Marsh, Bob Guccione, Jr., by request Jack Thompson), the hideously corrupted moguls (Jann Wenner), the self-aggrandizing characters starring in their own private dramas (Greil Marcus), the inhuman databanks (Jack Rabid), and the mass of faceless, check-collecting, opinion-for-hire keyboard bangers we may refer to generically as Parke Puterbaugh.

I don't want to defend them but paradoxically I don't like seeing them attacked either, particularly by someone so obviously self-serving as Joe Carducci. We can't name names here because we really don't know, but the SST record label where Carducci worked was long notorious for yanking names of freshly disfavored writers off their promo lists in retaliation for unflattering reviews. Carducci, in his capacity as A&R hack for SST, at least had to be aware it was happening, even if he wasn't the one who was up late at night hunched over a desk drawing lines through names. *Of course* it's fine and entirely within SST's prerogative to do this, just as it's yours to kick your bare foot repeatedly against the wall and then complain about the state of both your foot and the wall. No one has to send rock critics product. It's just that it doesn't leave a lot of room for complaining about getting the wrong coverage. Because even if those rascally rock critics sell your product to the used record store sooner or later anyway—unheard as likely as not (and I agree that's a mighty small "if")—still there's no way to listen to your product, let alone review it, if they don't have a copy of it. Write?

Time for a reality check. There's a certain cachet attributed by Carducci to being a rock critic that just doesn't exist. Where, in the first place, does he get the idea that anybody *ever* bases a marketplace decision on what a rock critic thinks or says? Does he really think a rock critic does what he (far more often than she) does for money and glamour? What money? What glamour? And if Carducci is mad because most rock critics are still caught up in the sociopolitics of high school, he's not doing much to make his case with all the gratuitous homophobia, feigned or not. That's *pure* high school.

Carducci's buddy macho clearly has its appeal. The work of his most ardent supporters shows that. For them, for all of us who can sense how right "feeb-rock" is to describe Pavement and its progeny, Carducci's book serves as a critical touchstone and provides a vocabulary that many had been groping for. Carducci effectively formulated the rock aesthetic behind the *Forced Exposure* school (or "school"), an overdue task, and he has unified and provided focus to all those ashtray heart inarticulates you see in the clubs standing alone and together, clutching beers that slop as they bang their heads righteously. That's even been me at some of those shows.

But what's with the rock-crit abuse? Most of them that I know are just obsessed maniacs driven by their love of something they don't understand ... it's the love that drives them and the need to try and understand it, *not* the material or social rewards, which just don't exist (repeat: don't exist). Now of course I am happy for Joe Carducci that he can create a dichotomy (rock vs. pop) and a drama (*purist rock defiled by whore pop!*) that works for him. If there is a guitar or two and an amplified bass and a drumkit and everyone is playing together, he seems to be basically satisfied. To my tastes, he has made an apotheosis beyond reason of early-'70s prog impulses, which make me want to challenge him on a few points—like for example I don't understand his problem with Slayer if he likes Motorhead and Metallica so much. Did Slayer sneak a keyboard in when someone wasn't looking? I could have sworn that was fusion (dare I say prog) noodling I saw Metallica putting down. But never mind, rock critics are allowed their quirks, and make no mistake, a rock critic is exactly what we have in Joe Carducci.

As such, he is as infuriating as any of them. Rock is good, pop is bad—where does he get off with this? "I Think We're Alone Now" was every bit as life-changing for me as "School's Out," and *Very* vies with *Nevermind* as my favorite album of the '90s so far. Joe Carducci has never ached for some gorgeous, disposable piece of pop flotsam? I don't believe it. And I'm certainly not going to reduce the mystery of what I love and what moves me to something as simple as drums-bass-guitars playing together. In a way I envy Carducci's ability to do so. Well, I take that back. I think he's a horse's ass for simplifying it so grossly.

Carducci might not believe this, but a lot of rock critics understand exactly where his apprehensions are coming from. I've thrown magazines too. But I would like to invite him, now that he has written a very important book, to spend some time getting his word out in the rock press that he deems so deeply influential. No one can know what it's like to work in those environments until they do. This is the fact: You are required to justify, over and over, the painfully obvious. Like why Hüsker Dü should be covered instead of the band Limited Warranty (Minneapolis winners of "Star Search" circa 1984), why Sub Pop should be covered instead of Duffy Bishop (white R'n'B covers band), why the drag theater renaissance in Seattle should not be overlooked (circa 1992), what's wrong about Tom Grant and what's right about Courtney Love (circa 1995). It's like reinventing the wheel every week.

Eventually it becomes easier to cave, because even when you win the battle of story selection, then you get the battle of story slant and line-by-line language. And *then* publishers can just go ahead and kill the story anyway, and if you're lucky you get a kill fee, which is usually about a third of what you were supposed to get for the story in the first place. Let's see, a third of $50 for two or more days' work already done is... Plus of course then you get an A&R hack on the other end of *your* long-distance line (reimbursement for which does not happen often enough), asking why you *said* you would write a story about Saint Vitus, and now you're not.

Look, at least the radio people get cash and drugs. Rock critics get intermittent free product and virtually no money. They basically function to boost morale for industry people and other professional scene-makers. Nobody pays attention to them except to complain about the lousy job they're doing. I think a lot of what Carducci says is true, but bottom line he's more part of the problem than the solution. And you wouldn't believe how often this is the case.

But you have to give Carducci credit. Even more than the Monkees, he's got something to say. His aesthetic and his judgments seem kind of weird to me—sorry, I just can't get with Montrose. Plus, loath as I am (for shallow generational considerations and other obvious reasons) to defend them, I really have to say that if your formulation of

rock doesn't have room for Bob Dylan or Neil Young, then your formulation of rock is wrong. Still, for better or worse it's all in a day's
work for a rock critic and should be taken as such. Because the bad
news and the good news is that Joe Carducci is a rock critic. Live with
it. (1996)

Chills, "Song for Randy Newman, Etc." (1992)
I like how Chills songwriter and mainstay Martin Phillipps tries so
hard to make this as particular to a concrete place as he can, to
bucolic New Zealand. "In New Zealand our volcanoes and towns /
Rest together in peace, keep their roots in the ground," he noncha-
lantly leads with on one verse. New Zealand, yeah, right. This song
contains one of the most universal themes I've ever heard, laid out
and rendered flat and stripped down to the essentials of a singer
and keyboards, masking itself in them, charting the dark night of
the creative soul behind private choices and pains. All of us are
implicated one way or another. Even the desperate name-check-
ing—Randy Newman in the title only the most obvious, perhaps
because those are his piano licks providing accompaniment. But
there's another handful or so of usual suspects lurking and dart-
ing about the passageways of this deceptive three-minute ballad
("Wilson, Barrett, Walker, Drake," Phillipps reels them off at one
point). It's so full of humility and yet so arrogant and so certain of
what it knows and resigned to it that it transcends and leaves behind the downer vibe it carries like a cross. I seem to keep saying
things like that, making excuses perhaps for a bunch of downbeat
songs. I can see it fits a pattern. There's self-pity here (as there is
in "Nightime" and "Someone to Lay Down Beside Me" and others I like). Certainly self-obsession. But all of them, from Martin
Phillipps to Alex Chilton to Karla Bonoff to Linda Ronstadt and
all the others, also make a case, simply by doing what they do, for
dignity and for cheer too, for staying engaged with the best of all
things, however one may find them, and whatever pains they may
bring with them. Because the one thing we know is that there will

be pain. Martin Phillipps makes that point here, but he also describes as well as anywhere I know the rewards, with his elegant description of a songwriter's powers: "Can you hear sounds forming in your head / Do they say more than you've ever said." (2012)

Robert Christgau, *Christgau's Record Guide: The '80s* **(1990)**
It's possible that Robert Christgau's second volume of his record guide is actually better than the first. Some irregularities of tone and depth of consideration weakened the '70s volume a little, and were likely as not the result of Christgau still feeling his way into his ultimate format of the letter-graded, pellet-sized assessment. The writing is markedly improved and more uniformly focused in the second. It has a better sense of what it can do. If this volume was never going to feel like the breakthrough of that first one, it's also arguable that the '80s albums he covered just weren't as good, in the overall aggregate, as the '70s albums—arguable, I say, though I would not necessarily want to be the one to make the argument. What I know for sure is that whereas keeping the '70s volume around only gradually disclosed all it has to offer, with this follow-up, armed with exactly that information, I felt justified in sitting down and reading it like a novel, front to back, Introduction and Gregory Abbott's *Shake You Down* ('86, B+), to ZZ Top's *Afterburner* ('85, B), and all the useful and provocative lists in the appendices. *Then* I put it in one of my more convenient stacks of reference books with the '70s volume.

If I say I am very fond of the range of reaction Christgau provokes in me, I mean it sincerely. He is a pleasure to read, to browse, and to compulsively poke through. He can also be annoying, gnomic, obtuse, and full of himself. He is the first to note that the sheer mass of industry releases, whose growth has continued unabated throughout his career, finally ran him to ground at some point in the '80s or '90s. But if he can't realize his ambition, which is to have a little something to say about everything within the narrow range of the contemporaneous rock album, he is also as reliable as gravity, examining a daunting amount of cultural product by metric ton as only a few others can (the only ones I can think of are in other areas or more general ones, such as David Thomson's encyclopedia of film, or Montaigne). I am humbled and grateful just thinking about all the stuff I came to know about via Robert Christgau. He is strong in a number of areas where I am weak: folk music, African music, certain select New York City acts (Dolls, Blondie, Chic, Talking Heads, Sonic Youth, Yo La Tengo, Amy Rigby), lots of funk, dance, and hip-hop, and all the boomer icons. Plus Al Green. You could do much worse than to assign a certain portion of your shopping dollars to tracking down his A's. He is the consummate professional in this regard, delivering what he says he's going to deliver, a consumer guide—even if he remains pointedly skeptical of the commercial infrastructure breeding and nurturing the objects of his (and our) adoration. It's exactly that ability of his to work within this tension that might make him so worth visiting and revisiting. Oh, and wow, I just now noticed how beat up my old copy of this is. (2012)

Petula Clark
Most people now associate Petula Clark solely with her mid-'60s hit "Downtown," and perhaps for the soundalike follow-up "I Know a Place." A one-hit wonder, in short. But between 1965 and 1968 her releases landed in the top 40 no less than 15 times, in the top 10 six times, and went all the way to #1 (for two weeks) twice. Petula Clark articulated the various private fantasies of workaday Londoners, putting the material over with a tone-varnished voice of gleaming clarity and a small, odd note of weary knowingness. She was Julie Andrews yearning to become Dusty Springfield. Somehow she became my personal favorite woman pop vocalist of the decade, which I treated as guilty pleasure for a long time. Revisiting her catalog one sentimental weekend, I am more convinced than ever it is actually filled with a dozen or more great songs. (2010)

Patsy Cline, "Walkin' After Midnight" (March 2, 1957, #12)

The easy comment here, one I've made myself a few times, is that this stands in as a fine divorce or breakup song. It has served me well at such times. But Patsy Cline's sweet, nagging, ever-so slightly nasal performance delivers a good deal more than an opportunity for self-pity and crocodile tears. In fact, it's not even particularly sad. Instead, it digs into the softly evocative mysteries of an inability to let go of someone, and does so with a perfect image, encapsulated in the title. Speaking strictly for myself, I know when I've found myself taking to the streets late at night (or "along the highways," a notably chilling image from a woman singer) that it may not always involve relationship grief. But it usually does. The singer's ostensible mission, to seek out that missing object of love, is futile on its face. If he's not with her at 1 a.m. he's not likely to want to be found even if she could—even if she knew where to look. *Especially* if she knew where to look. This is one of Patsy Cline's specialties, a kind of theme that surfaces over and over again in her work, casting it almost into the shadows of noir: a simple idea that becomes stranger and more deranged the more one thinks about it. It's that voice of hers, partly, and the tunefulness, and the homely country (going on countrypolitan) trappings that lull you. But think about it. How insane is this for a nighttime scenario: "I stop to see a weeping willow / Cryin' on his pillow / Maybe he's crying for me." Or this, the heart of it: "I go out walkin' after midnight / Out in the moonlight, just hopin' you may be / Somewhere a-walkin' after midnight / Searching for me." That's not right. It's the image of a zombie. Nothing about that is right. (2010)

Coasters, "Poison Ivy" (Sept. 7, 1959, #7)

Perhaps the most comical line in all of Wikipedia is about this song: "In a recently published biography about Jerry Lieber & Mike Stoller, the song's authors, it was revealed that the song's lyrics are about sexually-transmitted disease, not the illnesses previously thought [measles, mumps, chickenpox, common cold, whooping cough]." Good to have that cleared up. And now that we're all done laughing I should probably mention that I didn't exactly realize that myself back when I first listened for it on oldies weekends. No, what I liked were the insistent rhythms, the infectious melody, the weird way it twists the words around, plays with the themes of disease and flora, making them hooks all in themselves: "Measles make you bumpy / And mumps'll make you lumpy / And chicken pox'll make you jump and twitch" and especially the flat declaration, "You're gonna need an ocean of calamine lotion." Later on, as an adult, I figured it out, but on those early encounters when I fell into its orbit so naturally, it was just bewildering and transfixing what they could be going on about. This was the first hit by the slick novelty specialist Coasters that arguably wasn't a novelty, though you could certainly make the case that it is. But it's sly as opposed to the broad strokes of "Charlie Brown," "Yakety Yak," or "Along Came Jones." Not that there's anything wrong with them—the Coasters are one of my favorites. But there's something special about this one, I think. Listen to it a few times and see if it doesn't get under your skin. (2010)

Eddie Cochran, "Summertime Blues" (Aug. 25, 1958, #8)
I'm young enough that I came to this song first more or less through the bizarre filters of the Who, Blue Cheer, and T. Rex, none of whom got it particularly right. Even with all its rockabilly signifiers, it's always struck me more as a Coasters type of song—it has that exasperated wiseass teen griping nailed down to fine shtick, notably in the flat booming intonations of the walk-on grown-up parts, e.g., "Now you can't use the car 'cos you didn't work late" or "I'd like to help you son but you're too young to vote" (and I love that he takes his "problem to the United Nations" but ends up talking to his Congressman). But in the end I think the appeal here is all sonic, compressed expertly into a scant two minutes: the rolling bass that sets it in motion, the neck-snap guitar chords, the highly inflected yelping of the vocal, counterpointed by the wry, cartoony admonishments, and the

way the sound of it opens and closes, on oiled hinges. At this point I think I won't ever get tired of it. (2011)

Cocteau Twins, *Heaven or Las Vegas* (1990)
This was the bestselling album ever for the Cocteau Twins, in a career that spanned from 1979 to 1997, and it was their last for 4AD. All I knew at the time was that it was gorgeous and enchanting if alarmingly vaporous, difficult to remember very clearly when I was apart from it. In fact, I had a habit for several weeks of putting it on daily with the intention of getting to the bottom of it once and for all. Then that chopping, plodding attack to "Cherry-Coloured Funk" would start and about 30 seconds in Fraser would swoop to the lovely note and join herself in lilting counterparts and my concentration scattered, distracted or buoyed or both by the ineffable. It's hard to say whether this is exactly comprehending music, or whether it's rather more something like finding a suitable background soundtrack to ignore. But now when I hear it again I know perfectly well, like muscle memory, what dodges and feints each song will take in the seconds before it does so and all the hooks and notes and various tricks. And it's indelibly connected with the feelings and experiences of the time when I was listening to it so slavishly, a mostly unremarkable period yet with its triumphs and disappointments and unique whatsits, the like of which I shall never again, etc. I always thought of this as the one from their well-stocked catalog that I just happened to land on, all of the rest of it equally distinguished based on what I heard, which just might be to say equally undistinguished, except by the force of what's brought to bear.

An anonymous visitor to my blog left this comment the day I posted the review above:

> I associate this album more with the concert tour that accompanied it. I had the album of course, at the time. In 1991, living in Minneapolis I had my life shattered irreparably by a girl who dumped me. I scraped

together what sanity I had left and continued to attend concerts, art shows, movies, etc. Alone every time. I felt strangely at odds with life and disconnected with it... like it didn't mean anything anymore. The concert was beautiful. I remember spotlights on motorized gambols that would wave around and radiate in sync with Elizabeth Fraser's voice and the (three) guitarists. A girl sat next to me during the concert who lived around the corner and was killing an evening. I exchanged a few words, she immediately spouted off about her boyfriend in Montana. She didn't have to worry about me coming on to her... I was beyond feeling anything besides emptiness and remorse. When the concert finished and the lights went up she leaped up out of her seat and ran away from me (!).

Anyway, the girl who dumped me lived in Boston. It was when I was making arrangements to be with her that she put a stop to it... months of planning wasted. I instead moved to San Francisco 'cause I figured I could hide the fact I was such a loser from everyone for a while. It worked, until about three years ago when my ex-wife divorced me.

Anyway, to sum it up I remember this album as one of those things that was there for me when everyone else was not.

(2010)

Paula Cole, "Where Have All the Cowboys Gone?"
(April 12, 1997, #8)
"It is not, truly speaking, the labour that is divided; but the man: divided into mere segments of men—broken into small fragments and crumbs of life, so that all the little pieces of intelligence that is left in a man is not enough to make a pin, or a nail, but exhausts

itself in making the point of a pin or the head of a nail" (John Ruskin). (1997)

John Coltrane, *A Love Supreme* (1964)

More time than John Coltrane's entire lifetime has passed since the release of this one. It seems to stand now outside and astride of time, fresh as a spring day, ancient as the earth, massive and gentle. Nothing and everything about it is familiar and well-worn, the grain of the horns, the sighing chants, the heights and depths risked on a path of spirituality. Yet, as the black and white cover signifies, it's composed entirely of grit and reality. Passion burns white hot and almost blinding, but the grit and reality are in the service of beautiful vision, naked vulnerable and endlessly present. It makes someone like me say things like this. (2007)

Elvis Costello, *Spike* (1989)

Elvis Costello's final dispatch from the '80s was every bit as accomplished as the two that had preceded it by three years. And sad too—life must have been dealing him a lot of lemons. As it happens, it was dealing me lemons as well, so I found something here that was at once familiar and yet foreign and strange, seductive and off-putting too, and really quite welcome. With this set of some 15 songs, Costello, aka God's Comic, retreated so far into British repression that he decided one song, an instrumental performed by the Dirty Dozen Brass Band called "Stalin Malone," does not even require words. Why bother? Just cursory glances at this and other titles give hint of the agenda here: "Let Him Dangle," "Deep Dark Truthful Mirror," "Tramp the Dirt Down," "Last Boat Leaving." Listen close and you can hear the sound of a soul chilling to rigor. Play it in the background and—you can't play it in the background. As temperate and considered as all the music stubbornly sounds on close examination, it's not music that will recede with any grace. It will only go away and that is achieved only by turning it off and putting it away. Otherwise it is the glum world of God's Comic, where humiliation and cuckoldry are the order of the day and "despair" is just another word for nothing left to say. I think it's humorous that this was Costello's idea of putting his best foot forward for a new label, Warner Bros., after leaving Columbia. I guess the singles are there if you want to look—"Veronica," a Paul McCartney collaboration, which even made the U.S. top 20. For me, it's in for a penny in for a pound—if it's going to be dark, let's make it coal black, as, for example, on "Tramp the Dirt Down," which is about a visit he envisions to the grave of someone who has not yet died even as I write, 21 years later: Margaret Thatcher. He can't wait for her death to happen, you see. I know that feeling, or something like it, though mine are related more to others, or at least to localized political figures of the United States, let's say, than anything to do with British politics. That's just there for the universality. After all, Costello takes nearly all of six minutes to consider the Thatcher graveside matter closely, which is perhaps above and beyond by anyone's measure of civility. Bitter, I'm trying to say. Very, very bitter. (2010)

Douglas Coupland, *Microserfs* (1995)
I have probably read enough Douglas Coupland by now that I should be able to make up my mind how I feel about him. In some ways it's tempting to reflect back his own tone of studied disaffection and shrug my shoulders. His novels read quickly, almost effortlessly, the narratives studded with the kinds of details and bric-a-brac of popular culture that it makes you happy to understand, but resentful not to—here a Popeye coffee mug, there some programming code, everywhere a lot of self-conscious irony and acute insight vying for supremacy. Ultimately I like Coupland most for his sweetly sentimental air, which might be the wrong reason. There's a gallantry to him that desperately wants the human race to do the right thing, honors father and mother and home, thinks there's more to a relationship than just sex, and never starts eating before everyone else has started. It's the one thing about him

that always surprises me. I should start with *Generation X*, which is probably the better book in most ways, but I lost my copy in a hotel room, and anyway, I love the first hundred pages of *Microserfs* so much that I'm willing to forgive the larger novel the wandering aimlessness into which it drifts. It's not, I'll say it right out, particularly redeemed by all its remarkable prescience, not only for the dot-com bubble but also for a good deal of the way we now live and orient ourselves toward the world, so heavily mediated by our sophisticated computer devices. Technically it's not supposed to be a book about Microsoft, except those first hundred pages quite patently are. And having been at the "Lazy M" myself, in years not far beyond those depicted here, I remain impressed with how swiftly, completely, and ruthlessly he captures it. Not everyone agrees, including any number of Microsofties I know, but I've never seen anything else close. Coupland did work there for a brief time, that's true, and that would help. But he's also got the wit and self-awareness to see it plain, and he brings a good many illuminating insights into the strange mix of arrested adolescence and precocious aging that holds sway around there, or did. The various quirks of the kind of people (and I would have to include myself here on some level, for better or worse) who gladly slave 60 to 80 hours a week because they're smart and the work is easy and fun and because someone has offered them unlimited amounts of free soda pop to do it. (2012)

Culture Club, *Kissing to Be Clever* (1982)

Boy George turns 50 next month, a statement of fact I am not entirely prepared to get my head around. To me, the "boy" part of George O'Dowd's self-selected appellation is still and will likely always be the most relevant descriptor. The arc of his career starts here, when he was barely 21. Culture Club stepped in, with Spandau Ballet, Visage, and Duran Duran, as one of the main players in the so-called New Romantic flavor of British New Wave in the early '80s. Perhaps more than any of them, Boy George and Culture Club drew convincingly on reggae and soul sources, with everything polished up to a high sheen of production, even as provocative titles such as "I'll Tumble 4 Ya," "White Boys Can't Control It," and "Do You Really Want to Hurt Me" promise a sultry garden of sadomasochistic sexual pleasures. Boy George has got a pretty good voice, and he figured out how to mimic enough of Smokey Robinson's sweet croon to transcend all the character flaws, starting with the willful outré manner and, especially, the coy transvestism. Right out of the gate Culture Club started scoring hits, and for my money the first of them, "Do You Really Want to Hurt Me," remains the best, a bruised and whimpering declaration of love in the face of unnamed threat and/or potential rejection that soars on the chorus. In many ways Boy George has gone on to live out the lifestyle he romanticized, even as he has found ingenious ways to make it work to his advantage—who else, for example, could possibly have been tapped for the theme to the movie *The Crying Game*? It proved to be his biggest hit since the salad days of Culture Club, and there he was again, charming as ever, on the TV talk show circuit. More often, however, he appears to have lived out the dark side, with lurid episodes encompassing heroin addiction, secret love affairs with straight men, and imprisonment for drug use, theft, and kidnapping. Nevertheless, in interviews he remains as charming and self-effacing a celebrity as one could hope for. A man of mystery, in other words—and with the potential still, I suspect, to surprise us all at least one more time. (2011)

D

erhaps because stupid people by reputation are prone to
saying "duh" (but more likely because of the letter grade),
the letter D comes with a deceptive reputation as a dolt-
ish underachiever. Note Tweedledum and Tweedledee, for example. But the letter grade, in fact, deserves a moment all to itself.
Think about this: "I got a D." What does it mean? Is it not a cruel
way of failing without technically failing, more on the order of a
humiliation, incidentally saying more about the system that designed the grade (duh)? But I'm sure it's also due to the way the
letter D also stands for things like down, done, don't, dirty, disgusting, depraved, denigrated, deranged, and degenerate. Well,
somebody has to do it! It appears to be a self-esteem problem of
some kind, always tending back again toward that familiar sem-
blance of underachievement. This raises a question. What were
the Greek alphabet makers thinking when they put D fourth in
line? Is it something about the mouth noise, the voiced brother
to the plosive T? And if so, what? As we have seen already with A,
B, and C, it isn't frequency of use that's winning this contest. The
letter D ranks only #10 on that scale—and that, no doubt, mostly
for its ability to throw verbs into the past. And doesn't that also, in
the end, actually make the letter D something of an *over*achiever?
Well, it does make a bit of a silly, pot-bellied figure, doesn't it?

All military posture on the left and then the flab on the right (or vice versa, approximately, face right, with the lowercase d). The letter D also belongs to the large family of letters that rhyme with E, their spiritual progenitor as it were: B, C, D, G, P, T, V, and Z. Represent! (I understand those with stronger ties to the British mother tongue are wont to say "zed" for Z, but that is a topic for another time, duh.) Another question: Does anyone *like* the letter D? Why? It seems unassuming to the point of bland neglect, somehow not quite there. And then somehow paradoxically it always manages to overachieve again. Consider: The strongest fingers on our hands are, as everybody knows (after the thumbs, duh), the middle fingers. And look who's sitting there under your left-hand middle finger with pride of place, waiting to take the punishment. None other than ... well, duh. Man, sometimes I think the letter D just sits there and waits to get everything handed to it on a platter. It's the spoiled, practically worthless brat of the alphabet. But wait a second now. It's also an honest letter, doing an honest day's work, with a single unique sound that no other letter uses. What's more, it's widely common among many, many languages, if not all of them. Somebody stop me from actually typing, "So credit where due." All right, we're done. (2013)

Damsels in Distress (**Whit Stillman, 2011**)
Director and writer Whit Stillman's first movie in over 10 years is silly and shrewd from beginning to glorious end, with other agenda items signaled in various ways: The title bears a close resemblance to *A Damsel in Distress*, a Fred Astaire vehicle from 1937 that also featured George Burns, Gracie Allen, and Joan Fontaine. Our modern-day damsels are named Heather, Lily, Rose, and Violet, a guileless bouquet that strides the campus of the elite Seven Oaks University like giants, attempting very hard to sort things out. Their distress is on the order of too much student body odor, too many suicides, and not enough compassion for fraternity house members.

"We're trying to make a difference in people's lives," explains the ringleader Violet (Greta Gerwig) to new recruit Lily (Analeigh Tipton). "One way to do that is to stop them from killing themselves. Have you ever heard of the expression 'Prevention is nine-tenths of the cure'? Well, in the case of suicide, it's actually 10-tenths."

The closest models are in Whit Stillman's other movies, with his unmistakable erudite dialogue—*Metropolitan* (1990), *Barcelona* (1992), and especially *The Last Days of Disco* (1998). After that, there's obvious affection for the '30s portmanteau, mixing up fanciful elements of comedy, romance, and drama, lathered over with musical numbers. Violet's greatest dream is to be responsible for starting a new international dance craze.

It's a great role for Greta Gerwig, who always seems a little strange and unnerving, with her impeccable sense of timing that constantly surprises. After rescuing a random girl named Priss (Caitlin FitzGerald) from an "attempted suicide in progress," Violet takes her to a coffee shop for cocoa. Priss opens up about her affection for the boy who just dumped her, speaking tenderly of a loving way he had of looking at her. "Do you know what I mean?" she asks Violet. Gerwig's response is a gem of subtle face movements and timing.

She's the star and deserves it but she is well supported by the others. Heather (Carrie MacLemore) does not speak often but listens well, with ever-varying displays of expression only now and then appropriate to the moment. Her face is a show all in herself, scene to scene. Rose (Megalyn Echikunwoke) has affected a British accent since a high school visit to England. She defends herself: "I was there, now I'm here … I'm *from* London." She is a childhood friend of Violet, which among other things is blatantly convenient for understanding the mysterious Violet. Rose is suspicious of everyone and everything, continually attacking people as "confidence tricksters" and their behavior as "playboy or operator moves."

Being a small independent film, it's packed with bunches of odd characters and developments. One of the frat boys, Thor (Billy Magnussen), has never learned the names of colors, a source of profound shame for him. Others, such as Rose, dismiss this as impossible to understand, which only adds to his suffering. "Ed students" have begun to attempt suicide by throwing themselves off of a two-story building, not understanding it isn't high enough to kill them, only maim them (therein lies the tragedy, according to Rose). Lily takes up with a French graduate student, Xavier, who teaches her the ways of Cathar lovemaking.

People are remarkably open in *Damsels in Distress* about grave or typically private issues such as suicide or anal sex. Violet falls into a depression midway—which she prefers to call "a tailspin"—and goes wandering randomly. In search of her, the others wander randomly too, or ride in golf carts, calling her name. Violet ultimately finds herself at a diner where the patrons and staff are observing her closely. They ask her if she's one of those college students who come down there to commit suicide by stepping into the nearby blind curve in the road.

So it goes. These are good, weird jokes, and they never really stop coming. As with all Stillman pictures, they are aimed directly at buffooneries of the American white-bread upper class, concocting characters who are eloquent and incoherent and hilariously foolish all at the same time. Here Stillman may even have topped himself with ludicrous exaggeration—the stupidity of the frat boys (remarkable), the suicide attempts (with nice sound work), Lily's naivete, Violet's many annoying ways of being presumptuous.

What saves it—if it's saved at all, because you pretty much have to be on board with Gerwig's style to get this far—are a couple of things. First, it's obvious that everyone is having a great time. The four principals, preening and prinking away, love the camera and it loves them right back. Watching MacLemore wrinkle up a smile as Echikunwoke high-handedly dismisses one more person as a playboy or operator, while Gerwig gazes off blankly the way a cat does when tracking something invisible, or how Tipton anchors everything as the sensible, bemused one who understands more or less they are insane (though ultimately she comes under the sway of Violet)—it's no less than intricate clockwork.

Then it all ends on not one but two big musical numbers, the first a rehearsal that transmogrifies into a song and dance performance of "Things Are Looking Up." Which is "swellegant" and everything, though suffering maybe a little from the obvious implicit comparisons to Busby Berkeley, Fred Astaire, etc., against which it inevitably falls short. I wish someone would give Whit Stillman the budget to try a few big movie musical numbers, because I think he could do it (he's as good as ever at disco, by the way, as the party scene here with "Another Night" makes clear). Then the Sambola, the attempt to launch an international dance craze, sends the movie out in high style. It doesn't really stand comparison with the "Love Train" ending of *The Last Days of Disco*—not much does—but it will do. (2013)

Destroy All Monsters, *To the Throne of Chaos Where the Thin Flutes Pipe Mindlessly* (1975)
This third of a 1994 box set sponsored by Thurston Moore, composed of studio and otherwise scrapings from Destroy All Monsters, is the one I can come closest to saying I "enjoy." Before Ron Asheton and the enhanced musicality of the band's later history were these children playing with their toys with the tape recorder running. Some of it, for example "It's Just Your Mind," which clocks in at 0:36, seems to be from a microphone pointed at a TV set. "Boots" is a cover of the Nancy Sinatra hit with a guitar break guaranteed to rip every face in the house off its head. Free jazz jams with wailing saxophones and feedback. Improvised percussion and sound effects. A lot of echo and reverb, clumsy double trackings. Kids giggling and

goofing around. Home tape recordings from a reel-to-reel, I presume. I don't know exactly what makes it so unnervingly creepy. But a cold patch you can't ignore passes across even if you just play it quietly as background. *Especially* if you just play it quietly as background. I think they mean it with that title. (2007)

Philip K. Dick, *Martian Time-Slip* **(1962)**
Martian Time-Slip is the first novel by Philip K. Dick that I can say blew my mind. On later rereading I isolated the effect essentially to one chapter, featuring an example of the title concept, which is only explained tangentially, by recourse to various significant words that are not exactly as we understand them, today or then. The most important is "schizophrenia." One key character here, Jack Bohlen, is described as "ex-schizophrenic." The paranormal abilities of another important character, the autistic boy Manfred Steiner ("autism" also gets a Dickian treatment) are equally grounded in terms of "faux" mental illness. Then there are the native Martians—yes, the book is set on Mars, in the 1990s—called "Bleekmen," who are similarly able to unplug from the perceived time stream. As a plot element, the Bleekmen remind me a good deal of aborigines in movies by Nicholas Roeg and Peter Weir. Finally, there is a can-do American spirit of the '50s, crystallized most in the person of Arnie Kott, a corrupt union official and small-time despot.

In the background are the harsh conditions of Mars and the bored empty lives of the humans living there. Arnie—he insists everyone call him "Arnie," coldly correcting anyone who calls him "Mr. Kott"—wants a schizophrenic who can predict the future (more accurately, project into the future) in order to get a leg up on his business competition. He drafts first Jack and then Manfred to his cause. The results for Arnie play much like a situation comedy or Rodney Dangerfield scene. He just can't catch a break, he can't win for losing, what's he gotta do, etc. Through random and often unmotivated betrayals, snafus, and setbacks, Arnie finally settles on a single point in the past to go back to in order to attempt to change the course of future events. The book is chronological, so that means we can see the moment of time and Arnie's attempted interference with it before we really understand what is going on.

Dick pitches his tone at the blandest levels—his language is rarely heightened but almost dead, which provides a rich loam for his bizarre and troubling ideas. Thus the particular chapter I'm talking about, 10, plays like a malfunctioning machine, resetting itself over and over. It is subtle, and terrifying, and no level of rational explanation later (which is neat but ultimately not enough, in terms of credibility) even comes close to a weird new sense of reality that never goes away. Or maybe probably that should be with the scare quotes: "reality." This is a great one. (2014)

Joan Didion, *The White Album* **(1979)**
Named for the Beatles album that does not actually bear the name, and about which it is anyway entirely silent, this may well be Joan Didion's best book. In many ways it plays like the album (or certainly side 4), an ostensible collection of essays that of themselves stand only arbitrarily as discrete units, often composed rather of fragments. They are tangentially related to a brooding sense of "the '60s," a concept forever maddeningly just out of reach. The title piece, for example, which opens the book, runs some 40 pages, touching on southern California life, rental homes, mental illness, serial killers, the ubiquitous dread of a knock on the door, the old Hollywood, the Doors, Huey Newton's health plan, traveling tips, Ezra Pound, campus unrest at San Francisco State College, the song "Wichita Lineman," Linda Kasabian, synchronicity writ intimate, and the afterlife according to the manager of a motel in Pendleton, Oregon, who happens to be a Mormon. Elsewhere, Didion attempts to establish the distance she's incapable of in regard to her homeland, California, about which she remains endlessly absorbed

in spite of herself. She examines women and the women's movement through the lenses, implicitly, of Doris Lessing and Georgia O'Keefe (the latter reminiscent of Didion's sincere regard and esteem for John Wayne, both as an icon and as a person). She travels to Hawaii, Colombia (foreshadowing some of her best '80s work), and the Hoover Dam. She attempts to explain the movie industry, authoritatively, from the inside. She apologetically breaks down the marketing physics of shopping malls. She takes to her bed with migraine headaches. If this is not her best book it's certainly the beginning of a string of them that continue to impress. The cryptic, elliptical style is first perfected here, the compression and poetic precision of her language, the nagging sense of dread balanced by attempts at irony, understood as insufficient and vain even in the act of making them, and the eternal yearning for a sense, any kind of sense, of this baffling kaleidoscope of American culture—inside of and beyond "the '60s," which haunt her. (2010)

District 9 (**Neill Blomkamp, 2009**)
It's probably no coincidence that the aliens in this Peter Jackson-produced feature film debut for director Neill Blomkamp, late of "Halo," look an awful lot like Alan Moore's old comic book antihero the Swamp Thing. They are certainly at once as ugly and as sympathetic, in this story of space travelers disabled by some equivalent of a flat tire on the shoulder of a galactic roadway. They have appeared here on Earth, and have been marginalized and abused by our good friends the human beings. If you can get past the fast-paced verite chaos of the handheld pseudo-documentary style, which is not that much to ask with a story as forward-propelled as this one, your heart will not only find its way in, but may break as well. I appreciated that, and also the spectacle of its conception. The giant spaceship hovering over Johannesburg (yes, Johannesburg) maintained an impressive brooding presence, not least because, as the narrative found ways to inform us, it had done so for decades, with no explanation (hence the response of

fear and hostility on the home planet). As for the allegory, well, it's about as obvious as it gets (I remind you its Johannesburg), but that doesn't mean it doesn't work. If the whole thing gets a little squishy in the second half—that's literally as well as figuratively—there's still an awful lot of functioning pathos on display here, and sadly believable, too. (2010)

Doors, "Waiting for the Sun" (1970)
Wikipedia covers the main points on a disambiguation page regarding any initial confusion: "*Waiting for the Sun* is a 1968 album by The Doors.... 'Waiting for the Sun' [is] a song by The Doors from their 1970 album, *Morrison Hotel.*" This oddness did not matter to my brother and his friends, who introduced me to *Morrison Hotel,* and especially "Waiting for the Sun," which they championed tirelessly. They recommended listening to it with headphones, an exciting new consumer electronic product at the time—and loud, needless to say. It was a galvanizing reintroduction to the Doors, following the hits I knew from junior high days. There's a context for it, I should mention—Jim Morrison & co. fighting for counterculture integrity after the disgrace of those pop hits, taking on the blues late, and incidentally in more trouble for alleged self-exposure antics on the part of Morrison in live performance in Miami. Talk about identity crisis. But the various shuttlings about between proto-gothy poets of doom, teen heartthrobs, and drunken white blues boys were surprisingly seamless, partly because they managed it by distending to embody the contradictions. And what a fine example we have in this song. Taking care of the teens is the easy part, with equal parts California sun worship and the skeevy Lizard King persona already well established. Then they proved surprisingly adept as a blues band, starting with *Morrison Hotel* particularly (the Doors as musical enterprise remain underestimated at one's peril). As for the poets of doom shtick, well, that's actually what makes this work. "Can't you feel it now that spring has come? / That it's time to live in the scattered sun." Key word here, I think,

being "scattered," which torques it just enough in a certain direction that it amplifies the effect of the band coming in so hard, lending it an almost majestic quality. Especially if you are listening to it on headphones. (2013)

Drifters, "Fools Fall in Love" (1957)
Jerry Leiber and Mike Stoller wrote this originally for the Drifters—a 1957 model of the Drifters, that is, which featured Johnny Moore on lead vocals. To me it's one of the purest pieces of rock 'n' roll to be heard. Elvis Presley recorded it a decade later and came as close as anyone to getting a hit out of it, but of course missing the charts only cements the case on some level for its purity. Brash and supple, uptempo with a vengeance, entered into on a brushed drumkit and gently choogling sax, Moore's clarion yelp is all over it in a matter of seconds, powered by doop-a-doo-wop background moaners and chatterers, interrupted briefly only for a solo in which a guitar plucked on the lower strings carries on a conversation of some erudition with the aforementioned sax before Moore retrieves it again and drives it to a glorious sunset. Over and done, 2:30. It's not a typical Drifters song, although, to be fair, it's not exactly easy to defend the idea of a "typical Drifters" song in the first place. Does that mean the Clyde McPhatter style typified by "Money Honey," or the Ben E. King style typified by "Save the Last Dance for Me"? Rudy Lewis was the singer for "Up on the Roof" and "On Broadway." Johnny Moore was back for "Under the Boardwalk," but that's not very much like "Fools Fall in Love." I'd say you're better off looking at the Leiber & Stoller songwriting credit, because they've got the credentials and they're the ones who knew their way around this kind of bright easy-rollicking sound with such supreme confidence. This is one for the ages. (2011)

Bob Dylan, *Highway 61 Revisited* (1965)
In 1965, "Like a Rolling Stone" was all over the AM dial when I started listening close to top 40 radio in the summer. Our babysitter

brought her own radio with her during the day that summer, tuned to the stations that mattered (in the Twin Cities, in 1965, that was WDGY and KDWB). I recall the rapid-speaking DJs were all excited about the song, and about Bob Dylan generally, hyping it and all the Dylan covers making it around that time (by the Byrds, Cher, Turtles, etc.). But I did not care for "Like a Rolling Stone"—it seemed to me too long, whiny, aimless, and sour, and already I resented pressure to like something by way of heavy word of mouth. As I recall, my own first purchases of 45s that summer were "Save Your Heart for Me" by Gary Lewis & the Playboys, "I Got You Babe" by Sonny & Cher, and "Help!" by the Beatles (as much for "I'm Down" on the flip as anything).

In 1970, on a garage sale outing with my father, I found a cheap reel-to-reel tape recorder in perfect condition. My best friend in high school, Peter, had a hip older brother in college, and Peter seized the opportunity to make tapes for me of things he thought I should hear. The first batch included albums by Miles Davis and the Mothers of Invention (Peter would also steer me to great shows by Captain Beefheart and Miles Davis in 1971 at the old Guthrie Theater in Minneapolis, my first concerts). One tape had *Highway 61 Revisited* on one side and *Are You Experienced* by the Jimi Hendrix Experience on the other. That was the one I could not stop playing.

In 1985, I moved from Minneapolis to Seattle, selling most of what I owned until I could get the rest to fit into a U-Haul trailer (which as it was barely made it over the third mountain range I had to get over, the Cascades). I knew I would need furniture, a kitchen, clothes, and other essentials, but I allowed myself the extravagance of room for a crate of albums. Half the fun there was the agony of picking and choosing, one of the ultimate lists I have ever made, and a welcome distraction from the ongoing upheaval in my life. It's exciting to move but also stressful, as you may know. I was just numbly going through it, one step at a time.

Highway 61 Revisited still mattered a lot to me, so its inclusion in the crate was a given. What surprised me, at the other end, in my new tiny studio apartment, with a view of the Puget Sound harbor, and the Olympics, and the spectacular sunsets of that September, was how the tremendous dimensions of the album somehow unfolded even further for me at that point. It wasn't so much a geographical connection between the Upper Midwest and Pacific Northwest, but more about reaching for and grasping certain high points in life. *Highway 61 Revisited* wasn't any longer just something I had liked a lot in high school. Now it sounded more fresh and vital than I had ever heard it. My days were spent wandering a strange new city, worrying about money and the change and finding work and what I was doing. In the late afternoon I shopped for food and beer and went home and played the album loud, baying at the sunset and often half-drunk or better by the time it was dark.

OK, so fair question, what's the connection among these events? What is the appeal of Bob Dylan? And/or *Highway 61 Revisited?* From my biased view, first, it seems as good as any litmus for one of the longest musical recording careers in all history (not least because the history of musical recording careers is not that long—but even so, no one has made more albums). If your opinion of *Highway 61 Revisited* is that you only tolerate it, I can see how some other Dylan album might seem better or even much better, *Blonde on Blonde* or *Freewheeling* or whatever. But if you don't like it at all, I have to think you may not like Bob Dylan at all. Interestingly, I understand that too, as I have also found myself deeply alienated from him, during the Jesus period of the late '70s and early '80s, and mistrustful for many years beyond that. He really can be so fucking annoying when you're on the other side of it—on the outside looking in.

But that's part of his game, isn't it? He has made a career of setting up polarities—in case anyone wonders how he got tagged as a protest singer, for example, there is "Masters of War." He implies his support for one extreme ("Masters of War" again, on the military industrialists: "And I hope that you die / And your death'll come soon"). Then, most often in some kind of media glare, he elaborately rejects those who have followed him to the point, and then it's on to the next circus crisis—working through this with folk, protest, rock, country, divorce, makeup (glam), Sam Peckinpah, Jesus, Daniel Lanois, death itself. So it goes.

That dynamic is core to *Highway 61 Revisited*. It's heard perhaps most explicitly in "Ballad of a Thin Man," which is more cutting than most of the loopy word salad and inspired punch lines of the rest. That dynamic is also the outstanding feature of "Like a Rolling Stone"—which, yes, of course I changed my mind about in time, as I grew up. In fact, it now seems to me compelling and irresistible, perhaps the first and one of the best examples of Robert Christgau's "semi-popular" pop music, neatly captured another way in its enduring #2 chart performance (do not miss it in Martin Scorsese's 2005 documentary *No Direction Home*). It's totally of a piece with the core Dylan dynamic I'm talking about and one of the most interesting and strangest hits in all of U.S. top 40 history, with way too much of everything—too long at six minutes, too smug and insular and wordy, and definitely too mean.

I'm pretty sure half the appeal of Bob Dylan is something about flattering oneself. I say this with all due humility. There is something you like about the idea of yourself in being able to get it—whatever "get" means exactly and whatever "it" means exactly. But a smug feeling of complacence, of course, of being safely on the inside, is not much reason for anything, as I learned when I grew up some more. It is, in fact, a deplorable way to proceed, tribal, primitive, and merely self-reinforcing. But I suggest that it happens anyway and we all do it on some level. And that it's arguable Bob Dylan is perfectly well aware of this—whether or not consciously so is another question, which I won't touch—because it explains the practically slapstick dimensions of his ever-hopscotching career, which has now lasted more than 50 years. He cannot escape it and frankly neither can his followers.

So here we are. I realize I have probably explained nothing. But I can talk about the album, as this is such a natural point for it. So much is so well known (again, see *No Direction Home*). It does not hurt that it is yet another amazing band among the many, many that Bob Dylan has assembled for the studio, this one led by Mike Bloomfield, and with Al Kooper famously faking it for all time playing an organ. The pastiche of roots Americana is singular and superb. But the main point for me about all nine of these songs, always, is how crackling alive and *funny* they are. It's word salad, it often doesn't add up, and the lampoonish assertions within the songs even negate one another. But the images are stark and swift, swimming up and flashing by, for example in "Tombstone Blues," which happens to be playing at the moment I'm typing this: the famous "sun's not yellow, it's chicken," one of the early surprises, a turn to King James with "death to all those who would whimper and cry," and the eloquent complexity (complete with punch line) of "Now I wish I could write you a melody so plain / That could hold you dear lady from going insane / That could ease you and cool you and cease the pain / Of your useless and pointless knowledge." I would not even necessarily call "Tombstone Blues" one of the "better" tracks, but it's hard to judge when everything here is as good as everything here is. The first side of the album has the greater contrasts in highs and lows, with both "Like a Rolling Stone" and "Ballad of a Thin Man." But somehow the four-song suite of side 2 has always opened me more to the extraordinary purities here, notably in "Queen Jane Approximately" and especially the epic "Desolation Row," which lasts nearly 12 minutes, going verse after verse after verse, and continually working its narrative points of view from new but contiguous angles, and featuring tremendous, amazing harmonica playing. Maybe now I'm just remembering the ends of those half-drunken nights new to Seattle, but "Desolation Row" seems to me still one of the greatest and most signal of Bob Dylan's many great songs, that has tremendous resilience and appeal and depths. As I say elsewhere, it's "at least 75% joy," title notwithstanding.

Highway 61 Revisited is nearly 50 years old now, so everyone has had fair opportunity to know what this artist, career, and album are all about, and, as always, in all things, it comes down to a matter of mysterious taste anyway. As for me, it's my favorite. (2013)

E

The letter E is the most frequently used letter in the English alphabet by a wide margin—12.7% of all letters. No other letter cracks even 10%. Without it, we would have to speak Nglish. There are some who want to do without it, you know. They're called lipogrammatists, and spend their time doing things like concocting entire novels specifically omitting it (*Gadsby*, a 1939 novel by Ernest Vincent Wright, perhaps the best-known example). Elvis Presley, of course, recognized E as the king of letters and used it for his first initial. (In fact, Elvis is arguably the more supreme king because he could have dumped it and gone as Lvis, whereas the letter E really needed the support in the 20th century, before electronics breathed new life into it. More on that in a moment.) The letter E is highly intelligent. Everyone knows that $E = mc^2$. As a vowel, not only does it take on all the usual burden of these overworked signifiers for vocal intonations—playing it long, short, and all manner of gentle keening and/or ape-like grunting sounds in between—but it furthermore signs up for a giant portion of work in a "silent" role, sitting at the end of a word to drop a hint about elongating the vowel in front of the consonant in front of it, as in "wide," "entire," "have" (kind of), "done" (well, not exactly), "gone" (oh, forget it). This busy beaver is also seen taking position behind certain consonants to soften (examples: "gently," "certain"). We liked the lowercase version of the figure so much that we turned it upside down to indicate the schwa, an "uhh" sound that could itself be the most frequently occurring vocal sound in the English language. Well, the electronics industry really did the letter E a big favor, didn't it? In the past 20 to 30 years it has taken on a high profile as one poster child for computer and online culture, perhaps most notably in "email" (does anyone spell it with the hyphen anymore? that would be an N-ormous relief). I've even had periods when I've personally considered E among my favorite letters. I might be having one now. Certainly it's my favorite vowel by a good sight. Because of the mysterious Great Vowel Shift, which set in along about the 14th century, and proceeded inexorably across the next three or four centuries, it sounds more like the I of most European languages and less like the way we presently pronounce A, which is the sound other European languages make with E. So confusing. How *do* these things happen? Something about the Black Death, I understand (note to self: avoid). Now here's something strange. The letter E does not appear in the standard letter-grade alphabet, which of course goes A, B, C, D, F. I recall hearing an explanation once that it was formerly used to indicate "E for effort" but was still a failing grade, a kind of de facto F+. After the way I complained about the D, can you imagine what I would have to say if that was still going on? (2013)

The Elephant Man **(David Lynch, 1980)**
It's possible *The Elephant Man* is overpacked with intriguing sideline elements that obscure how good it is. It's a key milestone in the career of David Lynch and his tormented relationship with Hollywood—his first mainstream and arguably breakthrough movie (with Mel Brooks quietly pulling the strings in the background to make it happen). It's photographed in black and white at a time when that had begun to imply artistic pretensions (and/or ambitions). And its lead player, John Hurt, is obscured (somewhat ludicrously) by pounds of makeup. It was popular too, earning eight Oscar nominations, including Best

Picture and Best Director, and even spawning a minor controversy when makeup artist Christopher Tucker was overlooked (with the result that the following year there was a new Oscar category: Best Makeup and Hairstyling).

I was surprised by how much it impressed me again. I saw it when it was new, and liked it, but somehow never went back. It's sincere in a way that reminds one how sincere David Lynch is, at bottom, once past his petulance and passive-aggressive misgivings about operating within the Hollywood system, including its trained-in audience expectations. *The Elephant Man* might even capture the moment before Lynch became unalterably jaded. I think there's probably a better case for that happening with *Twin Peaks*—or maybe this is just what he does every 20 years or so, as *The Straight Story*, from 1999, has a similar openness and vulnerability—but *The Elephant Man* is flawed in ways that feel like studio oversight and compromised screenplay decisions. At the same time, those decisions are also the foundation for what makes this movie capable of soaring.

As a monster movie, which is what it is first and primarily, *The Elephant Man* is capable of powerful moments, genuine shocks, and a true miasma of the queasy. It owes much to the aesthetics of horror films of the 1930s, in turn rooted in the strictures of Victorian era morality and central European fascinations with the lives of gypsies. It looks most explicitly to both *Freaks* and *Frankenstein* (and is not unmindful of Jean Cocteau's *Beauty and the Beast*), mixing up the elements of grotesque carny life and the monster movie pure. Based on real events (always a risky basis for anything in a movie because it is always an implicit promise of things that will be hard to believe), it doesn't properly clue us in to the realities of its particular monster, John Merrick, the "Elephant Man" (John Hurt), until very nearly the halfway point.

The Elephant Man is an early case of Lynch going to his extremes. It is, in fact, an extraordinarily beautiful picture, on many levels. The photography is luminous, high-contrast black and white with deep shadows and detail in every frame, warm and glowing. More than that, the narrative feels its way to fairy-tale conclusions that somehow convince, because the sources for despair in this picture are so equally convincing. Thus, the theater is redemptive, civilization constantly affirmed, and love conquers all—it's a first-rate 19th-century wet dream.

From the hideous being whose appearance gives us early chills and thrills, whose deformities are dryly cataloged in a presentation by Merrick's Victorian champion, Dr. Frederick Treves (Anthony Hopkins)—"... varying fibrous tumors that cover 90% of the body ... congenital skull exostosis, extensive pappillomatous growth, pendulous masses in connection with the skin," etc.—Merrick evolves into an exquisitely sensitive gentleman of society, that rare thing, a truly civilized man. And it is not only believable, it is achieved at speeds unimaginable, effectively transformed within the space of a single scene, a tea with Dr. Treves and his wife Anne (Hannah Gordon).

It is a tremendously powerful scene, but also the point where the story begins to stray into elements that strain credulity—an abusive night watchman with easy access to Merrick, and some things that develop from that. They are hard to believe, but they are also necessary because they are the part of the story that creates tension. It's not hard to go along with them for the sake of getting on with it. Paradoxically, it becomes easier to take then as more or less harmless fantasy, even as these events may actually be the historical facts, and even though there is a profoundly humanizing "message" driving them (indeed, this could be argued as David Lynch's most blatant message picture, though it's open to debate).

A transcendent night at the theater, which caps off this picture in style, unifies everything in a stroke, and the objective is achieved. It is practically a clinic, and certainly a masterpiece. Within the space

of two hours, a monster is created and then thoroughly humanized
in front of our eyes. As we come to know John Merrick, his monstros-
ity, his "monsterness," disappears almost entirely. The sight of him
is always hideous but we somehow come to not notice. The performances that surround him, Anthony Hopkins and Hannah Gordon
and especially Anne Bancroft as a kind of angel of the theater, simply
rub the edges of the repulsion away with warmth and love, until the
repulsion is gone. It is remarkable, a skillful blending of '30s horror
and Disney impulse all at once, with absolutely top-rate magic at the
end. Sublime. (2013)

Brian Eno, *Another Green World* **(1975)**
Brian Eno's best album is a quiet and gentle affair, though it opens
with a rasping guitar noise and goes on to entertain various pop
flourishes (e.g., "I'll come running to tie your shoes") and an almost comical range of textures, all in service of the high concept
signaled in the title. Once I might have been more eager to argue
the merits of *Taking Tiger Mountain*, which preceded it, or *Before
and After Science*, which followed it. But this is now the one I would
keep. It's seductive and sounds as fresh today as it did 35 years ago.
It's something that can be played several times in a day, for many
days in a row, in practically any context: alone, with others, first
thing in the morning, last thing in the evening, on a lunch break,
taking a long hike in the mountains, on airplanes, or as pre-show
music for practically any band in the land (now I'm getting carried
away). Some of the 14 songs here are quite short, less than two minutes, though in memory it's hard to remember which are short and
which are long, or even to come away with any precise sense of their
lengths at all. They seem to exist outside of time almost, embracing and immersive. Many are instrumentals. A few are straight-up
pop songs, complete with hooks, chorus, verses, and melodies fit to
sing and occupy one's head. Many are explicit about what they intend to convey: "In Dark Trees," "Sombre Reptiles," "Little Fishes,"
"Golden Hours," "Spirits Drifting." And while, as promised, it is

indeed otherworldly as a whole, it never feels particularly cerebral or overly detached or as if it is trying to be anything more than what it is. A number of the usual suspects are on hand here and there for the festivities, most notably John Cale, Phil Collins, and Robert Fripp. Solid. (2010)

Everything But the Girl, "Wrong" (1996)
Everything But the Girl is a long-time collaboration between singer Tracey Thorn and keyboard / guitar player Ben Watt, a British act much in the vein of other couple acts from the '80s such as Yaz or Eurythmics. In many ways EBTG got lost in the welter of '80s synthesizers and bombast, but lived on to play another day in the '90s, when they found themselves more or less naturally, if somewhat surprisingly, aligned with trip-hop flavorings of electronica. As with the Pet Shop Boys or Madonna, much of their best later work exists in the form of multiple mixes, much of which is worth chasing down because it nearly always has a sturdy foundation of songwriting, with memorable vocal performances gliding across the top. Thorn has a big voice, with sources located equidistant between soul and lounge, a place she occupies well. The 1985 album *Love Not Money* was my introduction, a fine album. By the time "Wrong" came my way, they had turned more toward the electronics. But Thorn's voice is what it is, an old-school instrument, and so everything she records comes with a certain amount of warmth and stirring depth. This is my favorite example of how they work those tensions to their advantage. I've mentioned elsewhere my theory about becoming the singer once you're learned to sing the song (with Buddy Holly and with Prince, though not quite yet with the Velvet Underground). Thorn's phrasing here, her timing in and around the soft-pedaled furry and metallic beats, is deceptively tricky business, harder than it seems, and I was pretty happy with myself once I got it down and could sing along note for note, notably when I figured out how to get the "'cos I was wrong" right. (2011)

Eyes Wide Shut (**Stanley Kubrick, 1999**)

A telling fact about *Eyes Wide Shut*: Ultimately it earned $55.7 million in the US on its release in July 1999, four months after director Stanley Kubrick's death, but $31 million of that (well over half) came just in the first week of its release. A transparent story of high expectations thwarted. One contingent had been excited to see the first Kubrick film in some 12 years, and the last ever, while others were excited about the "it couple" of the moment who star in it, Tom Cruise and Nicole Kidman. Still others knew it was going to be naughty and dangerous. What little these audience cohorts had in common came to include reviling the movie. I took them at their word and, on that basis (and also *Full Metal Jacket*, Kubrick's previous movie and perhaps his weakest), decided to skip it.

When I finally sat down with a copy of it on DVD years later, my expectations were as low as everyone else's had once been high. My primary concern was how I was going to get through the two and a half hours I knew it lasted. But two and a half hours later I was barely aware any time had passed, and I started it up again. It is that kind of movie for me. Even when it is at its most ridiculous—and it becomes very ridiculous—I can't look away. It gives me shocks of fear, pleasure, recognition, panged confusion. I consider it now as among Kubrick's best, one whose mystery just seems to open wider and go deeper every time.

At its heart it's about sexual anxiety—not the performance concerns that curdle into neuroses, but rather the gnawing misgivings about the desire itself and what it may lead one to do. It is about that coiled thing inside us we live with from adolescence. It has betrayed us all, probably, getting us mixed up in things we regret forever. It will likely betray us again. It is the answer to a question we're always asking of celebrities, "Why did they think they would get away with that?" Upper-middle-class Manhattan residents Dr. Bill Harford (Tom Cruise, deployed perfectly) and his wife Alice

(Cruise's wife of the time, Nicole Kidman) are put through the eternal drill of *desire / act / regret*, and once again the humiliating, punishing lessons of sexual ethics and morals are administered without mercy. Sex and "great danger" are conflated over and over. Encounters with death, however direct or incidental, only ratchet up the weird.

It's based on a short novel published in Austria in 1926, Arthur Schnitzler's *Traumnovelle*, which has been translated as *Rhapsody: A Dream Novel* or *Dream Story*. I don't know the book, but the movie proceeds very much like a dream, the source of much of its eerie power, moving with through-the-looking-glass contours of fantasy stories, and bearing sexual charges that come unexpectedly and at random, like earthquakes. Set at Christmas time, the darkest time of year but mellow with gauzy liquid lights and emblems of love and sanctity sincere and insincere alike, it is impossibly warm and ripe, with velvety overlays of blue and yellow and deep reds and oranges. It feels in moments like decadence itself, or, more literally, decaying-ness.

The story is propelled by a late-night post-party conversation between Bill and Alice in their place on Central Park West, sharing a marijuana cigarette, a conversation that spins off into a senseless argument and finally a confession by Alice of a mild infatuation she experienced recently, one she never came close to acting on. Something about the story gets its hooks into Bill's most vulnerable insecurities, setting him up for a series of strange incidents that will last nearly all night and beyond. They start when he is called away from the argument on a medical matter (or shortly after he falls asleep that night?). Using a strategy Kubrick also used in *A Clockwork Orange*, every scene Bill visits before a looming transformational experience he will revisit again, suffering his punishment.

One of the most disorienting (even annoying) aspects of the picture is the lugubrious pace of many of the scenes. A lot of these characters are marching to tunes only they (and Kubrick) can hear. Kidman delivers nearly all of her lines ... with ... implied ellipses ... between ... every few ... words. This is not poor direction, let alone poor acting, it is just another tool in the arsenal assaulting us every step of the way, knocking our sense of things cockeyed and adding to the overall effect.

The movie is set up to disorient. It's true of the famous New York soundstages (the movie was actually filmed mostly in London), which supply a good many of the exteriors and a gnawing sense of fakery. There's a little three-block radius "in the Village" we come to know well, as one does certain places in dreams. It is true of any number of scenes—a woman's unexpected and inappropriate declaration of love for Bill practically over the body of her dead father, a Russian costume shop operator and his nubile daughter, not one but two cheesy girl-next-door prostitutes, and, of course, the big kahuna of *Eyes Wide Shut*, the elaborate masked ball in the mansion, with all its strange sights and sounds. Nothing makes sense here and yet somehow everything does, at incoherent levels.

The masked ball truly seems to be what separates the believers from the nonbelievers on this movie, and so the obvious place to throw out a hearty "your views may differ." I am too intoxicated with the sensation of it to be bothered by how outlandish it is. I know that's there, even in the hour or so it goes on, but I don't care. It is what I love most about the whole thing, the point when it reveals itself as essentially a horror movie filled with phantasms. I can't take my eyes off it. It is masterfully done. It feels overwhelmingly dangerous, toxic, decadent, thrilling, and a little sickening all at once. In the moment, I believe absolutely that those people in those cloaks and masks possess and wield great power. This is beyond the almost proletariat Greenwich Village Satan-worshipers in *The Seventh Victim*, the Val Lewton thriller from the '40s, and even beyond the unmistakably sinister and malevolent kindly-senior-citizen midtown version of *Rosemary's Baby*. The Vegas showgirl style of nudity and sexuality so ostentatiously on display in that gothic palatial mansion located somewhere in the New Jersey countryside is deliberately and lasciviously grotesque and repulsive—and, I think, even plays knowingly to that reaction in us. It verges precariously on camp. That's true of the whole movie. But it walks that line skillfully, not once tipping over into it by my sights. It takes its time to get to this and then just lets it all unfold naturally, the way one prepares for and engages in sex itself. It's very close to perfect. Play loud. (2012)

F

orrect me if I'm wrong, but it seems that even within my lifetime the letter F has become best known as the euphemism for the heavy lifting of the single most reprehensible, offensive, not to mention the raunchiest, rawest, and dirtiest word in the English language. I hear people saying things like this all the time: "I told him to get the F out." "What the F are you talking about?" "It's none of your F-in' business." And so forth. It's possible this is mere misperception on my part, as I recall similarly believing once that "motherfucker" was a term invented in the '70s, which happened to be when I came of age and adults started swearing around me. (Which reminds me—children, please stop reading this now.) Indeed, so common is it that more and more now it's rendered as "eff" (get the eff out, none of your effin' business, etc.). I guess there's always been a whiff of the lewd in the way that F makes you bite into your own lower lip, however gently. Consider: five fuzzy French frogs frolicked through the fields in France. There's a degree of erotic play embedded in the sounds of those words (mitigated by the presence of swamp creatures), focusing on the things one's mouth must do to say them. That's F all over for you! It's a fine, sturdy specimen of a letter. I like how straightforward and unpretentious it is about doing what it says it will do. Stands up straight and tall, points east. It's got a spine, balance and poise; no need for the lower bar of the capital E. No nonsense, no exceptions. It's the life of the party too. F makes such a popular sound that G and P have thrown in with H to get a piece of that action: "laugh," "phlogiston," etc. But F plays no such shape-shifting pronunciation-changing games as those, except winsomely doubling up on itself now and then (off, gaff, miff), which is the only hint that it may suffer any insecurities at all. Now and then it pretends to be V, as in "of." Is there any such thing as a ludicrous "silent" F? No, I think not—it is always that touch of the front teeth on the lower lip. F represents not only the dirtiest word ever invented in the history of humanity, by the way, but also serves as the disgrace of failure in our education system. F is for failure. F is for flunk. F is for you're fired dumb fuck. But F is also for forget, helping with the kindness of putting all of that behind us and moving on. F is also for flute and it is even a musical note itself (the one, as it happens, for those who know *The Sound of Music*, that is a long long way to run, on the C major scale anyway). F—for fine folks everywhere. (2015)

William Faulkner, *Light in August* (1932)
Of the handful of great William Faulkner novels (and keeping in mind that even the second tier of his work is probably above the top of all but a few others), *Light in August* is probably the most fun to read, a big juicy pulp-fiction style of melodrama that swoops about among its elements like a bird of prey. There are elements of this degree of storytelling power in *The Sound and the Fury*, but then there is also that novel's first hundred pages. *As I Lay Dying* is studied experiment. And both "The Bear" (which it's probably more accurate to call a novella because it's so short, so make that the *Go Down, Moses* story cycle) and *Absalom, Absalom!* have long passages in which the language must be parsed slowly and patiently. By contrast, *Light in August* tends more toward simply introducing its themes and players and setting them in motion, working everything with facility and seeming ease. I think it's closer to the

lurid gothic template into which he wanted so badly to fit *Sanctuary* (which, I will say, nonetheless remains very nearly one of his great ones too). To be sure, *Light in August* is not without the Faulkner trademarks of ornate brooding passages and elliptical structures, with long sentences and some tendency to favor the Latinate. The flashback, for example, to the troubled childhood of our antihero Joe Christmas (one of the great literary names) starts Chapter 6 with: "Memory believes before knowing remembers. Believes longer than recollects, longer than knowing even wonders. Knows remembers believes a corridor in a big long garbled cold echoing building of dark red brick sootbleakened by more chimneys than its own, set in a grassless cinderstrewnpacked compound surrounded by smoking factory purlieus and enclosed by a ten foot steel-and-wire fence like a penitentiary or a zoo, where in random erratic surges, with sparrowlike childtrebling, orphans in identical and uniform blue denim in and out of remembering but in knowing constant as the bleak walls, the bleak windows where in rain soot from the yearly adjacenting chimneys streaked like black tears." But that kind of thing is generally more for the effect here, and doesn't constitute the bulk of it. Me, I find this language utterly hypnotic, particularly once fully under Faulkner's sway, but I understand it doesn't work for everyone. As a study in racist anxiety, a continuing underpinning theme all through Faulkner's work, *Light in August* veers more toward the clinical (not to say Freudian) understandings of "hysterical"; but also toward the connotation of "very funny," in which regard it may sometimes seem almost badly dated. On the other hand, some days I look around at things happening all the time in Southern politics even now and I have to wonder how dated after all the kind of grotesque, deep-seated racism documented here really is. (2011)

Roberta Flack, "Feel Like Makin' Love" (July 6, 1974, #1)
Not to be confused with the Bad Company song of the same name one year later. Although, with the ongoing corporatization of rock

'n' roll in those years, they perhaps stand equally as heralds of a new way to sell, sell, sell w/ sex to undazing hippies and other children—"adult contemporary" and "classic rock," by name. I was less aware of that at the time, with all the other breakdowns going on. Indeed, I have wonderful memories of this song on the air in the late summer of 1974. I mean literally on the air. I heard it swelling from apartment windows and cars most unexpectedly, most welcome, as walking with friends on the Nicollet Mall in Minneapolis one night, on one of those gorgeous, still, warm but not hot August nights, coming from a taxicab puttering along. I'm prude enough that the frankness of the song made me blush a little—have always thought "making love" an awkward way to talk about sex (with or without our friend the gerund-friendlyin' apostrophe). But that's me. On the other hand, Roberta Flack sounds like a woman in love, not in heat (again, compare Bad Company for the dopey male version of the usage), and that is what makes this song particularly beautiful and affecting in spite of my efforts to resist it. It is indeed a harbinger of adult contemporary to come (more often than not a problem, I admit, though I like surprising amounts of it from the '70s still), with its sultry, swirling, softly treading electric accompaniment. The lyrics unfold a wonderfully romantic and domestic scene that sounds as healthy as a walk on the beach, with a happy ending. Winner. (2014)

Flamingos, "I Only Have Eyes for You" (June 8, 1959, #11)
The Flamingos were a doo-wop act out of Chicago who kicked around the various alleyways and lonely streets of rock 'n' roll for much of the '50s. Then, finally, came this, their big moment—and what a moment. Written originally for a Depression-era movie musical and also recorded in 1950 by Peggy Lee, the Flamingos turned it into one of the most gorgeous confections of the rock 'n' roll or any other era, powered by soft Chopsticks-style playing on a piano, layers of echoing shimmer on the imposing backing vocals, and a tender melody and lyrical preoccupations to die for. "Are the stars

out tonight? I don't know if it's cloudy or bright," warbles lead singer Nate Nelson, softly and carefully landing on each note. "I don't
know if we're in a garden, or on a crowded avenue." "CH-BOM CH-
BOM," his accompanists respond, which clarifies nothing but its
own stunning effect. You might hear it a thousand times and then
one time—perhaps in the many movie scenes where it has been
used (*A.I. Artificial Intelligence, American Graffiti, Heart Like a Wheel,
The Others, The Right Stuff,* and many more), perhaps on an oldies
radio station when you are making a quick trip to the grocery store
for a red pepper—it finally catches you unexpected and strikes you
dumb with the pure beauty of it. For how many fortunate couples
does this stand as an "our song"? Many. It would have to be. Many,
many, many. After all, this version alone has been around more
than 50 years, and it sounds as fresh today as it must have to the
class of '59. (2010)

Foreigner, "Waiting for a Girl Like You" (Oct. 17, 1981, #2)
Following the playbook of hard-rock / metal bands of the late '70s
and early '80s, Foreigner breached top 40 charts with this "power
ballad," by which is meant a soft-rock or adult contemporary ballad performed by a band with a stake in continuing to appear hard
and macho, though the song isn't at all. Consider "Beth" by Kiss
as primary model, or "Love Hurts" by Nazareth. Also note: that's
Thomas ("She Blinded My With Science") Dolby on the cascading synthesizer keyboard, which as much as anything makes this
song—in the break leading to the chorus, when it wells up into the
grinding, plodding, and impossibly beautiful doo-dee-doo-dee-
doo-dee-doo-dee, etc. Sublime moment. Evidently I was waiting for
a song like this because it struck hard. I'm not a Foreigner fan, but
"Waiting for a Girl Like You" arrested me totally and completely.
If pressed, I would probably still have to categorize it as that most
useful and evasive pleasure, the "guilty" one. It's certainly a coincidence—I would swear to this—that I had just taken up with
a new girlfriend at the time, someone I considered very special

(though no one else I knew then, including her, particularly liked this song). It came late in my career as a dedicated follower of top 40, when radio stations in the US were already busy carving up hits across new and different formats. It came pouring out of the radio in the delivery van I was driving at the time, echoing through parking garages where I made my stops, and it never failed to stop me short, moody, sweltering, and so fine. (2014)

4 Months, 3 Weeks and 2 Days (Cristian Mungiu, 2007)
This small-scale and ferociously intense story of late-period Communism, set in 1987 Romania toward the end of the harsh regime of Nicolae Ceausescu, made such a terrible impact on me the first time I saw it that I wasn't sure I wanted to see it again any time soon. When I finally did return to it recently I was interested to see just how much the sophistication of its aesthetic contributed to my first experience—how carefully and deliberately the whole thing is put together.

The premise is simple, but calculated. Gabita (Laura Vasiliu) is pregnant and wants an abortion, which is illegal. Gabita enlists Otilia (Anamaria Marinca with a disaffected nonchalance that is often brilliant), her fellow student, roommate, and friend, to help her. The picture is a chronicle of their efforts to accomplish this on the day set for it—borrow the rest of the money they expect they will have to pay, connect with the abortionist, find a hotel room in which the procedure can take place, dispose of the fetus, and so on. All of this is set against a stifling inertia of bureaucracy and queasy numb apathy that hovers and penetrates all.

The movie has no political agenda about abortion, I suppose I should say. It could never have been made in present-day America (or even America of 1987), which is a telling point. Rather, it takes the need for some terminations of pregnancies as a given of the human condition, of youth and of sexuality. It finds the subject a useful way in to a larger theme: the pervasive intrusions and humiliations of a society that does not particularly value privacy. At the same time, it appears perfectly comfortable with how much discomfort it knows it is likely to provoke. Always the approach, paradoxically, is with a light hand, bearing the mask of a finely tuned thriller.

Director and writer Cristian Mungiu's filmmaking is fresh and confident, even though this is just his second feature. He relies quite a bit on long takes, with the camera equally willing to move or to hold still and watch. When the camera moves it's evident someone is there, holding it, or walking just behind Otilia as she goes from place to place. This contributes even more to the sense of the picture's constant assaults, large and small, on privacies we take for granted. There is a baseline acceptance among all of the characters that one is always watched, one way or another. Part of daily life is to accommodate that.

As the picture goes on, Mungiu begins to cut off people or parts of their bodies with the frame. We see their chests but not their faces, for example. In a dinner party scene, we hear the voices but don't see the faces of people beyond either side of the frame. Again, this adds to the sense of violations of privacy. The camera and we by proxy are physically *too close*. In the last third, after dark, Mungiu is unafraid to let the frame go mostly black, as Otilia wanders the streets and up and down alleys and into the stairways of buildings, trying not to draw attention to herself when she encounters strangers.

More than anything, however, and ultimately what makes it work, *4 Months, 3 Weeks and 2 Days* is a sharply drawn character study. As Gabita's irresponsibility and unwillingness to confront her situation continually lead to further and further dire consequences, with which the vaguely cynical Otilia just persists in coping (albeit fraying), it veers toward becoming a kind of carnival-night hell house ride, an over-the-top exercise poised to explode unpleasantly at any moment in some potently visceral way. Once started, the skin never stops crawling, and the picture remains steadfastly believable even as the most outrageously unbelievable things begin to occur.

With Gabita and Otilia grounded so naturally in their environments as college students, they bear a certain familiarity, within which they seemed like people I've known. And just when I was coming to realize, remembering them, that I had maybe better stop caring so much, that's when it's too late. I cared. The screenplay is a marvel of efficiency, hooking one in helplessly, operating in fast strokes at unconscious levels.

Though it often feels clinical and studiously free of emotion itself, this is a film that knows well the reactions it expects to provoke, and they are not cerebral. The narrative here is so insanely compelling, so effortlessly a claw-the-armrest suspenser, that it can be easy to miss the art, and so, as if to remind us of the art, Mungiu picks a way to end it that is so sharply abrupt it can't help calling attention to itself. In that moment of confusion, even as the relief of its being finally over sets in, it forces you to look again and think and realize what an impeccable moment of timing it is—as, indeed, the whole movie, from start to finish, can fairly be characterized as a series of impeccable moments of timing. (2012)

John Fowles, *The Magus* (1966)
John Fowles's thick slab of high concept now seems more pulpy to me than literary, playing successfully to the obvious tropes of a thriller more than to finely wrought conundrums of human psychology, which it seems to be after (let alone the kind of literary pyrotechnical sleight of hand Fowles would attempt later in such fare as *The French Lieutenant's Woman*). Its gender politics are central to the story and, unfortunately, badly dated, likely a fatal problem for it now. Nevertheless, it makes for a fun and baffling romp through a confusing world of illusion, paradox, and deception. Inspired, according

to Fowles, by the strange and appealing novel *Le Grand Meaulnes* by Alain-Fournier, *The Magus* tells the story of Nicholas Urfe, an unpleasant Oxford graduate student who finds himself washed up with a teaching assignment on an isolated Mediterranean island. There he meets a mysterious wealthy recluse, Maurice Conchis, an older Greek man with a shrouded past, an intellectual bent, and sadistic tendencies, who has a predilection for staging scenes for something he calls "The Godgame." They are elaborate and often cruel set pieces designed to teach their target, usually Nicholas, some kind of lesson. As the games become more oppressive for Nicholas, they grow from a strange diversion that preoccupies him while he is on the island into a consuming, potentially dangerous obsession that even begins to have dire effects on his life back in England. For the most part Fowles plays fair. Even as the action remains as straightforward as it is weird, the real motivations behind it—who is who, who knows what, and why these things are happening at all—remain the enthralling mystery that carries all the momentum. The first time I read it, in my early 20s, I had a copy that was missing the last 120 pages, which about drove me batty and which I wasn't sure for some time wasn't just another trick engineered by Fowles. The second time through, more recently, I made sure ahead of time that I had a complete copy (recommend that you do too), and while it remained as diverting as ever I found it more difficult to enter into the fantasies whole. The resolution is not entirely free of disappointing cheats—mostly the kind of "you decide" ambiguities that more typically indicate an author who couldn't. Still, if the payoff is a bit of a letdown, the trip there is anything but. (2011)

G

With the letter G we reach the end of the musical scale, but most of the alphabet is still ahead, and that's something to sing about. G is another consonant that presumes more than a single sound to itself. There is the "soft" G, which sounds like a J, as in "judge" (there's also an even softer G found in "rouge"). And there is the "hard" G, a sound only this letter makes, which is a vocalized swallowing sound, a kind of spasm of regurgitation, as in "gulp." Go to the phrase "beige garage" for a look at this busy letter in action. Go "garaging" for a look at another sound G is involved in, in combination with N. This sound is fairly common in English (it's right there in the name of the language, you see, and even in the word "language"), as among other things it denotes the gerund form: singing, bringing, binging (wait a sec). As with so many letters (e.g., F, X), G has found a way to be sexualized, in this case by its association with a woman's so-called G-spot, the mysterious source of non-clitoral orgasms. (Side issue: Does "orgasm" count as onomatopoeia?) G is certainly related to babies, who by reputation are wont to say, "goo goo, gah gah," though I suspect relatively little documentary evidence exists for this. G is thus elemental and profoundly human, though it also seems somehow negligible. There are also times when it sits there and goes silent, as in "gnostic." K and P also volunteer for this psychologically unknowable "function," whatever it is. And then there is the pact of silence G also holds with H, as in "right." Aaand it can also makes an F sound, again when combined with H, as in "laugh." When does this letter sleep? In many type fonts the lowercase G is among the most beautiful of all letters, with its sense of the descender as a kind of liquid coiling pool. For all the work that it does, G doesn't have much significance on its own. Well, sometimes it can mean "thousands," in terms of money, viz., "That new boat set me back nearly 80 Gs." G-men came along with the FBI in 1928 to hunt gangsters, as we will see shortly. Astronauts seem to like G too, the way they talk about their peculiar intimacies with gravitational forces. Somehow the letter seems a little old-fashioned now. Gee ... golly gee ... gosh golly gee ... gosh golly gee whiz, and so on. Poor old-fashioned G, a letter already set back too far in the alphabet to distinguish easily. No one gets a G in class, and no one anywhere needs to know their GHIs. From here on out letters are more and more going to depend on the sequencing of the alphabet for their immediate identities. The second tray of letters in the alphabet the way I learned it is F, G, H, I, J, and K. It's the only line with six letters; all the rest have five, probably because I and J are reasonably thin, even when they are capitalized. By contrast, G is among the biggest of all letters, so go figure. (2015)

William Gibson, *Neuromancer* (1984)
I was happy to take another blast through this much praised pioneering science fiction classic, and came up about where I expected. The byzantine multilayered plot, its inheritance from hard-boiled detective fiction, lost me pretty fast, as these plots will, while the imaginative near-future visionscape impressed a good deal as always—and even more, the gray dense metallic language Gibson uses so skillfully to suggest that visionscape. *Neuromancer* seems to me now to move much more like a graphic novel, image by image, word balloon by word balloon, piecing together the complexities of its plot and its ideas, even though it was ahead of most such formal

novel-length illustrated enterprises. The action here arrives almost entirely on spindle legs of concept, which is its deeper inheritance from science fiction—so fully realized, in fact, that it invented its own subgenre, "cyberpunk," stories of infinitely cool, vaguely Asian, technologically superior, anonymous youth, living and sur-viving in a world of smoldering disaster zones and sophisticated communication. Even though I'm not always 100% certain I know what's going on here (along with a good many of the characters to keep me company), and even though the narrative sometimes is so elliptical that all detail of plot points is lost in the blinding edgewise views, I always feel like I know this world on some natural level, and that is what remains most eerily seductive about it. It feels convincingly like a place, a time, a way to live and perceive, some-where that existed. On the other hand, times change and so do perceptions. I find that I understand less now than I ever did some of the basic animating concepts, such as "jacking in." It seemed so intuitive at one time, so exciting and mysterious, but now I associ-ate it more with browsers that won't load. To that extent, at least, *Neuromancer* may be suffering some tarnish to the gleam. But not by much. (2012)

The Godfather: Part II (Francis Ford Coppola, 1974)

I understand too well the irresistible idea that more equates to better. If one is good, two is better, and three even better. *The Godfather: Part II*, Francis Ford Coppola's large-scale sequel to *The Godfather*, followed the original by a couple of years and comes with more of everything: more minutes, more cast members, more locations, more budget for more production values. It's bigger in just about every way imaginable. The result has produced a spectrum of strange, beguiled responses. Many flat-out call *Part II* the better movie. Others make an argument that at first seems reasonable that it is all a single film. This is likely because Coppola has on more than one occasion obligingly edited them together with footage not in either movie (and thrown *The Godfather: Part III* into the mix too, after that came along), creating giant interwoven amalgams whose last incarnation approached 10 hours. (I have seen none of them.)

I'm here to complain so I'll be complaining in a moment, but I want to be clear. I have little quarrel with the broad critical consensus which treats *The Godfather* and *The Godfather: Part II*, as two separate movies, and/or hailing *Part II* as the greatest sequel ever made. I think I agree on sequels with Roman numerals; but I may be more partial to *The Good, the Bad and the Ugly*, which is actually the third of a series, or perhaps to *The Bride of Frankenstein*. My problem is that I don't think *Part II* ever manages escape velocity from the almost perfect gravity and moral clarity of the first. It seems more content to wallow in that picture's hard-won accomplishments, taking good advantage of the greater resources afforded the sequel in reworking them. But there's a great emptiness to it other than what's intended. Coppola has rarely been in better form; and with a much bigger budget and more cooperation from the studio than he had with the first, he's given his head here to simply go forth and work out very fine sequences. The period detail is richer and more convincing than in the first. The screenplay is nearly as full of lines that have become coin of the realm: "Keep your friends close, but your enemies closer." "I don't feel I have to wipe everybody out—just my enemies, that's all." "I'm smart and I want respect!" Numerous fine performances, large and small, appear all through, and the scenes are expertly staged, blocked, and executed, with the players at the top of their games. Gordon Willis's photography is every bit as good—better, even, elaborating a trick I didn't notice done nearly as well in the first, which is to shoot his figures in interiors against the outdoor light from windows, rendering them as black shapes yet with identifiable profiles, the very epitome of dark actors.

But in the end, *Part II* is remains an echo and lumpy extension of the original, returning to the same ground and treading the old footprints. In fact, *Part II* rehashes in obvious ways many of the most memorable moments from the first. Kick off the picture with a lavish and grotesquely overdone party even as "the Godfather" conducts business behind closed doors—check (in the first it's a wedding, in *II* it's a birthday / confirmation party). Intimidate public figures with gruesomely elaborate extortion tactics—check (in the first it's a bloody horse's head in the bed of a powerful Hollywood movie producer, in *II* it's a dead, and bloody, call girl in the rented bed of a U.S. senator). Juxtapose a religious event with cold, efficient violence—check (in the first it's a baptism ceremony cross-cut with a series of assassinations, in *II* it's an Easter parade cross-cut with Vito Corleone's first assassination).

There's no denying the strengths of *Part II*—it's dark, beautiful, repulsive, and so well appointed. For a movie that lasts over 200 minutes it does flash by. But a recent misunderstanding I noted at the Wonders in the Dark blog helped clarify my problems with it again. Someone mentioned their favorite scene in the original *Godfather* was when Michael closes a door in Kay's face. Someone else gently reminded the first person that that scene occurs in *Part II*. The first person then gently pointed out to the second that he had actually been talking about the famous ending of the first. But a door in Kay's face does recur in *Part II*, and it's one of the best scenes in it.

For me, *The Godfather* actually tells a dramatically dynamic story with a narrative arc that unfolds naturally across its events. Michael Corleone, a World War II hero, has rejected his family's old-world Sicilian values, but he is inexorably drawn back into their orbit out of events that occur in combination with his love for his family, and finally he is corrupted. *Part II* starts with that corruption already in place and plays a three-hour-plus game of "how low do you go?" It essentially starts on the moral level in the original of the baptism scene and takes us ever darker and deeper in.

Eye of the beholder, and all that. It could be as simple as that I have little interest, or maybe the word is "stomach," for machinations of power, which in the end is all that *Part II* is about. Men with power (yes, *men*) go to extraordinary lengths to hold, maintain, and expand that power. This is news? No, but then, in fairness, neither is "people who love one another often don't treat each other well," which is the kind of story I myself am always ready to watch another version of. So if *Part II* seems to me too often to go well off the rails and wrap itself around the thickets of a byzantine plot involving the brutal calculations and gamesmanship and betrayals among three men I simply don't find that interesting—Michael Corleone, Hyman Roth, and Frankie Pentangeli—well, that might be just what the doctor ordered for others. And the 200-minute running time? The longer the better. (2011)

Goodfellas (**Martin Scorsese, 1990**)
As brash and kinetic and sustained as anything director and writer Martin Scorsese has done, *Goodfellas* is personal, defiantly anti-formal (all rules governing voiceover narration and freeze-frames summarily tossed, for example), and a critical twist on the operatics of gangster pictures as we had understood them until then. If, like *Pulp Fiction*, it now has much to answer for in terms of setting in motion clichés and other noxious pop culture memes still calcifying, this original suffers none of their deficiencies.

In fact, that is one of its great surprises of *Goodfellas* again and again: its pure crackling energy. Somebody in the special features on the DVD remarks that no one flipping through TV channels and landing on *Goodfellas* ever changes the channel again until the movie is finished. It's true that it is insanely engaging, with a powerful narrative current. Part of the trick is the shift in focus, which moves away from the wood-paneled and predictably corrupting counsels of power of the *Godfather* franchise (or even De Palma's *Scarface*) and instead concerns itself solely with the foot soldiers of the criminal enterprise, out hustling to earn. It's the same sickness of the soul, but now it's Chekhovian rather than Shakespearean.

The other part, and the great power of this picture, lies in the voiceover narration, which emerges as the most pungent character in the film. I'm not exactly talking about the gangster Henry Hill, whose story this movie tells, nor Ray Liotta, who plays Hill and provides most of the voiceover (one more rule broken: while there's mostly just one main narrator, another voice does almost impolitely intrude). That nervous, jittery voice that propels the story is charming, repellent, vital. It is as much as anything co-writer Nicholas Pileggi's contribution, based on his extensive taped interviews with the real-life Henry Hill (who says in one of the DVD special features that the events of *Goodfellas* are "95% to 99% true"). Ultimately, it is Henry Hill's actual spoken words that we hear much of the time. That makes this, in many ways, effectively a documentary embedded inside a lot of basically familiar cinematic gangster tropes.

As part of the process for making *Goodfellas*, Scorsese would work with Robert DeNiro, Ray Liotta, Joe Pesci, and others on improvisations that he recorded and transcribed and used to patch together the script. For example, the set piece scene in the nightclub where Tommy DeVito (Joe Pesci) tells a funny story, Henry tells him he's a funny guy, and Tommy has a strange reaction. That was all worked out as scripted lines more or less by the time the scene was shot, but once again the weird amalgam is there of the cinematically expressive and the documentarian, which compresses a tremendous amount of energy and tension into the scene.

It is a little tour de force in its own right, in fact, in a picture full of them, large and small. The largest and best may be the one that occurs in the last third, in the long section headed "Sunday, May 11th, 1980, 6:55 am"—Henry Hill's very bad day. The movie itself seems to come untethered before our eyes, entering Hill's cocaine-fueled delirium and observing him closely as he tries to keep it together on what otherwise appears to be only a moderately more stressful day than usual for him. He zips around town on errands, with a helicopter often flying overhead above him. It is riveting with its freewheeling jump cuts, rambling breathless voiceover, bizarre panicked behavior, and dread as far as the eye can see, all of it powered by a truly remarkable sequence of soundtrack choices: "Jump Into the Fire" by Harry Nilsson, "Monkey Man" by the Rolling Stones, "The Magic Bus" by the Who, "Mannish Boy" by Muddy Waters, and others, which perfectly punctuate the images and narrative events swimming by.

In fact, Scorsese cements his reputation in this section and all through *Goodfellas* as perhaps the greatest movie soundtrack artist ever. The soundtrack could arguably be the greatest single thing about *Goodfellas* (vying with the screenplay, principal performances, and cinematography). He hand-picks hit singles from the '50s and '60s and tracks from rock albums with a judgment so singular and so apt that it almost works retroactively to redefine some of these songs: "Then He Kissed Me" by the Crystals, "Roses Are Red" by Bobby Vinton, "Sunshine of Your Love" by Cream, "Atlantis" by Donovan, and "Layla" by Derek and the Dominos. I found a list on the Internet with 43 songs, from "Rags to Riches" by Tony Bennett to "My Way" by Sid Vicious. That is approximately exactly the scope of this remarkable movie, truly one of the greats. It is gangster ethos straight up— nothing else matters except what you can get, and family (next stop, of course, *The Sopranos*). *Goodfellas* is exhilarating and repulsive and always mesmerizing. (2012)

Grateful Dead, *Live/Dead* **(1969)**
As for the Grateful Dead, I have circled back on myself so many times I'm not even sure exactly where to pick up the thread. But I can say at least, at long last, I have the decency to recognize this album for the stirring and mysterious set that it can be—notably,

"Dark Star," the 23-minute opener occupying the first side of the vinyl double-LP, which periodically reenters and rules my world again, often after dark in quiet rooms alone. Candles burning, etc. More recently, "Death Don't Have No Mercy" and the eight-minute feedback sculpture (capped by the tremblingly beautiful but very brief "And We Bid You Goodnight"), which occupies the fourth side, have emerged as stellar points in their own right. "St. Stephen" and "The Eleven," side 2, at one time were my favorites, along with similar passages from *Anthem of the Sun*. That leaves only the 15-minute Pigpen goof made out of "Turn on Your Love Light" left for me to make peace with (which, to be honest, would not seem to be coming any time soon as it still seems to me indulgent and unnecessary, though I know Pigpen has his partisans). "Dark Star" remains my chief way in here, truly one of the great album sides along with *Bitches Brew* side 1 ("Pharoah's Dance") or *Electric Ladyland* side 3. Partly for such reasons I was tickled to find a "single version" of "Dark Star" on the expanded version of this album now available—that such a thing would exist never occurred to me. But sure enough, there are all the singing parts polished and marshaled in a row, with even some flavor of the guitar breaks scattered in lightly, tidying up at a relatively scant 2:42. Interesting to hear it conceived that way, because I so much prefer what is done with the longer version, which feels its way into the many strange places it travels. It's a jam but not what I think is more often implied by the term, a sort of communal rocking out with turns at solos. Instead it operates like intuition, mimicking and anticipating daydreamy kinds of thought patterns in endlessly eerie ways. It's even hard for me to focus on it as music once it starts to play; it is much more like a place I move through, or that moves past me, familiar but never quite known. I lose my concentration somehow, as it produces a sensation of returning to a city long abandoned, but whose streets and sites I still know well, embedded into neural pathways but out of the reach of consciousness. I know where it's going, I sense the turns even as they approach, I never feel lost, and yet it is always beautiful in ways I can't anticipate. It still surprises me. (2012)

Norman Greenbaum, "Spirit in the Sky" (March 7, 1970, #3)
If it's possible, I love this song now more than I did in 1970. Actually, it's quite possible, because I took it so much for granted then. Notwithstanding, it was always mysterious. Who was Norman Greenbaum and why was he saying these things? I explained the religious bent to myself then by assuming he was a Jesus freak, as we said, for which I forgave him (my more generous years). But it never stopped seeming strange sitting there in the middle of the radio, the impeccable rock 'n' roll instincts as context for words about dying and a friend in Jesus and such, with handclaps, and all with no evident hint of worry about anything (and no irony either). Always, always irresistible and best played loud. With Wikipedia to help, we find out that songwriter and performer Norman Greenbaum, with connections to the Lovin' Spoonful and Dr. West's Medicine Show and Junk Band (not to be confused with Dr. Hook & the Medicine Show), saw Porter Wagoner on TV one day and decided he wanted to write a gospel song, a thought experiment on his part about what went into one. Obviously he took liberties because you don't usually hear that kind of raw fuzz tone electric guitar on a gospel recording, but that's exactly what makes it so special. It sounds so blasted powerful, vibrating and wrapping itself around your head, and his voice with a sound as big as outer space. No wonder I took it for granted he'd had a vision. In a way, he did. We need more visions of that kind too, the kind which result in raw fuzz tone electric guitars. (2014)

H

et's hear it for breathing. The letter H is a funny thing, funny peculiar not funny haha. It poses formally as an exhalation of breath, and even that is dropped at the start of words
in some dialects, such as British. But then it goes behind the scenes
and collaborates with other letters to pervert their purposes and
its own and produce a whole laboratory of mouth noises, many
of which, in a rational universe, would have their own unique letters. Take H with C as in, e.g., "church." Why couldn't that sound
be assigned to that fraud C? And what about H with S, producing a sound that has only one meaning in society, aka STFU. I ask
you, what does that sound have to do with either S or H (beyond
a certain sibilance)? Then there is H with T, another fundamental
sound element of English but also one not appearing everywhere
and thus notoriously difficult for native speakers of some other
languages. And more frauds: H with G and H with P, as in "laugh"
or "physiology," which are perfectly adequately covered by F. And
can anyone anywhere explain the pairing with W. Wut? Oh, H, that
sly ape-shaped letter, going on its rounds about the language, sow-
ing trouble and confusion wherever it goes. How about that debate
over the indefinite article? Some say in front of words that start
with consonants it is without exception "a," while others argue for
"an" in certain specific situations with H, such as "history." They

seem to believe that "an history of New England" somehow sounds "better," which I happen to believe is a classist reverse-engineered artifact of that H-dropping British accent we spoke of a moment ago, which also sounds "better" to some ears. Can you detect I am an absolutist on this question? It's "a," only, for words beginning with H. Except when it is absolutely silent, as in "honor." Oh bother. Speaking of foreign noises in foreign languages, I have the impression that H in Arabic and perhaps other languages of the Middle East and elsewhere, can take on that non-vocalized rasping throat-clearing sound of the German "ch." We don't have much of that in English, the way other languages don't have much of "th." I do like the simplicity of the primary sound of H, that little contribution of carbon dioxide. What else is close in terms of basic building blocks of the sounds a human mouth can produce? Perhaps S, or, on the vocalized front, U, by which I mean the schwa, "uhh." Hey, look, there are Hs aplenty to inflect solo vowel noises too: "ah," "eh," "oh," "uh." Which one of these things is not like the others? That's right, "eh," which is pronounced much less closely to its original vowel, usually rhyming with "gray," essentially a speech noise that asks either for confirmation of what was just said, or a request to another speaker to repeat something because the user is not sure he or she heard it correctly. H—busier with part-time work than you perhaps suspected. (2015)

Harptones, "What Did I Do Wrong?" (1957)
The Harptones, a mid-'50s vocal group out of New York, helped establish a whole wing of the music that came to be known as "doo wop." Along with the Orioles (probably the true originals), and various forays by others, they perfected an innovation of bending a droopy-dog tempo and gospel harmonies to the burden of a soaring, deliberate vocal lead. They had a coulda-woulda-shoulda star in Willie Winfield, plus an arranger, Raoul Cita, who was built into the act (piano player and baritone), and in their fleeting moment nailed a few good songs. The Harptones never had a hit, not even

on R&B charts. Their best-known songs include "Sunday Kind of Love," "The Shrine of St. Cecilia," and a version of "Life Is But a Dream." I don't think "What Did I Do Wrong?" is typically considered top-tier for them, but I think it's just wonderful, my favorite by them. It steps in with a good bit of deceptive pomp and dignity, then a pause, and then ladies and gentlemen Miss Carol Blades and the song is underway proper. As it moves in deeper, it proves to be almost a little frail, led by Blades's big voice wielded like an instrument piercing the swirl of harmonies, which alternate between thick washes lush as velvet curtains and more free-floating probing lines standing up and sitting down like big dogs yawning, and way off in the background a small band, tapped and brushed drums, a bass, a piano. It hits a real nerve on that big start particularly with the great line of the title, delivered so tenderly and with such naked heart. (2012)

Ernest Hemingway, *Green Hills of Africa* (1935)
I had the impression *Green Hills of Africa* was a novel, but it's actually nonfiction, a travel adventure dressed up in some of the clothes of fiction. It features the stark alternation between blocky paragraphs of description and pages of dialogue that is typical of Hemingway. A brief Foreword somewhat awkwardly implies he is working the territory we now call "creative nonfiction," the "nonfiction novel," and/or "new journalism." To be fair, Hemingway was there long before Truman Capote or Norman Mailer. It's possible to make the case for *Green Hills* as a species of novel, but chiefly it bears comparison to a Hemingway novel, which reduces its innovation quotient. My favorite parts were when he talked about, or showed people talking about, reading and literature. Some of the hunting scenes were good too. But as usual Hemingway's ego squats in the middle of everything and stinks up the joint a little. We find out about his petty jealousies over the hunting successes of another. Hemingway's girlfriend on this safari, unbearably referred to as "P.O.M." (we find out what it stands for at the end,

but I've forgotten and looking for it now is somehow too depressing), is a case study in what has been called—just as unbearably, I admit—"codependency." It's a creep show. I know I complain about Hemingway's stoic, long-suffering shtick, and I suppose I should be happy he is exposing himself warts and all here. But I'm not. And why? Because Hemingway seems so determined to depict these character flaws as unchangeable facts of life which must be borne up under, delving into overly detailed rationalizations. It looks uncomfortably to me like an abuser cycle of eruption and contrition, with no sense that it can be dealt with and changed, or even that it's particularly a problem to be addressed, except by way of confession. So we are back to the stoic and long-suffering, and this book of confessions. Even so, if one can look away from that (and you see it's hard for me), there are many lovely passages here, and I certainly enjoyed it more than recent revisits to a couple of Hemingway's more celebrated novels. (2014)

Jimi Hendrix Experience, "Third Stone From the Sun" (1967)
"Third Stone From the Sun" is at once so blown-open and so gentle, a weird mix of lush and inhuman, harsh and daffy, making a conceit out of the god-like perspective of the title and never shrinking from going as big as it can. Ceaseless wonder, that's big—bigger than anyone could have imagined for a little pop song. I use "little pop song" figuratively because this is mostly instrumental, all of 6:44, and is actually epic, big as worlds, a vast vision, encompassing and superseding the solar system and/or galaxy itself, and finally an end-of-the-world story. The words are fragmentary, with many long patches obscured and virtually indecipherable from the production, but the story is about aliens coming to visit the earth (in a "kinky machine"), disapproving of what they find, and destroying us. It is funny in parts: "Although your world wonders me, / With your majestic and superior cackling hen / Your people I do not understand, / So to you I shall put an end / And you'll / Never hear / Surf music again." Dick Dale wept. When the end comes it is strange and desolate, elegiac and moving. (2012)

The Hitch-Hiker (**Ida Lupino, 1953**)
"It is the only *film noir* to have been directed by a woman," *Halliwell's* says a little solemnly of Ida Lupino's gritty highway drama. It looks fine, with stark black and white contrasts and a wonderful use of Western landscapes. She has a sense for how to do this, that's for sure, perhaps from her experience in *High Sierra*, one of the great 20th-century Westerns (*Hud* another good example), of which there should be more. Enough already with the 19th century Westerns. William Talman (aka district attorney Hamilton Burger from *Perry Mason*) is surprisingly believable as the desperado, aided by some freaky eyeball work I don't remember ever seeing on the TV show. (2013)

Buddy Holly, "It Doesn't Matter Anymore" (March 9, 1959, #13)
I have long held the theory that learning to sing with this, note for note, hiccup for hiccup, and with every nuance preserved of the eccentric Texan accent that keeps poking through, is better than any séance for raising the spirit of Buddy Holly. You become him. (You think I'm joking. I have also studied the effect with Everything But the Girl, Prince, and the Velvet Underground.) The significance of this song goes well beyond painful irony and the usual "hear my train a-comin'" folderol. Those strings, which predated even the recordings of the Drifters from the Brill Building era, mark an innovation in rock 'n' roll studio work that, though it would also suffer great abuses later, nonetheless accomplishes what it's meant to here, sweetening the sound, classing up the joint, and implying a tremendous amount of unfulfilled promise. Like salting watermelon, those strings provide an ideal counterpoint, an unexpected balancing element between Holly's nerdy affect and his Texas twang. At the same time, there's not actually anything sad here at all except, pro forma, the lyrics and, ipso facto, the context of its release. In fact, the sound is positively exuberant—help me thesaurus: animated, bouncy, brash, buoyant, ebullient, effervescent, *life-affirming*—thrusting itself into the world, with the strings zooming up and down and all

over, going pizzicato and then all swirly, while the music and lyrics remain eternally and perfectly intended for one another. A genius product of poetry and melody, a glorious and happy accident to counter the unfortunate one that preceded it, and a really great note on which to go out. (2010)

Hüsker Dü/ Replacements, Minneapolis (1981-1985)

I don't like the term "Amerindie," it's nearly as ugly of a word as "blog," but it's the scope you need to start with for Hüsker Du, the Replacements, and Minneapolis in the '80s, which I was fortunate enough to be around for (until 1985 anyway). Hüsker Dü and the Replacements would make their lasting outsize impacts on pop music and rock 'n' roll currents, but there was another powerful stream of Minneapolis music in the '80s coming from the north side of town in the person of Prince Rogers Nelson, who contended with them for ultimate supremacy of influence, musicianship, songwriting, guitar playing, hip cachet, future of rock 'n' roll, what have you. It's clear now who made the biggest dent—and more importantly, by implication (especially when you factor in those Amerindie dominations of Hüsker Dü and the Replacements), just how much fun it was to be in Minneapolis at the time. Note: As a native more or less of the Minneapolis environs, I come with all the in-built prejudices. Please read "Twin Cities" or "Minneapolis/St. Paul" whenever I say "Minneapolis."

Within that Amerindie scope, there was a vaunted Minneapolis tradition that traced back to the Trashmen ("Surfin' Bird"), Castaways ("Liar, Liar"), and Novas ("The Crusher") in the mid-'60s, and then carried on into the '70s with acts such as Skogie & the Flaming Pachucos and the Suicide Commandos. Aided and abetted by a nightclub in downtown Minneapolis called Jay's Longhorn, all this led to the Twin/Tone label in approximately 1977 and a rash of often worthy acts: the Suburbs, Curtiss A, the Hypstrz, and others (*Big Hits of Mid-America Volume III* is the essential document here). Besides the

Longhorn, much of this activity was hived around a record store in south Minneapolis named for Skip Spence and Roy Harper albums, Oar Folkjokeopus. And here it was that arrived one day a fabled demo tape which became a record contract for the Replacements. An instant legend too good to be true, they were impossibly young—Tommy Stinson, the bass player, was 14 when the first album came out in 1981, *Sorry Ma, Forgot to Take Out the Trash.*

My own involvement, as usual, was late arriving. I knew many people who were very excited by the album but I've always appreciated it only in pieces—and insufficiently, as I think now that "Johnny's Gonna Die," for one, is much more an amazing song than I understood for a long time. I did not properly catch up with the Replacements until the EP follow-up of the next year, *Stink*, which opened with audio verite of Minneapolis police breaking up a rowdy party, and contained two instant classics by title alone (fully delivered on in the music) in "Fuck School" and "God Damn Job." Inspirational verse: "God damn it, god damn it / God damn, I need a god damn job." I wrote up a review of the EP and several other albums that also came out that summer in an attempt to get a god damn job as a rock critic, and somehow it worked.

At that point, I still had not seen the Replacements, but the editor at the college paper who started giving me review and story assignments was Dave Ayers, already an enthusiast. In 1982 and 1983 I started going out to see music more than I ever had, and soon enough I saw Replacements shows too. I think the first I saw was on a Friday night at Duffy's in south Minneapolis. It was a "bad night"—I think you know what I mean. They were reeling drunk. Guitarist Bob Stinson (Tommy's older brother) was wearing a dress and appeared to be feuding with Paul Westerberg. They were kind of bumping and muscling each other around the little stage, hitting at each other with guitar necks. It looked like rambunctious antics but then you'd catch their faces—they were really mad. The band would pull it together for a song, or for part of a song, sound pretty good, even great, and then they would blow it for the next two or more. I didn't find it very charming. I had a suspicion they were overrated.

Late in 1982, Hüsker Du's second album *Everything Falls Apart* came out. At that point, Hüsker Dü was somehow distanced from the buzzing around Oar Folkjokeopus, even though it was one of the principals there, Terry Katzman, who put out the band's first two albums on his Reflex label. By all signs Twin/Tone never had much interest in the band. Already there were concerns at the label that the Replacements' *Stink* was too "hardcore punk." Hüsker Dü was definitely hardcore punk, in the developing California and DC sense of the term. In performance, they were also more like macho acrobats of playing fast and loud. They were from St. Paul, or beyond. Something was not quite right about them. And I think everyone agrees still that the first album, *Land Speed Record*, a live set, was all but unlistenable.

But *Everything Falls Apart* was something else again. There was a cover—of Donovan! The title song was epic and layered. Lots of pop hooks and lots of good ones. Though still in the loud / fast / heavy vein, it appeared now to be a loud / fast / heavy vein they were actually authoring as they went. Later, of course, Hüsker Dü became the ones that got away. After SST signed them around 1983, their really remarkable run started, first with a very good EP, *Metal Circus*, followed by the double-LP concept album *Zen Arcade*, at which time their imposing ambitions and abilities became apparent.

In the summer of 1984, I interviewed Grant Hart and Bob Mould and published some newspaper stories about them. I'd seen them once or twice before the album came out and then started making a point of going to all their shows I could. In retrospect, by my experience, Hüsker Dü at the time looks more like an invention of the future than the Replacements. I'd never seen shows like theirs before, and it feels like I have seen a great many of them since. Hüsker Dü

109

set a certain template. I'm talking about the moshing specifically, the notion that the circle emanating directly in front of the stage, and perhaps about the size of the stage, becomes a place for the audience to rehearse rioting. Bodies fly in and out and all about—stage diving and crowd surfing were just later, further permutations. I learned that my favorite position at these shows is one or two rows back of the moshing—the sight lines are good and there are bodies to protect you. Sometimes the people in front melted away and left you exposed, even as the music, felt in the bones it was so loud, kept playing, and then you had to pay attention, with arms positioned loosely out front to catch bodies as needed.

These shows—in spaces such as Goofy's Upper Deck downtown, where signs on the walls advertised "businessmen's special" lunches for the strip club below—were loud, physical, exhausting, cathartic affairs, almost like a workout on some hot summer nights. Another interesting feature was reflected in the way Hüsker Dü was going about making a career at the time. Around *Metal Circus* or *Zen Arcade*, they started getting one album in the can ahead of their releases, and were working out the next album in performance. When I was seeing them regularly in 1984 they were mostly playing the songs from *New Day Rising*. Thus that element of deep familiarity with the music was precluded. You went to the shows to hear unfamiliar stuff they were working on, to get familiar with it yourself show by show. There weren't always that many crowd-pleaser chestnuts. There was a kind of survivor's kick about getting to the end of them, and lots of unexpected highs as the new songs became familiar.

By 1984, however, it was the Replacements who were the darlings of Minneapolis. The lively and inventive *Hootenanny* came out in 1983, and New York was onto them then. There the Replacements sojourned in the spring of 1983, hungry for a break, and had some good nights and bad nights and generated more details for the legends. In winter 1984 I saw them at the hippie-era blues club the Cabooze, on the edge of the West Bank neighborhood of Minneapolis, in what may qualify as legendary circumstances. The peaks they were capable of were mostly sustained that night. They sounded good as a band and when that was true anything could happen, because they always had an arsenal of great songs and an amazing hilarious taste in covers. Then, for whatever reason, they felt like playing that night, and they continued doing so—past last call, past the house lights coming up, and even with the bartenders and staff hanging around arms folded and looking somewhat annoyed (not all of them). Bear in mind that bars closed at 1 a.m. by law in Minnesota. Maybe the band was just used to playing later from being out on the road. They played until almost 2 as I recall. A great show.

Let it Be came out in the fall. I thought at the time that it was uneven, but it struck with a mighty wallop and became inevitable and inescapable in my world of Minneapolis. I saw a competent show at First Avenue but they felt distant and inhibited, and didn't appear to be particularly into it. For whatever reason, I never did see them do well in that venue, whether it was the "big room" of First Avenue, which functioned much of the time as a danceteria (Prince's stomping grounds then) and also hosted touring acts, or the adjoining small venue called 7th Street Entry, a tiny wedge of space (formerly a kitchen) that housed many amazing shows in its own right, in my time mostly variations of punk-rock. On a good night you could shuttle back and forth between the great dancing grooves and crowds in the big room and into the bawling squall immediacy in 7th Street Entry.

Interestingly, the last truly great show I ever saw by the Replacements was in Seattle, shortly after I moved there. It was in late November of 1985, at the Astor Park (since demolished), downtown near the monorail line. They were touring in support of *Tim* and they were just great that night, never better, generous and joyful and on fire. They held court in the grand style, mixing up all my favorite originals with lots of surprising covers. It's sort of a bittersweet

transitional memory for me now. Bob Stinson was a critically important part of the band, and for better or worse I don't think they were
ever the same after they kicked him out. He was that good—or he
was that good when he was good, because we know how the narrative of the legend goes, which also has the benefit of being somewhat
true: never a better band, but also never a worse, a schizophrenia
played out randomly. I have followed their exploits since with varying levels of interest—Hüsker Dü too—but all that is mostly beyond
Minneapolis, and after the '80s. (2015)

I

I t's not hard to see that the letter I is the single most egotistical of all 26 of them. This is even more true given the great vowel shift in the English language in the Middle Ages. And despite its deceptively modest appearance: a single vertical line, adorned formally top and bottom with little horizontal hat and shoes. Just a vertical line? Oh, please. I will leave the phallic implications aside, but look, it's the one letter that arrogates to itself the singular first person. When someone mentions I they are always talking about the most important person they know, every time. Then there's the little matter of the pronunciation, most especially that long I, again best exemplified in the singular first person. One vocal noise is not enough for this imp, at least not since the blasted muddling Middle Ages. Whereas once (and still, in most European languages) we were only required to bleat "eee" in order to sound it, now we must throw an "aw" in front of that, very nearly multisyllabic style. This is so firmly embedded that aw-eee, for one, find that aw-eee must take a moment and listen to what aw-eee am saying when aw-eee say aw-eee. Traw-eee it yourself. Note the jaw movement. Thirty years ago, the rock star Prince, in his still handy and often useful and even prescient compressions of the language, reduced "you" to the letter U (and U know we'll be talking about that again), now a favorite of smartphone users everywhere. Even more interesting for our purposes here, Prince complicated I in a wonderfully poetic way with the graphic image of an eyeball. I'm not sure how much I like it in practical use, because I'm not sure it registers properly in the reading. Yet it makes beautiful sense when viewed as the secret actual ego of the letter I, its id let's say, betraying its profound narcissism, looking "out" but probably looking for a mirror, right? Prince's I presumes itself to be the naked window to the soul itself. Nice one. It is otherwise unprepossessing, this phallic rod—9th letter of the alphabet, third vowel. But I say again: don't be fooled here. I has ambitions to be the all of everything. If you took a poll, you would find that a near absolute majority always agrees with I. These people have no scruples and fewer morals to clutter their terrible predispositions and inclinations. They only think of I. In its lowercase version it has planetary pretensions, the only letter in the English alphabet with a satellite detached yet forever attending it, that dot which you must dot as you also must cross Ts. Ha—when comes, at long last, the eclipse, I? I ask U. I blends with E to inflect the sound in either long direction—U say E-ther, I say I-ther—at random, willy-nilly, depending on the choice of the speaker. But that's neither here nor there, either. (2015)

Iggy & the Stooges, *Raw Power* (1973)
Aficionados will appreciate the decades-overdue remix supervised by the Ig himself over the weird (make that rank amateur) treatment from David Bowie the first time around. Me, I always appreciated the songs themselves more than anything. They remained ferocious even in Bowie's teacup. Of course a remix is going to bring out the, er, raw power, bigger and badder than ever, and so it does. It can right pin you to the wall. I'd like to think that if the job had been done properly first time around, the Stooges might have started crowding Led Zeppelin in the arena megaspaces. But then I remember that this was also when the principals became heroin addicts. (2006)

See also: Iggy Pop, Stooges.

I Love You, Man (**John Hamburg, 2009**)

As much as I enjoy laughter, I have to admit I'm not particularly versed in latter-day American film comedy. I think this one may fall loosely under the "Apatow" label. Director / screenwriter John Hamburg is more closely associated with the Ben Stiller industrial complex, carrying writing credits on all three Fockers travesties, *Zoolander*, and *Along Came Polly* (the last of which he also directed, and the only one I've seen that I liked even approximately). Stiller himself goes way back with Apatow, but more than anything I think it's the familiar faces of Paul Rudd and Jason Segel that are giving me the impression, along with the omnipresence of a congenial try-anything gross-out aesthetic.

I liked this movie when it came out and then I forgot about it, but seeing it again recently I was surprised by how much closer it is to classic romantic comedy than many comedies today (including, especially, what's marketed as rom-coms). Indeed, it is actually quite faithful to the formula, except the formula has been turned askew. The couple that marries at the end the movie, Peter Klaven and Zooey Rice (Rudd and Rashida Jones), are basically OK all through. It's finding Peter a best friend so he can have a best man at the wedding that's more the problem, and therein lie all the familiar "meet cute / break up / make up" dynamics.

The basic strategy of turning the tables is a stunt reminiscent of one Tina Fey pulled for *30 Rock*, in which she gave her character Liz Lemon one of the most amazingly well-adjusted and happy families ever seen in popular culture. Everyone here (except Jon Favreau) has not just good hearts, but glowing, golden hearts. That is one of the picture's great charms. They are all naturally and convincingly playing variations on Ned "Okely Dokely" Flanders from *The Simpsons*. The fresh-faced Rudd as a Los Angeles real estate agent is already a good match for this with his gentle manner, but he takes it up a notch. Now he's a nice guy who's not very funny but never stops telling dumb jokes, and somehow becomes funny that way. "Play a U2 record while you're there," he tells a group of his pals who are heading out for a weekend camping trip at Joshua Tree. That's about the level of all his jokes, and they are constant.

Rudd carries the movie for the first 20 minutes, and then Segel comes along as the would-be best friend and best man Sydney Fife. These names! Both of "Peter" Klaven's significant others, Zooey and Sydney, are carefully gender-ambiguous. With the appearance of Segel, the whole thing takes off. I'm not sure it's right to say Rudd and Segel have chemistry, but it's close enough. They are more like train wrecks on parallel tracks. Whatever it is, it commands the screen. They are funny—there's clearly a lot of improv built into these scenes (and/or scenes built out of improv)—but the screenplay is solid too.

The intimacy sought for here necessarily, of course, finds its most profound elements in side-by-side dynamics, as opposed to the face-to-face kind normally animating a rom-com. Peter and Sydney hang out, shoot the shit, get fish tacos. They talk about girls. They talk about sex. They banter back and forth with rhythmic nonsense phrases. They give one another nicknames. Sydney calls Peter "Pistol Pete" and Peter calls Sydney "Joban" and "Siddy Slicker," both of which fall flat of course. Eventually, perhaps inevitably, perhaps even predictably, they bond over jamming to the music of Rush.

Rudd and Segel are fine but there's also a great supporting cast, starting with the surprise of a glowering, overweight Jon Favreau as Barry, the asshole husband of one of Zooey's best friends. He stalks around and feels continually about to explode with rage or heart failure or both. Barry has a dorky raw sexuality and a "smokin' hot wife," as Sydney puts it (Denise, played by Jaime Pressly). The lives of Barry and Denise are endless rounds of fights and make-up sex. "Well, if I do this, we have sex with the lights on when you get home," Barry mutters to her, conceding a point in a fight. "Just like in Jamaica ... All night long." ("Fine, whatever," she snaps.)

   Peter frames the whole picture early when he goes to his brother Robbie for help finding a best man: "How do I meet friends? It's such a weird concept," he says. (One of the best quiet jokes in this movie is how no one ever thinks of Robbie for best man when he's so much the obvious choice.) There's an interesting tension created between the weird niceness parading about in front of us—Peter and Zooey are an absurd yet convincing ideal of a perfect relationship—and the ferocious pursuit of the gross-out set pieces packed in. The R rating "for pervasive language, including crude and sexual references," has it about right but misses the warmth. The contrast actually does work to make the constant swearing, projectile vomiting, masturbation stations, and whatnot reasonably amusing. But I think the real appeal of this is closer to the feel-good turns of the rom-com. It's likable probably because the three principals played by Rudd, Segel, and Jones are likable. (2012)

Impressions, "It's All Right" (Oct. 12, 1963, #4)
Here's the biggest single for the Impressions and for lead singer and songwriter Curtis Mayfield too, at least until his solo career got underway in the '70s and he matched the chart performance with "Freddie's Dead." But that was 1972 and this is 1963 and therein lies all the difference. In many ways you wouldn't even know it's the same artist. That was the year that gave us "Be My Baby," "Blowin' in the Wind," "Guantanamera," "In My Room," "I Want to Hold Your Hand," "Louie Louie," "Ring of Fire," and "Surfin' Bird," so it's easy to lose track of "It's All Right" in the shuffle. Built for comfort, it moves slow—"When lights are low / When you move it slow / It sounds like a motor," as the song explains—powered by luminous harmonies and inflected by a nagging guitar upstroke and the kindest horn section you may ever hear. It is at once earthly and celestial.

"When you wake up early in the morning / Feeling sad like so many of us do"—you will know just what to do, now that you are reminded of the existence of this song. It's pitched at such a level that when the handclaps start near the end they are the rousing equivalent of a guitar solo. (2014)

The Insider **(Michael Mann, 1999)**
At some point I had better own up to a certain middlebrow orientation. With movies, my focus tends to be on narrative. Imagery, music, performance, and all the trappings are fine and good, but I tend to start with demands of a story—organization, clarity, and purpose at the very least; stakes I can connect with and some tension would be nice too. Most problematically, particularly in these fictional ripped-from-the-headlines exercises "based on reality" and/or the message picture bald, I further expect that it comport with my sense of reality and values. When it doesn't, I start to have problems. I think, in fact, this may stand in as a reasonably good definition of the middlebrow.

I say this by way of introduction to my favorite picture by director Michael Mann, which is so comically right on target in its messaginess—who, in 1999, was left to defend the enormity of Big Tobacco?—that you almost have to laugh. Michael Mann likes to do things big and he's good at it. He's also an aesthete, practically an abstract artist using the big-screen canvas to paint glossy photorealist portraits of cityscapes, luxurious cars, long freeway lanes, beautiful women, and powerful men. It occurred to me when I was revisiting *The Insider* recently that it is also the only Mann I have seen on a big screen. It could be that's the reason it's my favorite. But there are many reasons to like *The Insider.*

It is filled with money and swagger, which are so seductive. Mann takes outrageous advantage of the opportunities afforded by having *60 Minutes* as a central part of the story. The two-and-a-half-hour movie opens on an exotic and mysterious encounter with a powerful figure in Iran. It's a viscerally rendered side trip that has nothing to do with the story at hand except to introduce us to CBS News producer Lowell Bergman (Al Pacino), who is the first of not one but two gutsy larger-than-real-life heroes who will come to occupy center stage. Parts of these scenes were filmed on location in Israel. Thus it is a wild (and obviously expensive) ride from the beginning.

The cast is all-star, confirming the prestige production, with poised veteran Al Pacino going at it next to the ascendant Russell Crowe as Jeffrey Wigand, the tobacco industry insider of the title, whose admirably stammering, raging gallantry ultimately vanquishes malevolent tobacco right before our eyes. And it is so satisfying. Pacino struts around as the self-righteous and ultra-cool gonzo journalist, but Crowe maybe has the much tougher role, as an almost spastic boy scout wrestling with monsters inside and around him—a man alone, utterly alone, thrust into wracking moral turmoil. Among other things, Crowe proves how good he is at being tightly wound.

So that sets up the basic operatics of a story that saws back and forth and all around the wheels of power and justice. Wigand wants to get the truth out about the tobacco industry, Bergman wants to get it on *60 Minutes*, Big Tobacco and its armies of lawyers will stop at nothing to stop them. Meanwhile, my last time through *The Insider*, Christopher Plummer is making the most of an extremely sharp-elbowed portrait in the screenplay of legendary CBS reporter Mike Wallace, and virtually stealing the show. He is devastating as a pompous, self-important buffoon and hypocrite focused narcissistically on his own legacy and little else. It is so hard on Wallace I almost feel sorry for him secondhand—but it is also delicious in execution.

The Insider is kinetic from start to finish, excesses and all. Yes, too much time in Iran, and please, stop now with the Unabomber thread, but it is always moving forward, advancing its story, finding surprising ways to please and disturb and resolve. It is done the way Mann usually does things, probing, tentative, allusive, one immaculately constructed scenes after another. The images and the dialogue are dense and studded with important detail, but it's frequently hard to know where to focus, you're always set back just a little, trying to keep up.

My favorite scene—or image, really—is also faintly ridiculous. It is when Wigand is returning to his home in Louisville from his deposition in Mississippi, one more tense skirmish in what has become his personal war with Big Tobacco. It is nighttime and he is riding in the backseat of a car from the airport, with his security detail of three men. He is happy and satisfied he has been able to give the testimony, but he doesn't know yet that even more and worse problems are still ahead. The silent car with the four men takes a freeway exit and we see a car fully engulfed in flames, in the field just off the roadway shoulder. No one is attending to it. It is just burning away. No explanation is given. No one in the car says anything or even noticeably reacts to it.

It is a stunningly beautiful moment in a movie full of them. At its best *The Insider* is swollen up big and round, full of the menace, portent, surfaces, and textures of modern life. As it happens, these days I prefer my megalomaniacal evil geniuses to be wizards of the corporate world rather than the government figures that populate other movies—more realistic, in our present circumstances, for one thing. But *The Insider* plays well to many of Michael Mann's greatest strengths. I can't think of anyone else who could take hitting a bucket of golf balls at a nighttime suburban driving range and turn it into a moment of such high swooning fever. And really, does anyone else do men in crisp suits quite as ominously intimidating as Mann? (2013)

It's a Wonderful Life (**Frank Capra, 1946**)
Since coming to terms with how much I like and admire and value
the cornball object known as *It's a Wonderful Life*, I have maintained
that it's because the picture is essentially fearless, and not just "for
its times," about going right at human depravity. For every saccharine declaration that "every time you hear a bell ring, it means that
some angel's just got his wings," there's someone mean and surly like
Sheldon Leonard standing there saying, "Hey, look, mister, we serve
hard drinks in here for men who want to get drunk fast, and we don't
need any characters around to give the joint atmosphere." It's almost
like the call and response in gospel music, these extremes between
sunny bright and foulest black, and this is one of the best films I
know, short of *The Wizard of Oz* and *Blue Velvet*, at sharpening such
contrasts and making you feel them viscerally.

I came to it late, finally catching a TV broadcast from beginning
to end at some point in the late '80s. I was surprised by how dark it is,
even the photography, which verges on noir in some sequences, and
Universal-style horror in others. It's not just that it's a story about a
man who has decided suicide is his best option (nor that it's unafraid
to use the word "suicide"). The fact is it's just good all through, with
a screenplay that expertly juggles its many extremities, and with great
performances. It rears back and lets loose a story in excruciating detail of lifelong frustration and disappointment, the story of George
Bailey (one of James Stewart's greatest performances), who keeps seeing his dream denied of escaping the small upstate New York town in
which he was born and has lived all his life, a dream that is so systematically denied him that his interior life shrivels to the point where,
in a moment of uncalculated despair, he can cry out to his wife, "You
call this a happy family? Why do we have to have all these kids?"

The storytelling is energetic and creative, finding its own
rhythms and feel for each sequence. The structure is confident,

with the first 75 minutes a lengthy pastiche of flashbacks that sketch in and then flesh out its many characters and their relations, many of whom we see grow from children to adults. Then it spends about 25 minutes in the present before embarking on the science-fiction ghost-story / alternate future imposed on George by supernatural sources. It's an amusement park ride, one that sends you spinning and sprawling with George, free floating into a psychic space without mooring, where morality is absent and identity is gone.

The basic operating environment of the picture is in the vernacular of the brash midcentury urban wise-guy American comedy—the Frank Capra style ever more purified, screwball matured and perfected, absorbing Preston Sturges and Damon Runyon, rollicking on a swaggering series of bon mots and sight gags with touches of romance, dear old Ma, and inevitably slapstick, drunks colliding into piles of junk, everybody into the swimming pool, naked in a hydrangea bush, pratfalls and mugging as needed, and any old gag will do. One character puts his thumb in his ear, cocks his hand at the wrist, and brays, "Hee-haw!" and insists that all respond in kind, even into advancing middle age. High-spirited high jinks and horseplay are the order of the day, and there are numerous scenes with groups of strangers suddenly showing up all laughing out loud as one of our characters makes a fool of himself again.

But opposing all this joie de vivre, injected into the loose spaces that it opens up, come scenes that are not as comical, as when, early on, the grieving and confused pharmacist, Mr. Gower, lashes out and slaps around the young George Bailey after George has declined to deliver the medicine that he (George) knows is actually poison, the result of a mistake by Mr. Gower. It looks and sounds like a vicious assault by an adult on a child and it's shocking in the moment. In one of the picture's best and most celebrated scenes, George declares his love to Mary (Donna Reed) by desperately denying it. It's more of a tortured, painful moment, with George grabbing Mary by her upper arms and shaking her violently.

So it goes. Comedy, comedy, and then a scene with George bawling out his uncle: "Where's that money, you silly, stupid old fool? Where's that money? Do you realize what this means? It means bankruptcy and scandal and prison! That's what it means. One of us is going to jail. Well, it's not going to be me." And again with the grabbing and shaking. Uncle Billy (Thomas Mitchell), weeping, puts his head to the desk sobbing. Then a squirrel climbs on top of him. This is what I'm talking about. This is the speed with which it switches back and forth between its polar modes.

The scene where George goes home on Christmas Eve thinking he is ruined, with Mary decorating for Christmas and one of their daughters monotonously practicing carols at the piano, is one of the great set pieces in movies. George is a terrifying figure in that house, a malevolent presence, kicking and snarling, and finally just starting to wreck stuff. If this is comedy, it's *still* a new kind of comedy.

There's a happy ending, of course—or it might be more accurate to say there's 10 minutes at the end, perhaps 10 of the most bludgeoning minutes of schmaltz in all cinema, 10 minutes that most people come away more or less remembering as the whole of the movie. It's truly one of the most grotesque displays of excess you are likely ever to see. The power of it is frightful—not a dry eye in the house is a mild way of putting it. I love it in spite of myself.

Or perhaps "love" is not the right word. I respect its power. If the whole movie was that I would not like it very much, but it is only the last 10 minutes. And the ride that got me there is such a thrill I'm happy enough to go along with the rather odd and stern edict and sit there for a few minutes bawling. I think of it as my own way of giving it the standing O it so richly deserves. (2012)

J

The more unusual a letter is the more attention it calls to itself, and thus the less useful it becomes in the language. The letter J has this problem like crazy. But I hesitate to criticize J too severely because it is the first letter of my first name after all. In fact, it is the first letter of many people's names, first and last, indeed of many names in general. Corporations, for example: Jamba Juice, Janus Capital, Johnson & Johnson, or JetBlue Airways. Or months of the year: June, July, January. There it is again. You probably know several people in your own circle of friends and family. Take a moment to think. Names just appears to be the milieu that J prefers. Consider Judy Johnson, who fell in love with Jacob Jesperson. Together they had two sons and three daughters, who in turn married and had families of their own: Jimmy, Joseph, Jamie, Julia, Jasmine the elder and Jasmine the younger (technically, a cousin), Johnny Boy, Jaden "the Jukebox," Jan, Jennifer, Jacob Jr. of course, Jason (a juvenile delinquent, sadly), Jessica, actually make that two more Jasons plus another Jessica, Jesse (a boy), Jesse (a girl), Josie, Josh, Jacqueline known as "Jackie," Jay, and little Jago. You remember that song you used to sing around the campfire about John Jacob Jingleheimer Schmidt? It should have been Jones for the last name, and I think you know why. J is a squishy thing, taking on the exhalation of

the H at times and otherwise requiring a complicated coordination of vocal sound with a specific positioning of jaw and tongue
and a forward-thrusting motion that produces something like a
brief vibrating hum. The primary function of J is already covered
by the soft G (as in "judge") or very occasionally by H. It's silent
in a word like "marijuana" or perhaps, arguably, poses as a W in
such roles (the *consonant* W, for those inclined to believe W is also
a sometimes vowel). Speaking of marijuana, a J at one time was
a joint, or marijuana cigarette; perhaps it still is in some places.
Pass me the J, man. I'm jonesin'. J is also a predatory bird with a
striking, severe, and handsome profile, colored blue. I see them a
lot in my neighborhood. Still and all, I keep coming back to this
one detail. Why is J such a popular initial—something about the
sound, perhaps? The proximity to vain I? Because it is available
as a relatively unused letter? After all, it sits way down in the lowly
position of #23 on the ranking of letter frequency, and brother,
that is low. Because it is such an important letter in my signature
I had to choose at some point, perhaps about age 12, between the
very different printed and cursive forms of the capital. At first I
went with the loopy balloon cursive, but ultimately I settled on the
printed fishhook shape, decorating it with a handsome crossbar
over the top, which I think gives it panache. (2015)

Jacobites, "It'll All End Up in Tears" (1985)
The Jacobites were a British band of the '80s consisting of Nikki
Sudden and Dave Kusworth with sometime support from Sudden's
brother Epic Soundtracks (one of the great pseudonyms), Mark
Lemon, and others. On a downloading tear a few years ago, after
hearing of Sudden's death in 2006, I foraged for everything I could
find by them and their various antecedents such as Swell Maps.
But my favorite remains the first album I heard by them, which
I knew in 1986 as *The Ragged School* (culled from their 1984 and
1985 British releases, *Jacobites* and *Robespierre's Velvet Basement*) and
which contains this, "Ambulance Station," "Big Store," and other

essentials. Taking the easy way out, here's an album review I wrote for a Seattle paper in 1986: "Naturally cliches are to be avoided, but what we have in the Jacobites is the source of some *beautiful noise*. Simple as that. The guitars are loud, deliberate and raw, sometimes spare and sweet, the tunes good enough to hum days later, and the overriding obsessions (love and death, what else?) communicated so perfectly, so powerfully, that beauty and horror are revealed as the same thing. Well, aren't they? They deserve success, of course, but it'll never happen. More likely they'll find themselves in the same position as fellow obscuros Alex Chilton, or Nick Drake, whose haunting sensibilities the Jacobites occasionally match, even outdo. But at least we've got 'Ambulance Station.' And the bruising attack of 'Big Store.' And the Mick and Keith vocal harmonies of 'Hurt Me More.' And Dave Kusworth singing, 'And she feels / dead for just one moment.' And, and, and." (2011)

Henry James, *The Turn of the Screw* (1898)
There's a powerful undercurrent of the modern in this deceptive classic American horror story of (and supposedly for) children. I remember reading it for school at some point, I think in junior high—it couldn't have been easy—the language is a heavy dose of James's parsing and shading. The more you look at it as a whole the more sophisticated and almost impenetrable it becomes. Perhaps the most modern part of it is the way it is actually the story, not of two children, or a possibly mad governess, or a haunted house and ghosts, but of a manuscript. The manuscript is in the possession of one "Douglas," who reads it for the entertainment of a gathering on a country outing, though none of them are ever heard from again once the governess's story begins, told in the manuscript, written by her. At that level, of course, one soon loses all bearings, occupying the fevered brain of a frightened and/or hysterical young woman in her first real job, which she has taken (or claims to have taken) under unsettling circumstances and conditions. She sees ghosts. No one else does. She thinks the children do too. But

that's not entirely clear. On the other hand, when the governess confides in the housekeeper about her experiences and describes the ghosts, who are strangers to her, the housekeeper recognizes them as people who have previously been involved with the children but are now dead. All this is gleaned from dense passages, a blizzard of intricate cross-hatching language with long tangled sentences in fat paragraphs that sprawl across most of a page, qualifying anything that resembles a direct assertion. It is a kind of narrative optical illusion which looks like many things depending on how you see it, but each with some flaw that throws the whole thing into ambiguity again: a ghost story, except only one person sees the ghost, or a woman coming undone, except she's not the only one. At the end, in one outlandish interpretation, she might even offer a flavor of the Jim Thompson psychopath, casually killing, but talking about it so elliptically you miss the horror show. And it's even possible to see the children themselves as rageful aggressors, manifesting symptoms of sexual abuse. It's practically anything you want it to be and it's just a real corker. (2012)

Jefferson Airplane, "Lather" (1968)
People will tell you that the early albums by Jefferson Airplane are good, better than you would expect. As it happens, I am one of those people. And here is one of those songs. There are a surprising number of good ones, not just the hits, on *Surrealistic Pillow*, *After Bathing at Baxter's*, and *Crown of Creation* (with the mushroom cloud on the cover), which is the home for this plaintive meditation, so deliberately constructed. By most standards *Crown of Creation* is a reasonably conventional LP: 11 songs, most in the range of two to four minutes. Grace Slick wrote two of them, including "Lather," Paul Kantner and Marty Balin collaborated on two others, and the rest are by others or other combinations of others (Balin has his name on four, Kantner on three). So a tremendous amount of diverse creative energy applies. As for "Lather," among other things it's an interesting choice for the album kickoff, with fully absorbed

'60s politics and values and loudly espousing them (basically, "don't trust anyone over 30" multiplied by "don't ever grow up" multiplied by reality). If this was supposed to be "acid rock," as touted, it didn't sound like anything I expected: mournful mostly, and slow, though full of tricks like typewriter keys and random vocal eruptions for texture, operating on parallel levels. The result with "Lather" is a weird ballad that is nonetheless affecting—not the story, which is a bit trite, but the focus brought to bear in making the music realize the story. In its outrageous way it is understated, and vice versa, and they make that look easy. I think for Jefferson Airplane it actually might have been easy, at least across those first several albums. (2013)

Elton John, *Goodbye Yellow Brick Road* **(1973)**
At one time, along about 1975, I was pretty sure Elton John was that decade's natural heir to Elvis Presley and the Beatles. Later I thought that was ridiculous. But the last laugh is on me when I look up the numbers in my *Billboard* book: There, on the list of 100 Top Artists 1955-2009, is Elton John at #4, behind Elvis, the Beatles, and Madonna (yes), and just ahead of Mariah Carey, Stevie Wonder, and Michael Jackson. Wikipedia pipes up, somewhat tentatively, that this iconic double-LP package "has come to be regarded as Elton John's best and most popular album," noting that it's his best-selling anyway, with some 31 million copies moved. Checking around, I see that's good enough to put it in the vicinity of the top 20 all-time bestsellers, no small feat. So when I call it my favorite I understand that puts me with the rest of the unwashed, but at least I've pretty much thought as much since the time it came out. There has always been something a little bit different about Elton John, and I don't mean just that he was practically the only rock star of the time pretending to be gay who actually was gay. From his various folkie-cum-country-rock-raver postures early to the glittering glamour and pure pop insouciance on display here to the range seen across his strings of hits, he's a tough one to figure out.

Me, I gave in entirely with this, a big pop confection that opens with an 11-minute suite in which you don't even hear his voice until nearly the 6:00 marker—that's "Funeral for a Friend/Love Lies Bleeding." It's followed by a valentine to Marilyn Monroe, "Candle in the Wind," so universally beloved and genuinely touching he was able to rework it 24 years later in memory of Princess Diana, shortly after her death, and a lot of people were grateful. Then the weird faux live glam of "Bennie and the Jets," a song I am still waiting to understand, but one that nevertheless continues to thrill me. Then the title song, which verily cracks it open: a big fat hosanna to beauty in the face of debilitating nostalgia. So it goes: the luscious piano textures of "Grey Seal," the sassy rock 'n' roller "Saturday Night's Alright for Fighting," something about a made-up cowboy, "Roy Rogers," something about a made-up Depression-era gangster, "The Ballad of Danny Bailey (1909-1934)," and something about "I've Seen That Movie Too." My favorite song has always been "Sweet Painted Lady," even recognizing all the execrable prostitute clichés it bears. It's so fucking beautiful it makes me want to cry in spite of everything, and that's how the whole album affects me, when the moment is right. (2011)

Joy Division, "Love Will Tear Us Apart" (1980)
As epitaphs go, you're hard put to find any more apt to chisel onto the gravestone of Joy Division's long lamented Ian Curtis, who wrote this song with mates Peter Hook, Stephen Morris, and Bernard Sumner, who would go on—improbably, or so I thought for a long time—to become New Order (and please don't miss the Nazi thematics bridging the two). Curtis poured a lot of himself into this, something you just know even if you don't know who he is or much about him. He even picked up a guitar to play a few chords. I have never found it as ruinously bleak as the first two albums, perhaps because I happened to acquire the single shortly after it was released and spent many weeks and months puzzling over it. As sonics go, it strikes an almost impossible balance between

robotic and organic, even as it brims with a sadness almost impossible to put one's finger on. It's also catchy as hell, with a melody that sticks. Often, in fact, when I find myself frustrated by something yet compelled to work away at it—a particularly knotty anacrostic puzzle, say—I have found myself singing cheerily to myself, "There's a taste in my mouth / As desperation takes hold," humming and even whistling. From title to tune to verse to chorus, this has long been a stone favorite, perfect, and surprisingly so, for so many occasions. (2011)

K

K is my favorite letter, not least because it is worth five points in Scrabble, and 5 is my favorite number. (You'd think with my interest in letters I would play the game more, but I don't have many opportunities, and besides, I've never been much good at it.) Except when K is acting like a perfect doofus sitting out at the front of a word, only to be ignored, as is only appropriate—in "knowledge," for example—it is entirely and always simply what it is: the hard, scratching noise from the back of the throat, and a letter with a lovely, intricate, angled shape in print. I am more sorry than I can say that it has been so villainously abused by the Ku Klux Klan, which has no intrinsic right to it. It pains me deeply. I would sue them for damages if I could. As you know, I bear the letter in my last name, and over the years friends have had one, two, or more in their names, so many that I have finally come to register it as "the sign of the K," which tends to make me even more favorably predisposed to them, perhaps unconsciously. Is K actually a common letter in names, much as J is a common initial? K is also a pitchers' stat in baseball for a strikeout and that's really kewl. In the '60s, filthy hippies with no respect set about systematically abusing it— "Amerika," and all that, which would have grown tiresome except I also associate that with Franz Kafka, who wrote a fragment of a novel called *Amerika*. Franz Kafka—there's the sign of the K again, double-strength. Ken Kesey. Check that out. Emily Dickinson. See, the K exerts a quiet and subtle impact as well. The long-established alliance between C and K appears to be here to stay, baffling as it is. It looks better than KK would. But really, have you ever seen such a crock? C, Mr. Third Letter in the Alphabet, the malingerer that doesn't want to choose between K and S, blatantly exploits K for cover on its K case. Back that up, "ck," trick it out, and thereby jack up the absurdities. These are the kinds of things someone who really cares about K may find themselves thinking about. I mean, you can't really call K elegant—more like spiky. It comes with elements of the honest working class (as an entirely irrelevant aside, have you ever noticed how "honest" is actually dishonest about having an H?). Make no mistake. K stands in as its sound with no fuss or ambiguity (except when, as previously mentioned, it sidles up to an N at the beginning of a word). OK, I'm not sure what else there is to say. (2015)

Nick Kent, *The Dark Stuff* (2nd ed., 2002)
Nick Kent, self-declared Lester Bangs idolator and star *NME* staffer when it counted, brings all the soft-pedaled erudition, unblinking cynicism, and dead-on wit we have come to expect and appreciate from him and his '70s (and into the '80s) generation of British rock critics. A glance at the table of contents quickly reveals the usual suspects in play (plus maybe a few ringers): Brian Wilson, Jerry Lee Lewis, Roky Erickson, Syd Barrett, Brian Jones, Lou Reed, Sid Vicious, Elvis Costello, Morrissey, Shane MacGowan, Iggy Pop (twice—and he also writes the foreword), Miles Davis, Roy Orbison, Neil Young, Kurt Cobain, Prince, Johnny Cash, Eminem, and some others. In compulsively readable pieces that comprise equal parts interview, thought experiment, and nicely observed detail, with revisions and second thoughts and perspectives that stretch across the decades, Kent goes one on one with all our favorites, or a good many of them, as he works to get at the music and the players and fans and the scenes that spawned

them. One of the most surprising portraits for me, though perhaps it should not have been, was his staggering wade through the torrents of Elvis Costello's head, with Costello stalking through endlessly spitting petty vengeance fantasies when he was not yet even 22, circa 1977. It was just at the moment when success seemed within Costello's reach but not yet quite within his grasp. He was focused so intently that the overpowering creative energy reads like a kind of infantile rage—not the mellow, kindly, slightly sour or acerbic old uncle figure he seems to cut now. But there it is, in black and white, along with Lou Reed as mid-'70s wastrel speed freak (yes, children), Jerry Lee Lewis *still* plotting a comeback bid and imminent takeover of the entertainment world *in 1989*, and Kurt Cobain all MIA, the ghost who haunts every performer from Seattle across a six-week period that ended in April 1994. I can think of some I really wish Kent had been able to get to, e.g., Boy George, the Thin White Duke always, of course, and maybe Ian Hunter or Pete Townshend or Bob Mould or Nikki Sudden? Some others. But this will do. In fact, it's a real page turner. (2010)

Carole King, *Tapestry* (1971)
Carole King's *Tapestry* was not the first record that I bought—hardly. In fact, I don't think I actually came to own a copy of it until sometime in the '80s, and then only because of a wife who loved her old copy of it to distraction. To tell you the truth, I don't even remember the circumstances of purchasing it or how this copy I now have actually came into my possession, or even whether it is the first or the second or possibly even the third time that I have acquired it. But I do have it now, it is sitting upright on my desk, and I am looking at it as I type. It's in excellent condition, which is what makes me wonder if I didn't buy it sometime in the last five to 10 years, when the vinyl market was closing down and I bought so much in a frenzy. A scratch mars the upper part of the binding, evidence of a cat I once had, a dear animal prone to such irksome habits. But otherwise it is in practically flawless shape, still shiny and smooth

and supple. The irony is that I can't even play it as my turntable has needed replacing for several years now.

Even so, I submit *Tapestry* as a first record under the thinnest tissue of rationalization, namely that it is my first inescapable album, of which I count only three others: *Rumours*, the *Saturday Night Fever* soundtrack, and *Thriller*. I'm sure other examples exist for other people in this admittedly vaporous category, depending entirely on one's circumstances and tastes (*Sgt. Pepper's Lonely Hearts Club Band, Born to Run, Murmur*, and *Nevermind* might be possibilities). My own inescapable albums were all mega-sellers that also happened to be perfectly fine records, though it's unlikely I would have considered them much if they hadn't been played ALL THE TIME on the radio. What unites them most of all is that, practically against my will, they insinuated themselves deep into my life.

Carole King's blockbuster was the first of them, and my first taste of it, of course, was "It's Too Late," a #1 hit for five weeks in the late spring and summer of 1971, when I was 16 and just finishing 10th grade. I hasten to point out, for the sake of that callow boy, that my professed tastes of the time ran toward rock and jazz and some blues, toward the Doors and Miles Davis and Bob Dylan and Frank Zappa and Johnny Winter—heavy, difficult, relatively arcane music, and the fewer who appreciated it the better, because it only afforded me more opportunity to proselytize and affect superiority. Yet in spite of myself I continued listening to AM Top 40 radio far more than underground FM, which typically bored me, unless it was albums I already knew. And in spite of myself I was still continually entangled with the AM fodder of the day, with "It's Too Late" and "A Horse With No Name" and "Alone Again (Naturally)" and "Me and Mrs. Jones" and "Crocodile Rock" and "Hello It's Me."

For most of that summer of 1971 you just couldn't turn on the radio and avoid hearing the strains of "It's Too Late" for long. And it always caught me up. It made me genuinely sad, even tearful on some occasions. Its details were so right, opening with "Stayed in bed all morning just to pass the time," its generalities so provocative ("Something inside has died and I can't hide"), its overwhelming conclusion impossible to refute: "And it's too late, baby, now it's too late." I tried once to identify the wan break and solo in the middle of the song as some sort of jazz-respectable thing (King herself may have been looking for that kind of credibility in a later song, "Jazzman"), but even as I blurted it out to my friend I could hear the bullshit larded through it. The truth is that I couldn't help myself. I just loved it because it was damn pretty and moving.

The song captures the essence of giving up, which I believe is why it struck so many deep chords with me and, obviously, others. This was the time, the early '70s, when head-of-the-class baby boomers approached 30 (that whole milestone so laughable now), when it was all basically over, "it" being the '60s. The time had come to put up or shut up, you heard a lot of that kind of sentiment, and a surprising number of people were opting to shut up, to stop waving their freak flag, stop rioting in the streets, shrug inward and isolate, retreat to normative values (even hippies headed back to the land, to farm), return to college, get married, get a job, make a decision, stop fooling around, and grow up—and so what if the war was still going on. It's not surprising that the other song of that time that reliably choked me up was Carly Simon's "That's the Way I've Always Heard It Should Be," another song of capitulation and quiet, if beautiful, despair.

But in another way, its most obvious, "It's Too Late" ran somewhat against convention. More than anything, it's a song about giving up on a deeply felt connection, for no obvious or good reason other than "Now you look so unhappy, and I feel like a fool." This was also a time, the early '70s, when separation was coming more and more to be preferred over battling through the difficulties of a relationship, a trend that would not slow for many years. There has since been some backlash to that, ringing statements that divorce is bad for children, and probably in turn there will be a backlash to that. The truth here will likely remain a painful puzzle for generations to come. The fact is that only in the past century or two at most have marriages for love (as opposed to marriages for social advantage and marriages arranged by parents) been typically accepted. Marrying for love is a beautiful theory but so far it's no more certain in reality than flipping a coin.

In that way, "It's Too Late" provides one of the clearest and most straightforward statements of giving up that may exist in popular culture, a realm where, for example, Little Peggy March's sentiments of a decade earlier are more common ("I LOVE HIM I LOVE HIM I LOVE HIM/And where he goes I'LL FOLLOW I'LL FOLLOW I'LL FOLLOW/I will follow him"). In her tear-jerker hit, King argues gently and persuasively in favor of simply leaving behind a relationship, that it's really for the good of all, and she delivers it with a healthy and untortured sadness that makes it convincing. Separate, cry and feel your pain, and then move on, she seems to be saying—"get on with your life," as well-meaning friends urge friends in the throes of break-ups of any magnitude. Break-ups never make any sense anyway, when people try to explain them, but everyone knows the feelings, and those feelings are all over this song.

I should say that I was prompted to this essay by a discussion of *Tapestry* I read by Rob Sheffield somewhere. "The songs were everywhere but so was the album cover," he wrote. "It was the first album cover I ever spent lots of time staring at. Carole's in her apartment, sitting barefoot and frizzy-haired on her windowsill, one foot propped up, wearing a fuzzy sweater and jeans and holding some cloth in her hands. It's a sad rainy day, but lots of sun is streaming through the '70s curtains. Carole's cat sits at her feet. They're both daydreaming, staring out the window. They've glanced at the camera for a minute, still lost in thought, and when the photographer leaves they'll go back to staring out the window, alone together. You have no idea what they're musing about. When I look at this photo now, I see things I didn't see before. Carole's wearing a wedding ring."

It drove me to my own stacks to dig out my copy and look for myself. The first thing I noticed about the cover, with an almost paralyzing sort of shock, examining it closely for perhaps the first time in my life, was how *young* King looks (later I looked up the numbers and did the math, and guess she's 28 in that picture). At the time of the hit I had thought of her as an "older" woman, which she would be to a 16-year-old, imparting hard-won wisdom. Then I went back to Sheffield's piece and picked up where I had left off, and found him talking about how much *older* she looked in that picture than he had thought.

Something about the discrepancy of our perceptions—is Carole King older or younger than you thought?—struck me as terribly poignant. It made me sad the way "It's Too Late" itself once made me sad, and for some time now I have kept the album cover out to look at, though of course I can't play the record because my turntable doesn't work. Perhaps it's as cheaply provocative a question as Greil Marcus's familiar Elvis formulation—did Elvis go to heaven or to hell? But I think it's worth considering: Is Carole King younger or older than you thought? Did you think she was some ancient hippie and were surprised to find the girl who wrote the Little Eva and Shirelles hits? Or did you think she was a waify Janis Ian / Lisa Loeb prototype and were surprised to find a woman?

And if you were surprised, does it mean you lost something?

It's an imponderable, this feeble zen koan—yet for me, tonight, it somehow only deepens the mystery of the effect that *Tapestry* has had and still seems to have on me, in spite of myself. I don't think I've ever singled it out as anything particularly special, yet I've always been glad to have it, and happy to hear the songs on oldies stations. Still, if I actually played the album I would probably soon lose interest because it's all so overly familiar now. I have been hearing the music for more than 25 years. Perhaps that's why the object itself seems to be weaving such a spell on me. I am fascinated by it, picking it up to look at it closely, feeling its textures, even smelling it. (It smells like most of my albums.)

The other hits and the rest of the album always struck me as only faint and distant echoes of "It's Too Late." But because "It's Too Late" had such a powerful effect on me for so many years, even its pale imitations held some interest... "I Feel the Earth Move" (the flip of the single, a "two-sided" hit), "So Far Away," "Home Again," "You've Got a Friend," "Where You Lead," and the genius stroke of re-covering "Will You Love Me Tomorrow"—each contained an unmistakable piece of what made "It's Too Late" burrow so deeply into me. The sound of the album is all of a piece, slightly abashed pop, light tinkly jazz-rock arrangements put to the service of a painfully sincere folk feel, buttressed by a perfect sense of melody and a knack for the phrase that works, and King's voice itself, all homely and achy and plaintive. Sometimes I feel like I could listen to it in great gulps, for hours at a time.

But it wasn't until I was involved with the woman who became my wife, and later my ex-wife (oh yes, we crapped out just like in the song, "It's Too Late" indeed), that I finally had that kind of exposure to it. She loved *Tapestry*, and played it over and over, practically every day for months and years, so that now it carries the added baggage of tiny moments precious to me and doubtless banal to all others—the way she let herself sink into the opening strains of "I Feel the Earth Move," parading the living room or the kitchen in her jeans and barefoot, or the way she sought out and found the notes of "Home Again" as she sang with it, or the annoying (and gratifying) way she smirked and carried on over her favorite, "A Natural Woman." As often as I explained to her that, in this case, the songwriter had been unfortunately exceeded by the chanteuse, she never showed much interest in Aretha Franklin's version, and in fact often set the needle down directly to this track, playing it over and over, unself-consciously, maybe lighting a joint or taking a drink of white wine and going back to her work on whatever project she had to hand, humming and yelping happily with it. Is that why I'm just as happy I can't play it, you wonder? No way. I wish I could play it right now, and get a hit myself off that baggage (though chances remain good, I insist, that I would stifle a yawn and find myself looking at the newspaper before even a side had played out).

Tapestry finally also played a minor role in the first assignment I ever had as a rock journalist, which was to review a Fleetwood Mac concert in 1982. In my lead for that piece I made a small joke, talking about how Carole King and Fleetwood Mac bracketed the '70s with super-popular soft-rock classics, and likening them to the famous hamburger franchise competitors their names resemble. My editor laughed at that, looking over it with me there, and I think that's when he decided that in spite of my somewhat taciturn manner, I might actually have a sense of humor and be worth giving a dependable schedule of assignments. So when I look into Carole King's face on the cover of this album, and note the details of lighting and the unfocused cat perched on its pillow and the wedding ring and the curtains and everything that Rob Sheffield saw and pointed out, I see that too, I see all of it, everything: my career, my marriage, my deceased pet, the transition from the late '60s to the '70s, the wrecks and the glories of my life, my place in history and beside it and without it. I feel the sky tumbling down, tumbling down, tumbling down; I've got a friend, etc. And I'm glad my turntable is broken because I don't think the music could possibly support all of this, and likely never did, but against all odds or expectations and perhaps only for tonight the album cover itself somehow seems able to. (1997)

Maxine Hong Kingston, *The Woman Warrior: Memoirs of a Girlhood Among Ghosts* **(1975)**
When I finally got to Maxine Hong Kingston's memoir it was nothing like I expected, and much more. Much more—and much less, too—than an ordinary memoir, the experimental flavor of it suffuses and carries away much of the factual material. This goes beyond showing how events felt to showing how the unconscious experienced the events, and invented events of its own to absorb the blows of deeply foreign experience. It is full of strange dreams and irrational fears set to maximum impact—the anger, sorrow, and impossibility of such a transition are preserved almost perfectly, even as the homely details are mostly left behind. Thus, surprisingly, it becomes a story of great spirit encountering the strangely physical. There's not a lot to hang a hat on here—very little directly about language adjustments, ethnic self-awareness and accommodation, neighborhoods, schools, kindly adults. They are there—but their context is fierce and fantastic. One of the great things Kingston does is put the focus on Chinese culture and her heritage. The Western sophistication she has achieved speaks for itself, and is the perfect vehicle for saying what she's got to say. The hardships and privations can be wrecking. A raid, as recalled by Kingston's mother: "The villagers broke in the front and the back doors at the same time, even though we had not locked our doors against them. Their knives dripped with the blood of our animals.... Your aunt gave birth in the pigsty that night. The next morning when I went for water, I found her and the baby plugging up the family well." Unflinching stuff, yet followed by a beautiful and complex tale spun out of her mother's "talk-story" that she lulled her children to sleep with, about a powerful swordswoman and heroine, a shiny brilliant character. A variation of Wonder Woman, to the Western

comic book reader. The story is bold and swift and absorbing. The whole book is great. (2012)

Stanley Kubrick. See *A.I. Artificial Intelligence*; *Eyes Wide Shut*; *2001: A Space Odyssey*

L

The letter L is impressively rational—square and regular, representing one sound only (in English), which no other letter represents. Yes, it retires to the silent mode in words such as "walk" and "could." You can't have everything. But it's interesting to me that the sound is not itself universal to all languages. Japanese and some dialects of Chinese do not use it, and attempting to teach it to adult speakers tends to produce the predictable comical results. To me, it seems a very natural sound, but when I start attempting to describe the mouth mechanics required to produce it I realize it's a bit complex after all, what with getting your tongue just so behind the front teeth. It's vocalized and it is also infinite, which we have seen so far among the consonants only with F and H, both largely unvocalized. It's easier to control the volume of the L than the surprisingly noisy hissing S. I'll tell you who really likes L and get prepared to be impressed. None other than Superman himself—yes, that's right, Kal-El of the planet Krypton, son of Jor-El and Lara. He had a thing for L the way I have a thing for K—Superman's two favorite women were Lois Lane and Lana Lang and his deadliest archenemy was Lex Luthor. Note also that his mother's name is Lara and his last name appears to be El. Now that I think about it for a second, however, why would anyone look for the sign of the L in an archenemy? Well, L is also for losers, as we all know (first finger and thumb against forehead), and Superman was usually helping some of them out, so that's probably part of the explanation too (but I'm not sure even Brainiac gets this one). I like the way L takes the 90-degree lower-left corner of a box shape, direct and no-frills, and I like the way it's at the head of lovely words such as "like" and "love" and "learning," and I don't even mind that pronunciation of the letter itself would seem to have some qualities of the frilly—making people flip their tongues around like that. It's a good-time letter, blending seamlessly with others such as B, C, and F (but not at all, in the second position, with D, M, or N). Combining consonants with L in the first position is slightly more problematic, but done: half (oops, that's one of those mysterious "silent letters" again, isn't it? kind of like an "irrational" number), talcum (two distinct syllables there, as in "almost," so perhaps doesn't count), alms, kiln, bulb, etc. And yes, I just remembered that combining form in words like "double" and "bubble." By and large an honest workmanlike letter. Indeed, the idea of letters itself must have liked L so much that it took L for the first letter in the word "letter." Ludicrously, the same is also true for "lying." LOL (2015)

Frankie Laine, "Rawhide (TV theme)" (1958)
Entirely unexpected point of view: "Keep moving moving moving / Though they're disapproving / Keep those doggies moving ... Don't try to understand them / Just rope and throw and brand them." Fascinating. So the cowboys try to understand the cows. And the cows can be disapproving. And it bothers the cowboys when the cows are disapproving. (2006)

Charles Lamb, "Dream-Children; A Reverie" (1822)
It must have been the night many years ago when I first read for the first time Charles Lamb's remarkable long paragraph, "Dream-Children; A Reverie," that I realized, with a kind of thudding reality, that I'm likely not going to be fathering any children in this lifetime

(fathering, that is, in the biological sense). This did not come as a particular shock. I had been divorced over eight years and unable since then to forge the kind of lasting bond that produces children. Nor did I happen to make anyone pregnant, the situation that may prevail more often in generating children. Not that it couldn't have happened that way. It just didn't.

The origins of my divorce were as rooted in differences over children as anything—I wanted them, she didn't, in a nutshell. The real problems ran deeper, of course, but that was the issue on which we foundered. I count that divorce, melodramatically perhaps, as the worst thing that has happened to me (knowing far worse happens to others). Afterwards I spent agonizing, bewildered years watching my opportunity for a family slip away. I remember occasions that seem slight now, and whose details have grown fuzzy, but that affected me enormously at the time. One happened when I was walking fast on a street one day, on an outing, headed for some movie theater down the line and over a hill three miles away. It was Memorial Day weekend. I was brought up short at the sight of a woman pushing a stroller. Another time I saw a homeless woman leaning against the Woolworth's downtown, begging money. At her side was a grubby child of perhaps three in dirty clothes. The woman asking money was pregnant. I cried suddenly, both times, the tears stinging my eyes before I knew it and the stupid ache of the divorce rearing once more. And in my head I noted my age to myself, counting (36, 37, 38), and I could feel it slipping away, when others had it who perhaps didn't want it or couldn't manage it, and I did and could (or so I thought, though now I suspect I was wrong).

Paradoxically, I had taken full advantage of the opportunity afforded me by my divorce to lavish on myself a second young adulthood. I lived like a person in his 20s again. I avoided stabilizing my life by working at a stream of temp jobs, I went out frequently to see movies and shows and live music and to dance, I spent most of my disposable income on CDs and books and similar fare, I hung around with people 10 and more years younger than me (the *real* people in their 20s). I was also more productive in my work than I ever had been. There was barely room in that for a wife, let alone a family.

The fact is that I have ambivalent feelings about children, and good reason for them—not just about the straitjacket responsibilities they represent, but about children themselves. They intimidate me, with their irrational outbursts and their heartbreaking vulnerability and their sudden turns of cruelty. I am afraid to touch them, afraid to curry favor or correct immature behavior or knowledge, afraid that they won't like me, afraid more than anything of looking foolish or pathetic to them, treated with contempt. I hate to find myself in the role of the grown-up, and I resent their superior claims to attention. All of my most ridiculous insecurities and neuroses charge to the fore when a child is in the room.

I'm told it's best to relax and be yourself around children. But "myself" is so adult, bewitched solely by the activities of my fellow adults. Not only their sexual adventures—but those too, those too—but more their poignant, exasperating failings, and their difficulties identifying and overcoming them, and their occasional successes at doing so. You know what I'm talking about—all those things about people that "go back to childhood." As a joke on myself, a way to make light of my little obsessions and incidentally pry loose more disclosures, I cheerfully label myself a gossip and beg my friends to talk of themselves and mutual friends, even of complete strangers. But the truth is that I'm not really a gossip, not someone who wants to know the movements of the rich and famous to approximate myself to them, or who wants to learn the dirty secrets of friends and acquaintances to slander or antagonize or hurt them. I'm just a naturally curious person.

And then there are the disquieting fears of death, and the untoward longings for it, and for the end to pain, and the pain itself, incessant and consuming. I marvel constantly at people who seem able to put aside their grief (I know it lies somewhere in their hearts, as it is with all of us) and carry on with energy and convivial demeanor. It has long struck me as one of the great ironies that those with the sunniest countenances often embrace so heartily the darkest, most insidiously deceitful aspects of our society and lives—the yellow and white visage of Ronald McDonald, the fruits of totalitarian Disney, the brisk business of professional sports, and the churches, always the churches—while I am marked as unnaturally gloomy for harking to art and literature that exposes all to the light, Dennis Cooper and Diane Arbus and Roman Polanski and so on. The seeds of our destruction are carried with us from the day of our birth, our deaths are inevitable and foreordained, but it is not until we are adults that we realize this. It only begins to dawn on us vaguely in our 20s (though some teens seem fascinated with death, on closer examination it is more often mere fascination with drama), and the knowledge deepens and broadens and finally begins to consume us as we age.

I've come to believe that essentially only three things happen to us in life, that all the rest—the great architecture and good food, the clamoring for fair play, and science and the arts and hobbies and play—are amplifications and distractions, bright and merry as they may be. The first is children, what we are born to be, a unique time of life like nothing else again. We are mammals, after all, drawn to care for the young. It's no wonder that we love kittens and puppies and colts. The young afford so much joy, they are so vibrant, unself-consciously alive, running pell-mell in every direction, chasing their own tails, willing to try anything, with their senses blazing and vital and open—painfully so, at times. Children's taste buds, for example, are so sensitive that they cannot tolerate the intense flavors we come to appreciate as adults, hot peppers and pickled fish and steamed greens. And no matter how much it hurts and scars us as we live it, something in childhood remains the experience that we seek and seek again, for the rest of our lives.

The second is sex, with which we are wholly consumed immediately upon leaving childhood, whose concerns in fact mark definitively the end of childhood. Along the way it helps us to produce more children, repeating the pattern and the process seemingly to infinity, and introducing still more intractable ironies, such as the razor-thin line between the pure abandon of sex and the most imposing responsibilities of our lives.

And the third is death, the preoccupation for which gradually replaces that for sex, as our sexual powers diminish, and we hurtle forward into the years, ever forward, our legs crabbing, our intestines clutching, and our heads aching. But in our minds we remain always on the threshold of childhood, wondering at that changed face in the mirror, peering out with puzzled fear, and now and then and almost always unexpectedly feeling real joy for the simple fact of being alive.

These are the things that preoccupy "myself," and I frankly don't think they make appropriate or even interesting topics of conversation for a child. It would be like asking him or her to share my broccoli.

There was a time when I thought all of this, my anxieties and discomfort and sadness in regard to children, would be different if it were my own children, of my seed and sprung from the loins of my beloved betrothed, etc. For all I know it might have been. Living with a child from its earliest animal stages through all its phases of development might have caused me to rise to the occasion, to assert my will with love and strength and judgment and to shape, or help to shape, another human being into something decent. I might have been too busy, my life too full of happiness, to sink into my brooding and morbid funks. Certainly I'd have enjoyed holidays more, and likely I'd have found more use for cameras and personal photos than I do now. But fulfillment guaranteed, by the numbers? I doubt that, and believe instead that like most I'd have muddled through the best I could, coping with the overwhelming responsibilities with equal parts love and fear, inevitably projecting my thwarted hopes and regrets and frustration about life's—and my own—limitations, like so much garden dirt spaded onto the heads of my children.

What saddens me is that I will not know, that I seem fated to stay on this side of the great gulf that separates adults, those with children from those without. To a person, with never a hint of dissemblance, the adults on the other side look me in the eye and tell me that children are worth it, worth all of it, worth the sacrifices of time and energy, worth the sacrifices of their youthful commitments to art or to justice or to peace. I believe them, even standing outside and observing them serve the jail term that is caring for a child in the first five years of its life, and the exhausting battles of will that follow, and the cold, scornful rejection so predictable of teens. I watch them quarrel with their children as if they were children themselves, see them plumped into a humiliating isolation practically total, surrounded by the detritus of the infantile, by primary colors and geometrical shapes and the cooing tones of children's television and the clutter of toys and the stench of urine and the ceaseless battery of inane questions. To a person, these adults swear their lives have been improved, and even if part of me shudders, I believe them.

But I can't ask for pity in my situation, and I don't. I reasoned out the obvious many years ago, even in the haze of self-pity that followed my divorce, which is that if you want children in your life, they are there to be had, and everywhere. Your friends, your neighbors, your community—all, and so many, are dedicated to raising children, with their resources stretched to the maximum and too often long since snapped. I have tried my hand at some of it here and there, like some dilettante taking an evening of adult education at community college. I volunteered for a literacy program. I dallied at "becoming involved with" the son of a friend—paying regular visits, helping him with a difficult phase of his school and homework, and talking to him about himself. And I have vaguely made myself available as a "male adult figure" to other children of friends. The chemistry, alas, never happens, or I don't let it happen. I realize that an involvement with a child will mean an unhappy involvement with the parent (of most of whom frankly I disapprove), leading to a situation in which I can have no real standing or ground. So I back away.

But isn't it a fact that, standing on this side of the gulf, I don't know at all what I'm talking about? Isn't that what you want to tell me? Doesn't this ring forth as a litany of excuses that reflects my own unwillingness to accept responsibility, or to assert my will and feelings? Wouldn't I, if I felt strongly enough, have a "child figure" in my life, which I may or may not need as much as they need a "male adult figure" in theirs? Is it really so important that a child be "mine," and that it be the product of a stable, loving relationship that retains its own primacy? Couldn't I just, figuratively speaking, snatch one of them off the street, give it a home it might not otherwise have?

An ongoing refrain of well-meaning friends suggests that I take comfort in the fact that I don't have the famous biological clock ticking, that I can father children at any time in my life. All right, I suppose that it's possible to meet and fall in love and make a good home with someone half my age. I have even, I must say, entertained that fantasy. But really, the question just becomes to what lengths am I willing to go simply to procreate? How important is that? Should it really be the first consideration in connecting with a life partner? Or shouldn't it rather be the degree to which we can provide one another companionship and understanding and emotional sustenance? Modeling a sound and working relationship, with equal parts of self-sufficiency and ability to support another, is the most important thing we have to pass along to children, or so I believe. And that, it seems to me in my worst moments, is what has been lost to me forever. Fathering a child when I am 56 is no compensation.

The child I am most concerned with today, perhaps selfishly, perhaps tritely, steps forward tentatively from the pages of self-help books and years of therapy. It is myself—the joyful rollicking youngster I was at seven, the shattered child of 10 marked for the first time by death and loss, the furiously angry teen and young adult, the married man who tried to convert his wife into his mother. This person needs love. This person needs caring and support. This person needs, not a good job and a better car and fine appliances, but reason and capacity to enjoy them. My belief, the conclusion I reach when I think hard about this, is that it would be a better world if more people went my route, lived simple lives and devoted themselves to quelling that raging, greedy, fearful infant inside of them. Instead, it seems to me, the majority choose merely to spawn, blindly, even as they channel most of their energies into being the most loved or feared emotional third-grader in their place of work. When they think of it, say at Christmas, they convert the attendant spoils into expensive gewgaws for their emotionally impoverished offspring.

This picture of myself judging others so harshly, isolated in my spiteful self-righteousness, makes even me sad, and I have not set out here to win myself a clan of pitying long-faces. But consider, for just one moment, the situation of Mikal Gilmore—horrific, yes, but capable nonetheless of putting the matter in perspective. In his moving *Shot in the Heart*, the story of his life and the "wrecked" and "ruined" family that produced him, Gilmore wonders if he ever should have been born. What a question. Yet he speaks convincingly in this book, at length and in detail, of the unimaginable suffering that is everyday life for so many (who nowadays may frequently be found on daytime talk television), outlining the Mormon origins of his mother and the dark criminal background of his father, who was 61 when Gilmore was born. His father beat his mother, and his brothers, and he disappeared frequently for weeks and months. He spent time in prison. One brother, an alcoholic, died from complications related to a stabbing. His most famous brother, Gary, was executed for murder by the state of Utah in 1977 in a celebrated case.

It raises the obvious question that, if you can't do right by your children, is it right to bring them into the world at all? But there is an equally obvious and even more terrifying question behind that one. Why do some children, from the same family and with essentially the same upbringing, turn out basically all right—scarred, but decent and kind and functional—while others become monsters? I know now, at last—and it has taken me some time to get here—that my parents are not to blame for my problems. They made their mistakes, of course, as all parents do. But in modeling a steadfast and in most cases a kind and gentle love for one another they provided a ray of hope for me, a feeling that there might be shelter in this world, there might be a place where I can go. The rest, everything else, is my responsibility now.

In the meanwhile, my questions and doubts about children and myself will likely continue to plague me, until some day they finally fade, if only because I fade myself, and die. Though I have never dreamt of the children I do not have, I dream often of the house in Minnetonka, Minnesota, where I was raised and which my father sold in 1987. I am seduced by the women of my life there, terrified

JEFF PIKE

by a ghost there who seems to want something but only moans, and stalked there by strange criminals. Once I shot baskets with the Chicago Bulls there. Another time I shot holes of golf with Vijay Singh. My family is often there of course, and occasionally a grade-school chum. I have seen my ex-wife there many times. Who are these people, and what do they want? Do I return to that house time and again because it's the last and only place I will ever live with children?

Charles Lamb, the British essayist whose "Dream-Children; A Reverie" prompted me to write this extended note to myself, witnessed, at the age of 20, his mother's murder by his sister with a knife. His sister was temporarily insane and also wounded their father in the incident. Eventually she was remanded to Lamb's custody and they lived together and took care of one another for the rest of their lives. They also had a brother, John. A lifelong bachelor, Lamb wooed for seven years but never won the hand of a woman named Alice Winterton, who married someone else. John and Alice are the names Lamb gives his dream children in his reverie. (1997)

The Last Days of Disco (**Whit Stillman, 1998**)
There are thing to complain about in *The Last Days of Disco*—it's not flawless. But I was compelled to revisit it after seeing screenwriter and director Whit Stillman's first movie since, 14 years later, *Damsels in Distress*. Not only did I adore *Damsels in Distress*, but I also find that I like *The Last Days of Disco* a lot more in its glow. As a matter of fact, in many ways *Damsels* picks up where *Last Days* left off, certainly in terms of the never-ending search to find truth and meaning in popular dance crazes and the social upheavals that attend them. Nothing, in fact, prevents *The Last Days of Disco* from being a complete winner start to finish, a broad farce playing our superiors in New York City's Upper East Side ruling class for witless buffoons.

I think I didn't comprehend before how funny Stillman is at sending up these people—or, more specifically perhaps, their children. Making privileged WASPs into caricatures of the vicious and dumb may look easy, but making it work is probably his best trick in a whole magic bag full of them—he's gentle and yet shows no mercy. To a person, no one here is likable (or, in fairness, entirely unlikable either). There's a lot of skill to the way Stillman renders them as well-educated, well-mannered, well-spoken, and well-dressed preening nincompoops, alternately strutting about or cringing to perceived authority. It may be class warfare, but it's deliriously fun.

Never mind the plot—something about the downfall of Studio 54 in the early '80s. It just plays in the background as a way to keep its many moving pieces organized for a tidy finish. Above all, this picture soars on the music, where it has power to provoke absolute swoons. All the most energizing scenes are on the dance floor, just music and costumes and bodies writhing, with a preternatural sense for timing the arch emotional turns of its story, such as it is, to the music, as when "Doctor's Orders" swells up big in the early moments just when Alice (the Betty, played by Chloe Sevigny) and Charlotte (the Veronica, played by Kate Beckinsale) have gained access to the nightclub. Gorgeous moment.

In the alternate universe of this movie, disco is lionized and glowingly extolled as a heroic moment of youth culture. Maybe I thought it was punk-rock denied its place in those times, but *The Last Days of Disco* finds ways to remind us that disco was actually one of the most publicly reviled episodes of popular culture ever. The name "disco" itself had to be discarded, marginalized to this particular era, even though keyboard-driven dance music has never gone away, just traveled under different names ("urban," "house," "club," "second British invasion," "electronica," etc.). The dichotomy is explicit here, even including out-of-time-frame news footage of the 1979 Disco Demolition Night at Chicago's Comiskey Park, a record-burning event that turned into a near riot. The snark is thick, as this is a picture filled with irony and strategies of distancing. But it's hard to miss the genuine affection (and feel) this movie has for the music.

On top of that, I can't help myself. I do end up loving these dopes it calls characters, forever saying things like, "Have you ever noticed how people who look just alike never seem to know each other?" Or, "One thing I've noticed is that people hate being criticized. Everyone hates that. It's one of the great truths of human nature." Or, "The way I see it, Brutus was a good friend to Caesar." It's talky and wordy and New Yorky, which count as plusses for me.

Thus the absolute heart of *The Last Days of Disco* turns out to be ... just another conversation at the club. But an acutely key one, a discussion of the 1955 Disney feature *Lady and the Tramp*, which becomes an earnest—ridiculously earnest, of course—undergrad English classroom type of discussion. The deeper they get into their explications the more apparent it becomes that they are actually using *Lady and the Tramp* transparently as a way to talk about themselves with one another. It's a unifying and profound formative experience they all share, this Disney movie, a neat symbol of privilege in its own right, even though they cannot agree on it any more than they can on anything else. *Bambi* also comes up in an earlier conversation, now that I think about it, and in many ways *The Last Days of Disco* perversely occupies that same imperturbable bubble as Disney movies.

The players are fine—eloquent, unintentionally self-revealing, and with the vague manner of animals trapped and considering chewing off their own legs. Kate Beckinsale is shallow and bitchy and delightfully lame-brained. Chloe Sevigny brings her usual intriguing presence, a kind of indie brand of its own, careful and self-regarding, a dense walking discomfiture and a chilly vision of beauty. I think Stillman has arguably cast and directed her as well as anyone ever has. She's not likable, as few here are, but even so one reads her and feels her at every step.

As with *Damsels in Distress*, *The Last Days of Disco* manages to have it all ways an outrageous amount of the time: poking good, hilarious fun at the empty rich people, swooning it up with musical flourishes, and then probing with precision for secret vulnerabilities and humanity. One of the best moments in the whole thing, funny and shivery good all at once, is entirely unexpected, when Charlotte rears back and peals off a beautiful reading of "Amazing Grace" from a hospital bed. She's the least likable person here—that's mostly for laughs though it's not always that funny—but for that one moment it's hard not to fall in love with her a little.

The movie ends on a speech, a closing argument from Josh, who is also a prosecutor and the greatest lover of them all of disco—"Disco was too great and too much fun to be gone forever," etc.—and then, as if to prove the point, and to assert one last time that it is actually serious about all this on the deepest levels, the picture heads off to a scene on a subway train car for the credit crawl, a beautiful and strangely moving music-video style interlude based on the O'Jays' "Love Train." Once again, you don't know whether to laugh or weep at the sheer beauty of the spectacle of it. Now that's entertainment. (2012)

Peggy Lee, "Is That All There Is" (Oct. 11, 1969, #11)
Peggy Lee's tender parable of nihilism is so artfully done that even still, all these years later, it can leave me feeling a little exhausted and weepy. Part of it likely stems from the cabaret elements of the arrangement, a piano, a banjo, some strings, eventually a horn, and Peggy Lee's smoky voice, which retain a whiff of the Weimar decadent. Peggy Lee could be Greta Garbo's secret daughter. The song picks its targets carefully, building for maximum effect: fire, circus, love, finally death itself. The trick is not just the choices, though they are important (watching the house burn to the ground was

disappointing? and yet, on some level, who doesn't know that feeling?). No, even more important, I think, is the way she (and/or Jerry
Leiber and Mike Stoller, who wrote it) frames them to be so convincingly inconsequential as experienced. Circuses, for example,
are something that adults have always appreciated more than children—my own visit to one as a child was at least as disappointing as
reported here. And who doesn't know the disappointments of love?
But there's something uniquely awful to contemplate in the chorus,
where the dagger is really slipped in—that croaking "Let's break out
the booze, and have a ball" never fails to chill me, perhaps because
boozing itself so inevitably produces the reaction documented here.
Meaning, in short, that there's no escape at all, is there? And that's
why the last thing considered in this song is the last thing to be con-
templated at all, ever. Good night. (2010)

Elmore Leonard, *City Primeval: High Noon in Detroit* **(1980)**
Elmore Leonard is a writer anyone who cares about good writing
needs to look into sooner or later—he's easy to read and amazing
at his craft, his words washed bone clean by narrative momentum.
His dialogue, in particular, can make brilliant miniatures, as he
simply takes out the words that people don't say and leaves only the
rest, which is remarkably different from how most people recon-
struct conversations, even in memory, let alone writing them down.
Yet his lines ring like fragments of melody. Leonard started out
writing westerns (with a day job writing advertising copy, maybe
how he got so pithy), then moved on to crime novels set in Detroit,
in Florida, and finally in Los Angeles. He might even have one or
two set in New Orleans. Most people's favorites by him seem to
be the first one or two they've read. It's true for me anyway, and
for that reason probably tend to favor his Detroit novels. The subtitle here makes that setting clear and also underlines the lasting
influence westerns had on Leonard, both the ones he wrote and
the ones he read and saw at the movies—the profound influence,
indeed, that westerns have had on crime fiction generally (and

American detective fiction particularly). Raymond Chandler's image of the man headed down a mean street, after all, has always been basically a 20th-century urban scan on certain frontier stories. Here Leonard simply elaborates on that, as much as he ever "elaborates" on anything, with a nerve-jangling confrontation between a depraved, soulless criminal, a young kid named Clement Mansell, aka the "Oklahoma Wildman," and Raymond Cruz, the Detroit homicide investigator who is determined to take him down. Mansell is enough like Billy the Kid, and Cruz enough like Gregory Peck, to make the overriding conceit work. And Leonard never has to spell anything out in even that much detail. He just sets the players in motion and lets things roll; the subtitle is there for the clue. The landscape is quickly littered with victims and potential victims, including perhaps most memorably Mansell's own attorney, the hard-as-nails Carolyn Wilder. It can get to be a pretty rough ride, but at least it doesn't take much more than an airplane flight, or single late night, to polish off. (2011)

Daniel Levitin, *This Is Your Brain on Music* **(2006)**
Author Daniel Levitin put in time as a studio session player before going on to college to become a neuroscientist, which gives him something of a broader view than one normally expects, able to discuss Stevie Wonder, Beethoven, and rigorous scientific inquiry with equal facility. The results in this pop science book are often illuminating. Among other things I found some support for my (slightly weird) contention that learning to sing note for note and vocal tic for vocal tic enables one to momentarily become that person, or persona (see Everything But the Girl, Buddy Holly, Prince, and Velvet Underground). Music, it turns out, is not just universal and ancient among human beings but, biologically speaking, requires massively complex coordination across many different regions of the brain, which are all active all at once in the presence of music. Music becomes a kind of externalized essence of being fully alive. What's more, the unique patterns of brain activity produced

in someone hearing a piece of music are virtually identical to the patterns of brain activity in the musicians playing it. This suggests a profoundly intimate connection among people that is caused by music, which certainly confirms my experience in live settings at shows. Dozens, hundreds, thousands of brains firing simultaneously, in parallel, together. No wonder people get off on this stuff. Where a contrarian like me persists in seeing differences—I would like to register a minor complaint about Levitin's tastes, for example, which often seem to run to the predictable classic-rock / NPR sides of things—Levitin more convincingly makes the case for music as one of the most characteristically human of all activities, rivaling even language. And he flatters us by noting that very few people are anything less than expert music appreciators. As someone who is often flummoxed by the paucity of ability I have to sing or play instruments, but who insists on writing a good deal about the experience of hearing music, I find that an appealing point of view, incidentally helping me to explain a little better a part of myself that occasionally baffles me—this fierce clutching at music for meaning and identity. Also, Levitin is very good on Joni Mitchell. (2014)

Life Is Beautiful (**Roberto Benigni, 1997**)
Glad I waited 16 years to see this. For one thing, it afforded me the useful perspective that Roberto Benigni has turned out to be no classic comedy player of cinema after all, as seemed to be widely believed (or hoped, or hyped) at the time this came out (*The Great Dictator*, etc.). Once this movie arrives at the concentration camp, and it does take some time to get there, I found it possible to imagine it as some kind of psychotic break on the father's part, particularly the way he was able to hide his kid in the barracks. So that was interesting, but ultimately not sustained. On the other hand, for all its cloying air, it does not cheat. I think it neither minimizes nor grotesquely distorts the Nazis, it's reasonably good on the fog of war, and it has a moment that shocked me. So you could do a

lot worse with a war movie. I fully expected to hate it. Respecting it a little might reflect only that I found it better than mortifyingly awful. (2013)

Little Richard, *The Very Best of Little Richard* **(1956-1964)**
The original wild man of rock 'n' roll, accept no substitutes. In his prime—oh hell, even now—there is no one like Little Richard [Penniman], of Macon, Georgia, though plenty have tried. James Brown, Paul McCartney, and Otis Redding all started their careers dazzled by and frequently imitating him (Redding also hailed from Macon), adopting his vocal stylings if not sartorial (few before the '70s were willing to so publicly attempt such transparent light-in-the-loafers foofaraw). Bob Dylan wrote in his high school yearbook, circa 1959, that he aspired to play with Little Richard. Jimi Hendrix once said he wanted to do with his guitar what Little Richard did with his voice, by implication his performance. Prince reaches all the way through James Brown to get to the essence of Little Richard. This is no matter of simply paying lip service to a hoary rock 'n' roll cliché or legend. A listen to what Little Richard accomplished in his prime, and maybe a look at what he contributes to the movie *The Girl Can't Help It*, should serve to answer any further questions. "Tutti-Frutti," "Long Tall Sally," "Rip it Up," "Keep a Knockin'," and others—the excitement is irresistible to this day. Penniman, like so many of the early rock 'n' rollers, may be driven as much by mad flight into and out of the arms of Satan—which, at least in his case, could be more exactly a matter of refusing to accept his sexuality, though arguably that amounts to the same thing. His career itself has been marked by a similar dynamic. Rock 'n' roller, minister of the church, star on the oldies circuit, hallowed communicant, *Hollywood Squares* regular, servant to Jesus, Geico pitchman. So it goes. Fortunately for us (if perhaps less so for him), all of that tension is compressed into his music, which, as the saying goes, will never die. That's the art of it, and his never-ending accomplishment. (2010)

Living in Oblivion (**Tom DiCillo, 1995**)
The title for *Living in Oblivion* refers to a state of working on a project, working so intensely that time, reality, and life seem to fall away, leaving a binary existence, working inside of nothing and trying to make something. There's a kind of creeping self-pity just around the edges. Yet in spite of all the booby-trap plot points that threaten to blow it to smithereens of artsy indie cliché it is an exhilarating ride, one of the best movies ever made about making movies—admittedly a sketchy category. But *Living in Oblivion* works. And it's not just a movie about making movies, but commits many other sins as well: extended dream sequences, a wanton mix of color and black-and-white film stock, and for God's sake Steve Buscemi, Peter Dinklage, Catherine Keener, James LeGros, and Dermot Mulroney, an early flush-out of talent in a new post-Tarantino era. So self-conscious is this that at one critical point Quentin Tarantino is name-checked (a late-breaking substitution during the shooting for Oliver Stone). There's a generational changing of the guard for you.

Buscemi as indie film director Nick Reve and Keener as his leading lady Nicole Springer turn in matched and subtly mysterious performances. The strange, swirling story this movie wants to tell, that it tries three separate ways to tell, revolves around the humdrum matter of getting a shot, and all the things that conspire against it. It expands from there to regions of Kafka and Sisyphus, and then on to redemption, managing a scope as big as the world with a handful of scruffy players acting make-believe in a New York City warehouse space.

I missed it. I came to it a few years late—much like the characters it's built around, I don't think it has yet seen much of the recognition due it—and then it reminded me of nothing so much as *Run Lola Run*. Both movies exist in strange alternative realities, with formal redundancies and repetitions outside of time, told in triptych form, and they end on similar unlikely upbeat notes that feel more like genuine salvation than empty cheer. Even with the hipster trappings they are profound, convincing, and tremendously heartening.

But forget the big picture. Consider the small parts, because more than anything else *Living in Oblivion* is a great thing made out of very fine small things. Catherine Keener's performance, for example, where she is required to convince us, across multiple takes of a single scene (three separate scenes, actually), that she is a very good actress attempting a very difficult scene, capable of nailing it entirely but more often hitting her strongest notes only occasionally and randomly. Because that's the way it goes when you're making a movie, right? Buscemi is equally convincing as the film director who knows what he wants, can feel it at the furthest edges of his fingertips, and is totally committed to getting it, but is foiled in large and small ways again and again at nearly every point.

The first third of the movie was originally conceived and shot as a separate short film, and that is where the greatest sense of futility occurs, almost at the level of pure abstraction. The shot they are trying to get is a delicate scene between Nicole's character and her mother Cora (Rica Martens), who share a background of unresolved pain, and one thing after another keeps fouling up the shot. Reve wants to get it in a long single take but problems occur: a boom in the frame (twice), a focusing goof, external noise. Finally the players are so frazzled by the interruptions and stress they start blowing their lines. Reve stops everything and calls for a break and a run-through of the lines. In the run-through, something is triggered in Nicole and Cora and the great scene starts pouring out of them. But Wolf (Mulroney), the camera operator, happens to be sick in the bathroom from bad milk and they will never get it. Is that why it is so tremendously moving as it plays out? Yes, partly, but also Keener turns it on there, with a convincing depth I'm not sure we've seen from her anywhere else. It's a tremendously beautiful, isolated moment.

Everything else feels right too, starting with the integration of the second two parts with the original in the full version of the screenplay. While the narrative of *Living in Oblivion* is fractured by design, all parts have always felt coequal and organic to me, a seamless whole. And there are so many nice points here: the sulky but talented Wolf, the flinty efficiency of Wolf's girlfriend Wanda (Danielle von Zerneck) as the production manager, James Le Gros's hammy Chad Palomino, all the ways the crew interacts to get the work done. It's possible I like especially that latter point because *Living in Oblivion* often reminds me of another movie about making movies that I like, *Day for Night*. But I have never actually been on the set of a movie. That's not the kind of verisimilitude I'm talking about when I say it feels right. It seems truest to me about the frustrations and meager rewards of creative work, where nine-tenths of all effort can feel like soul-deadening waste of time and effort.

It was thus generous and shrewd of DiCillo to give us the 10% that makes everything else worth enduring—and to give it to us at the end, amounting to the "happy ending" that is ironically rarely the hallmark of the indie production (though it is, actually). Not coincidentally, it is also the part of the movie that is funniest, with Peter Dinklage taking apart the whole enterprise of using small people to signify dream sequences in indie-addled movies (though I like it very much, *Twin Peaks* comes to mind at this point). Dinklage's thunderous fit of pique takes place amid the greatest collapse yet of Reve's quest to get a shot. And just when all is lost, the magic happens—but that only makes you realize how much magic has been happening for the movie's entire 90-minute length. It's a little masterpiece. (2014)

L7, *Hungry for Stink* (1994)

L7 calls this rut a groove and goes with it. The only difference from its immediate predecessor (*Bricks Are Heavy*), and kind of a shame into the bargain, is that the mix too often swallows the vocals. But then, the lyrics this time are several clicks of the dial darker: rage about to detonate, the baggage that drowns, the vulnerable who are trailed down dark streets, depression gone too far ("the paint chips are kicking in"), and TVs that broadcast personalized messages. "I'm good at feeling bad / I'm even better at feeling worse." I suppose it's not really fare for the weak of spirit. But feel it: the punk is punkier, the heavy is heavier, and the metal metaller. Don't miss the throbbing cellos on "Can I Run." Those wanting a straight jolt of rock 'n' roll are referred to "Riding With a Movie Star." Headbangers of all stripes, down your antidepressants and start your engines. This one goes the distance. (2007)

M

I get the impression the letter M is particularly popular among Roman numeralist mavens, especially those in the motion picture industry, who have spent something close to a century confusing us with copyright dates. Perhaps it was all worth it when the year 2000 finally arrived with that elegant formulation of "MM." Small consolation, but incidentally reminds me of the attempted promotion of M&M candies at the same time. It seemed like a natural for the new millennium but never took off that I noticed. Maybe people just aren't that much into Roman numerals? The NFL finally figured it out with its idiotic Super Bowl numbering. As for the candy name, that finds its source in the business collaboration between Forrest Mars, Sr., who was the son of Mars candy company founder Frank C. Mars, and Bruce Murrie, who was the son of Hershey's principal William F.R. Murrie. That's an awful lot of chocolate, M, and class privilege there. M is the 13th letter of the alphabet, standing in as the termination of the first half. When I realized sometime recently that the postal abbreviation for my home state of Minnesota, MN, actually thus spans the two halves of the alphabet, it struck me as one more conceptual bifurcation of the area and my origins. MN, after all, straddles the Mississippi River at the center of the continent, and has radio stations with call letters starting with both K and W. Perhaps most obviously there is the "Twin Cities" of Minneapolis and St. Paul, but also, more personally, in a kind of primal ur-bifurcation, two specific western suburbs of Minneapolis: Minnetonka, which provided my family's mailing address, and Hopkins, whose schools I attended. There were clear class divisions between the traditional, garden-style suburb of Minnetonka, formerly a resort, and the small town of Hopkins, which skewed more working class, swallowed by encroaching big city growth. But that is a topic for another time, this bifurcation. We're supposed to be talking about M here. M is more or less a natural letter. Compress the lips, sound the vocal cords—what could be easier or more primal? In fact, the sound appears to be among the first grasped at all, associated with "mama," often one of the first words learned or spoken. As an aside, I have known people to train dogs to say the word. What's interesting to me in those cases is that even though the lip movements and vocal sounds are fairly good at imitating the sound of the word, it rarely registers as a dog saying a word. The intentionality or something is missing. If anything, however, that's more likely a problem with the vowel than the consonant. Those dogs are getting the letter M right. Speaking of growling, please don't remind me of the baseball team the Seattle Mariners, often commonly known as the Ms. They are hard at work competing for status as the worst team in all baseball history, and as such they are putting this letter into a terribly embarrassing predicament. Not even M, I suspect, can get behind the Ms. And I do not blame it. (2015)

M (Fritz Lang, 1931)

Back when I started watching late-night movies on broadcast television, this seemed like a natural when I read descriptions of it. I loved Peter Lorre from his iconic supporting roles in *Casablanca* and *The Maltese Falcon*, and I appreciated Fritz Lang particularly for *Metropolis*, which I also read about avidly and eventually had the opportunity to see at a nostalgia film club in the suburb where I grew up. That film club occupied the space above a storefront, furnished with folding chairs and a tiny screen, and it showed Max Fleischer cartoons and old movies in 16-millimeter (maybe even, some of them, 8-millimeter)—*Freaks, Reefer Madness, White Zombie,* comedy reels, various obscurities and curiosities, and, eventually, *M,* which by that time had assumed something of the role of a holy grail for me.

Thus I have to count *M* as the most disappointing movie I have ever seen, an experience I replicated a couple more times (for purposes of verification as much as anything) over the decades. More than once it has worked as a soporific on me, literally putting me to sleep. I've come to have more appreciation for it— the commentary track by Anton Kaes and Eric Rentschler in the Criterion DVD was helpful in pointing out its many virtues—but it remains a film that frankly mystifies me. It seems so promising with Lorre and Lang and especially with all its accolades: greatest German movie of all time (according to a good many), "the best of all serial-killer movies" (Jonathan Rosenbaum, who perhaps never saw *Shadow of a Doubt*), and way high on any number of lists of greatest pictures.

And it's exactly the kind of thing that ought to appeal to me— part true-crime exercise (even, arguably, police procedural) and part sensational thriller, it's the story of a man, Hans Beckert (Peter Lorre), who kills little girls after seducing them with candy and toys. It should be creepy and unnerving but it is exactly the opposite—it is talky and plodding and studiously removed from its most intriguing possibilities. I like it more than *Battleship Potemkin* but not as much as *The Searchers,* two more movies I find wildly overrated, but which I hesitate to criticize too energetically, cowed by the widespread regard in which they are held. What are others seeing that I am not? I suspect this is a question we all have, but about different titles.

There are things about *M* I have come to appreciate. I like the spindly way it enters into the story and opens it up, with kids announcing the premise in a playground rhyme (a trick later used to good effect in the *Nightmare on Elm Street* franchise). The alarmed response of the grown women responding to the rhyme elaborates the premise, and then there is a crime. The mother of the victim, Elsie Beckman, was the one who maintained her poise in the opening scenes, with her friends who were upset by the children's singing rhyme.

There are elements in *M* I can see should work, such as the familiar tune Beckert whistles, which identifies him (Grieg's "In the Hall of the Mountain King" from *Peer Gynt*). Elsie's abandoned ball rolling to a rest in a field. Her balloon, which Beckert bought for her, abandoned too, caught in a tangle of telephone wires (commentary track: "which suggest the world of modern communications"). But they don't work. They feel pro forma, or underdeveloped, or just clumsy somehow.

There are many great images, lots of great setups and shots. The edits can be positively cunning. The camera placements and the ways the camera moves are often interesting. The expressionist touches, particularly the use of shadows, are brilliant. Yes, it's worth studying all right. (Walt Whitman: "Have you reckon'd a thousand acres much? have you reckon'd the earth much? / Have you practis'd so long to learn to read? / Have you felt so proud to get at the meaning of poems?")

It's dated as much as anything. The insights *M* offers about paranoia and people turning on one another in such situations—a community paralyzed by fear because a serial killer is among them—are trite, on the level of *Twilight Zone* business. Ditto the concerns about the pernicious evils of mass media. *M* gets into more trouble when it opens up to a broadly sociological portrait of a city in extremis. It's all right on the police, and it's not even too bad on organized crime. But a formal organization of beggars, really? This is hokum. (It's also the point where the commentary guys start talking about "parables," which I take to mean they don't believe it either.)

It's mostly shot on soundstages and it shows. There's no sense that it takes place in a city of millions. It feels like the set of a TV production. By the way, nothing here makes me interested in anything about artificiality and constructed reality. It moves from crime picture to police procedural in the first half, moving on to the broader sociological profiling. Then the second half is a tiresome, protracted, and largely incoherent (though lovely) chase sequence, followed by an overlong allegorical criminal trial cum kangaroo court with Peter Lorre chewing the scenery.

Setting expectations is the name of the game here, because there's no question *M* is a handsome and capable production. Here is where the commentary guys were notably helpful. As they say, *M* is not a thriller, not even close, nor is it much of a mystery or police procedural. It is most accurately a message picture—the message being "protect the children" primarily, with strong daubs of "exterminate the brutes." This latter was largely because a few similar cases of serial killers had recently played out in Germany, and the death penalty had become a lively social and political issue.

Put in those terms, it's easy to see my problem. A message picture advocating for the death penalty—at a point in history when (in my humble opinion) Germans had more important things to be thinking about—is virtually guaranteed to be lost on me entirely in the first place. (2012)

Greil Marcus, *Mystery Train* (2nd ed., 1982)
It had actually been a good long time since I looked at this, when I brought it along with me recently on a cross-country train trip

(ha ha, get it?). I was really struck—chagrined, even—by seeing what a pervasive influence it has had on me (and, in fairness, on dozens if not hundreds of other music journalists, professional and wannabe alike). That whole stream-of-consciousness game of associations around favored artists and American cultural landmarks, taking a freewheeling intuitive style into one's arguments, along with some tendency to overstate the personal impact for effect, has virtually all been absorbed by me, for better or worse, not to mention various specific points of pungent observation, such as the one about Jerry Lee Lewis and Sam Phillips and pentecostal religion, or a few about Mott the Hoople. They are Greil Marcus's ideas, not mine. I have just chosen to live in that world. Over the years the artists he focuses on and lionizes here in his first outing have come to seem to me more eccentric than fundamentally central. It might be me, but I think it would be easy enough to pick and choose one's own favorites and make the cases for their various places in the cultural mainstream at large. For myself, I think of Jimi Hendrix, James Brown, the Velvet Underground, Jonathan Richman, Iggy Pop, and Big Star. There's a place for Brits here, of course—the Beatles and Stones, Marc Bolan, David Bowie, Mott the Hoople, the Pet Shop Boys. After all this time it looks like the only real naturals that Marcus picked were Robert Johnson and Elvis Presley. Harmonica Frank, the Band, Sly Stone, and Randy Newman are variously significant but second-tier or even more minor. I realize I could be out on a limb with that point, but I think anyone can agree that the Elvis piece is where Marcus is most original and most persuasive here. He focuses on basically one album, *The Sun Sessions*, with a focus no one has produced for any one album anywhere, figuratively speaking. All the warm-up exercises that precede it are rewarded, in the "Presliad," and it enables Marcus to roam even more freely and wantonly among his whims. In the extensive "Notes and Discographies," an appendix but fully a third of my tome (which is the 2nd edition; it comes to occupy more than half in later editions), there's a powerful sense of someone thriving and relishing the opportunity to read books and play music and turn ideas around in his head all day. That's when it's most fun. Marcus points to an electrifying way here to think about these things, tying together *Moby-Dick* and *The Pilgrim's Progress* and the invention of a nation and all this rock 'n' roll racket, and he communicates the excitement of making the connections with almost irresistible infectiousness. (2012)

Marilyn Manson, "Antichrist Superstar" (1996)
Parents, lock up your children, it's Marilyn Manson, scourge of a nation. Probably I never would have given any of this a second thought—too much concept in the naming schema, to start—except someone sent me a copy of the first album, which was way better than I expected. By the time of this follow-up the band had become a really great performing act. I attribute that to the influence of Trent Reznor and touring with Nine Inch Nails, and because Fort Lauderdale's finest, Brian Warner, has always been a decent songwriter. If I ever happen to make peace with the bombast of opera I believe it may be with Marilyn Manson pointing the way. Yes, this is formally and intentionally a rip on *Jesus Christ Superstar,* and no, I know, rock opera is another beast altogether. The tiresome Nietzsche thread in the *Antichrist Superstar* album does the service of locating the sonics closer to Richard Wagner than Pete Townshend (speaking as one who happens to love *Tommy*). I think you're supposed to care about the stories in opera but I don't care about the story here. What I like is the dense wallop, with a bottom that reaches to the molten core of the earth, where nothing is ever at rest. Even quieter moments (for the dynamics, see), with say a warbling choral sound straight out of Diamanda Galas, hover more as teams of wraiths and infernal termite buzz, alternating with football cheers, demon vocals, stepping down the scale into tumult, and a heavy riff that's ultimately quite satisfying. When it achieves full roar it's hard for me to see how you can call it anything but magnificent. (2013)

Joe Matt, *Peepshow* **(1992)**
Joe Matt's first foray into comic book autobiography (his self-declared career and raison d'etre from approximately the age of 24) is still so far his best. It's a collection of a few years' worth of the mundane adventures of his daily life in the late '80s and early '90s, opening an intriguing window into his development as an artist. That's not the only window it opens, of course—it's notorious for the occasionally grotesque candor of its revelations, which include shrieking fights with his girlfriend, repulsive habits of thrift and laziness, and, yes, too true, the inside view of a porn habit with particulars regarding fetish. It is a consummate portrait of ongoing clinical narcissism. He gets away with it (as much as he does) by strength of the comic book art, which is charming, by the fact that he tends to take ownership of his warts with relish instead of shame, blaming no one but himself for them, which is somehow charming, and because he's likable enough. In controlled doses. At a distance. And via the mediation of the printed comic book page. (Everyone who knows him reports that he's exactly as he describes himself, perhaps more so, and it's not like he doesn't catch on— he's often able to convey how others struggle to cope with him.) In the end he's not so different from you or me, just more willing to talk about his stuff and put it out there. What makes this worth it is the chance to trace the self-discovery as it happens. In the earliest pages you can see him feeling his way toward it. R. Crumb, Harvey Pekar, and many others by now have made careers of comic book autobiography, but no one does it like Joe Matt, who soon enough flails his way to a discipline he mostly manages to stay within: the single-page / tiny-panel installments he delivers at about a monthly rate. He explores variations along the way, but never drifts far from what can be done with a single page, a minimum of cross-hatching (it's nearly all line work), and plenty of black ink. And he not only bares his soul naked, for which he's famous, but also explores a good many other crannies along the way: the philosophy and practicalities of living cheap (some good tips!), his obsessions

with showering, with collecting, with walking, the strange cats with whom he has lived, and all kinds of aspects of his art, including comical abstract exercises. If I didn't know better I'd be tempted to compare him to Montaigne. (2010)

Horace McCoy, *They Shoot Horses, Don't They?* (1935)
Horace McCoy is another newspaperman of the Great Depression who turned to crime fiction after arriving in California, followed shortly by a career and steady work as a screenplay writer. His first novel eventually became a movie, but that wasn't until nearly 15 years after his death. As with a surprising number of the novels that series editor Robert Polito collected for the Library of America two-volume set of crime novels, it's as inventive and sure-footed as it is dour and gritty. In this case, some typographical stunts help ground the basic setting of the novel in a courtroom at the moment sentence is pronounced, with the context gradually filled in by a series of extended flashbacks. Robert Syverten, the narrator, and the defendant, is a bit of a Jimmy Stewart character by temperament, who has shown up in Hollywood to make his fortune. He meets Gloria Beatty, a few years older and far more chewed by the Hollywood grind of the time, with which she is alive with detail, even in her collapse. They both need to make money and Gloria suggests the marathon dance, an event that fortuitously is just about to start when they meet. It's a foolish idea, but desperate times call for desperate measures, and as the details of their participation slowly unfold it becomes apparent just how desperate those times and measures were. Marathon dances went on for days and weeks and months. Contestants here are allowed a 10-minute break every two hours and otherwise go around the clock; the break time must be used for eating and cleaning as well as sleeping. Contestants are required to keep moving to stay qualified, which necessitates partners taking turns sleeping on their feet while the other drags them around the floor. Periodic events such as footraces are also staged to liven it up, draw crowds, and cruelly to eliminate couples more

quickly. For something that may seem from our vantage as quaint and goofy as stuffing telephone booths or swallowing goldfish, it quickly becomes evident what these things really were. Gloria, for her part, remains resolutely a complete and relentless downer, bitter to the core—that has something to do with her eventual demise, an act perhaps more effectively framed as one of mercy than malice. The book is no marathon itself but rather quick, a pointed and sprint-like exercise that nonetheless seems to get well under the skin of its times. (2010)

Ian McEwan, *The Innocent* (1989)
Ian McEwan's deceptively straightforward novel of love and intrigue in 1950s Cold War Berlin brilliantly drops chunks and slices of various genres into the blender and purees. As romance, its core, it's most affecting, although that may be because its turn to horror is so surprising, unsettling, and ferociously unrelenting that the shock leaves one softened for human qualities—indeed, pathetically yearning for them. The appurtenances of spy novel, and rock 'n' roll coming of age tale, are there more as decoration, or blessed distraction. Maybe because they're both Brits playing along the borders of cruelty and sexuality, McEwan here reminds me some of John Fowles. But underneath all the crisp pluck and cheeky diffidence, I get the sense there's more of a heart here than in anything from Fowles. (2007)

Modern Lovers, "Pablo Picasso" (1972)
Before Jonathan Richman became the spritely endearing saint we have known today and for the past many decades, he was some kind of rock 'n' roll demon. Most of the surviving evidence exists on the essential album *The Modern Lovers*. It's true that the rock 'n' roll is still strong with him, and always has been, as I witnessed again for myself just a couple weeks ago. He was playing an acoustic guitar as he always does and accompanied only by Tommy Larkins on a cluttered drumkit, traveling the land with a compelling polyglot

message of inner peace and childlike fun. "Pablo Picasso," by contrast, is raw, frustrated, and gripping, with Frankenstein rhythms and a corkscrew electric guitar that drills for the skull. I love it insanely. I love it to pieces. Arguably it fits with Richman's series of latter-day songs about artists such as Vermeer, Van Gogh, and Walter Johnson, but not really: "Well some people try to pick up girls / And get called assholes / This never happened to Pablo Picasso." That's the gist. "Well he was only five foot three / But girls could not resist his stare / Pablo Picasso never got called an asshole / Not in New York." A few years ago, again with Larkins, I saw him do a version of it, but he's made it more family-friendly now, clipping off the swear word entirely, which I do think is a bit unfortunate. Or my inner rock 'n' roll demon thinks so. It's not like Richman would have to snarl or be surly or anything. But Jonathan Richman gets to do what Jonathan Richman wants to do. Those are the rules around here. (2011)

Modern Times (Charles Chaplin, 1936)
I saw *Modern Times* and Charlie Chaplin for the first time in 1972, when I was 17, and it was a pleasure. I don't want to overstate, but I think Charlie Chaplin was the first real star of the past that I understood. Not even the Marx Brothers or Boris Karloff had done as much for me, or Elvis, although within a couple of years I would go through familiar Humphrey Bogart, or "Bogey," gyrations. Maybe the Chaplin made its great impression because I saw it on a big screen, with all the fine points present (the dark room, the voluminous sound, the companionable strangers), rather than fighting sleep late at night on TV, interrupted by commercials. More likely it was because that day I happened to be caught up into a deep, black depression following an amphetamine run, a little one. I was crashing. Not to overstate.

My father, of course, was not aware of that when he took me to see *Modern Times*, driving me to the theater and dropping me off with enough money for admission and treats. He just had the impression I was a little down and he thought the movie might cheer me up. And he was right, not because the laughs chased away the gloom—though I did laugh, and registered the usual wonder at how brilliantly funny some of those sequences are. It cheered me rather, I think, because it provided the necessary space and time to let me get out of the worst clutches of the waning chemicals. It gave me something to do. I was discovering that pulling out of the tailspin that is the end of an amphetamine run, even a small one, is not easy and more than anything requires time.

It's fair enough, on some level, to say that amphetamine is my favorite drug, though I used and abused it only in one of its mildest forms and that only intermittently. I was never what you might call a speed freak. Mainly I took white cross, which I've also heard called cross-tops. They are small white pills grooved on one side with an "X." No benzedrine for me, no dexedrine, no greenies or needles or crystal meth, though even now, more than 20 years later, a part of me longs for *those* fucking jolts, yearns for them so viscerally that my heart actually flutters, sentient itself perhaps thinking of what would be required of it in the event, and a sickly feeling crawls up the back of my thighs and settles in my stomach, and I don't feel so good.

If my favorite drug is amphetamine then it's probably no surprise that my favorite carnival midway ride is the Roundup. There's a version of it seen in the French movie *The 400 Blows*. It's the ride that delivers pure centrifugal Gs; you stand there holding rails, facing into the center of a circle, and it spins round fast, tilting up sideways like a gyroscope when it gets going fast enough. I tried it a few years further on than I should have, in my early 30s, and I was almost sick to my stomach. But when I was 13 and 14 I could ride that damn thing all day. And tomorrow too.

For a period of about three years in my late teens, from 1972 to 1975, I gradually worked my way into a little habit of taking the white crosses in runs—burning through them by the hundred, forgoing sleep and food in favor of taking more, in larger quantities, for days at a time. I loved those wicked pills, fiendishly and with guilt, loved them. If I remember right, they went for a quarter apiece, five for a dollar, which is about as many as I was told to take, and you could get a hundred of them for 15 dollars. I don't ever remember it as a particularly popular drug, which did puzzle me. I seemed to be alone on this one. Perhaps its adherents die or become mute from the extremes of pleasure and horror, or maybe they just don't talk to each other—too busy, man—but in my high school it wasn't nearly as popular as alcohol or marijuana or LSD.

As for the effects of amphetamine, they reduce one more or less to the vernacular. Here is its appeal: it kicks your ass. It takes hold quickly, within 20 minutes or less of swallowing the pills, and it brings an insanely penetrating, bated-breath intensity to all things. You experience the illusion of the purest most focused concentration of which you've ever been capable, though the truth is that your fierce concentration is all too often spent on something like counting.

You might (or might not) get a lot of filing or typing or cross-hatching done. The real thrill lies in what it does to the body. It is the most body drug I have taken. According to science, amphetamine essentially goes to the cells of your body and releases the extra energy stored there for emergency use. There is a constant rushing sensation, a feeling of hurtling forward and changing mass drastically like one experiences on carnival rides such as the Roundup, but with utter poise and control. The skin tingles everywhere and even more intensely if it is felt or bumped or squeezed. The corridor along the spine, from the small of the back to the back of the head, glows and pulses. It is what I imagine immortality is like.

It is by far the best drug for listening to music. Every rush of pleasure that music provides is super-amplified along the spinal cord and

in the belly and back of the neck and head. The drug also suppresses appetite, its primary use as a prescription drug. On the upswing
that's fine. Who needs to eat when you feel like *that?* Some said sex
on it was not possible but my experience was exactly the opposite. I
found myself getting memorably hard and staying so and returning
again quickly to it, following orgasm after orgasm, each one incredibly intense. I have to think it would have been even better with a
partner. Ahem.

With speed, the tolerance slopes are steep. It is truly an unfor-
giving drug. Think about it. If amphetamine goes to your cells to
release the energy stored there for emergency, and at the same time
suppresses your appetite, then you are going the wrong way in two directions at once. You have quit your job and begun to spend your re-
tirement principal on peep shows. Diminishing returns doesn't even
begin to describe it.

Nights after taking it I could never sleep; after the first time I
didn't even expect to. I stayed awake and played Doors albums in
the dark, shivering under sheets and thin blanket. The next day
I had to suffer through, that was all there was for it, because the
drug was rarely available at school two days in a row. But when it did
happen to be around again, or after I had begun to buy as much as
I could when it was available, I found that the four or five pills I'd
taken the day before had a negligible effect. I needed more to get
off as good again. It was even worse on the third day, and that's how
it went. Sooner or later you had to face it. You fought the law and
the law won.

After high school, when I began to buy the pills a hundred at
a time, I saw the tolerance curve clear, or at least as much of it as
I could stand. Though I would always start with the usual four or
five or six pills, I often found myself taking the last 20 or 30 all at
once, along about the morning of the third or fourth day—"eating

them like M&Ms," I would say—and even that didn't have the effect of the first five. But I was hooked. I couldn't begin to conceive of taking that first handful, sweating out the bad night and day that followed, and then waiting a week or longer to take them again, after my tolerance had returned. You know, the rational thing to do. Not when I had them right there. No, oh no. And not when it felt so good to be rushing again. I had to have that sensation again as soon as possible.

Toward the end, not surprisingly, everything went out of control and it was frightening. It's hard to compare these things, but my guess is that the depression and all the physical and other symptoms that come with crashing, inevitable crashing, are more severe than the sense of well-being at its highest. Amphetamine doesn't give back as much as it takes, in other words.

I hasten to point out, lest anyone think they are reading the words of a drug fiend who should be locked up and the key thrown away, that there is likely some element of dramatization to what I say here. That is in my nature. The fact is that my use of amphetamine was limited to the pills, on some dozen or so scattered occasions over a period of three years, and that my longest "runs" amounted to no more than four days.

The day that my father took me to *Modern Times* it was in my head to kill myself, if only to end a painful bleak sinking feeling of monotonous nothingness. But sitting lumpen in that dark theater, soaking in the blast of Chaplin's amazing music, and watching the black and white antics of the Tramp and his sidekick Gamin (played by Paulette Goddard), gave me time to recover a sense of well-being, enough to restore my appetite and let me look forward to a good night's sleep, which so often is all that anyone needs to embrace life again, sweet life, strong and brave. Cue choir.

Later I began to cut the drug with valium when I could get my hands on both at once. Valium doesn't have the cultural resonance of Charlie Chaplin but in general it was better at getting me through, because the fact is that as bad as the day was that I saw *Modern Times* a little more than a year later I had the opportunity to buy speed again and I took it. And thus began the second half of my speed consuming career. You see, it goes on and on. It's really a very simple story.

As for Charlie Chaplin and *Modern Times*, I actually returned to them later, much later, and found that more or less they were as good as I remembered. *Modern Times* is "modern" in many different ways. The music, by Chaplin, is often shrill, staccato, and angular. *Modern Times* is also acutely aware of the strikes, unemployment, class conflicts, and labor unrest ripping into the fabric of the culture and economy at the time of its release, deep into the Depression. Explicit cocaine use is not only acknowledged but played as a joke, and a good one. Chaplin's mincing about, and his use of characters such as a prison inmate working on a needlepoint project, imply layers of hidden farcical sexuality. And when the vagabond couple is left alone in a department store overnight the first thing they do is go to the toys section and start playing. Or is that "post-modern" to treat the human condition and/or enterprise as one conducted essentially by immature children?

The next time I saw it, some 10 years later, I was married and it became a favorite of ours. We identified with the Tramp and the Gamin, making their way in a harsh world. What they wanted seemed so understandable, and also understandable, for us, was its being out of reach—a home to share breakfast in. They were willing to work for it! The indomitability of their spirit inspired me. "Buck up. Never say die. We'll get along!"—those words, silly as they, actually came to mean a lot.

Come to think of it, they are also a very fine prescription indeed for detoxing from amphetamine, or at least most of the difficulties associated therewith. "Buck up. Never say die. We'll get along!" Help is always right around the corner. Sometimes, like a train, you can even hear it coming. (1999)

Van Morrison, "T.B. Sheets" (1967)
Van Morrison was just 21 when he wrote and recorded this remarkable meditation on untimely death, which is stripped down to essentials even though it goes on a long while: a sparse open arrangement, moody distracted guitar licks, equally moody organ fills, a piercing harmonica, and the singer trying to deal with the fact that it's the middle of the night, his woman is on her deathbed, and the room is stuffy and smells bad. "I can almost smell your T.B. sheets," he says, muttering to himself, "Gotta go. Gotta get away." "I want a drink of water," he says. "I'll send somebody around later." Legend has it that Morrison broke down in tears after the session. That's no wonder. It's meticulously imagined and he is well inside it. The better question may be how a 21-year-old Irish rock 'n' roll lad came to dream up such a thing in the first place (which may or may not be answered in terms of psychic vibrations by the circumstances and events of Morrison's visit to the US during which this was recorded). John Lee Hooker covered this song five years later, and it's a worthy version as Hooker certainly has the doomy authority to put it over. But I'm not sure even so that he touches this Morrison original, which is so bold about its stark scenario and candid themes, so rooted in the sensory details of an overwhelming and horrific moment in the lives of two people, of whom we know only their immediate circumstances and nothing else. He finally flees the scene, leaving the radio on to play for her, and takes us in his mind with him, welcome respite. (2011)

Mothers of Invention, "Who Are the Brain Police?" (1966)
Here's a nod (if not outright shout-out) to my young high school self. It came along a few years before I was actually in high school,

but high school is when it spoke to me. The spooky paranoia and ham-handed production effects, with the obvious big-brother themes, suited my point of view, one of those things I recall I hoped I would always remember as a grown-up. I forget most of the rest now. It's from the auspicious double-LP *Freak Out*, which signaled all the elements to come in the entirety of Frank Zappa's career: the mordant wit, the humanist intellect, the compositional experimentation, the musical chops, and the belching and farting. Honestly, I miss the clichés and received wisdom on display here— "plastic" as perhaps the most devastating insult imaginable, deeply grounded resentment at corporate as well as government attempts to control intellectual honesty, and a willingness to let the vectors go erratic and the mix sloppy in emulation of chaos. Why not? I'm pretty sure the clichés and received wisdom of our current age are far more pernicious and feeble: the vapid tightness of cool, economic bootstrapping as viable strategy for improvement to character, material wealth as the unmistakable sign of God's grace, "government is the problem not the solution." You know what I'm talking about. Sometimes Frank Zappa's death in 1993 looks like Hunter Thompson's in 2005, a bad sign that times just got worse in ways we never could have imagined previously. But now I'm getting sentimental. (2011)

Mott the Hoople, "All the Young Dudes" (Nov. 4, 1972, #37)
This is almost surely the best song David Bowie ever gave away, and Ian Hunter and his mates prove in a matter of three and a half minutes they were just the ones for it. No one, not even Bowie, does or has ever done this song better. Mick Ralphs's plaintive guitar opens and already it's a heartache. Then Hunter arrives at the mic, mumbling about suicide and kicks in the head, with a melody line that falls face-forward in slow motion, and the sweet pathos is underway in earnest. By the time of the chorus, one of the great moments of '70s rock is pealing forth like doves released from a box. The song materialized in the glam era, and it's all about putting on a good

show, but it comes with its own bag of tricks, chipped in by people wearing their shades 24/7, doubtless up for days on end weary and ragged. They fit this song out with hand-clapping, a homely, rolling drumkit, and a lovely droning organ. The totality of it busies itself sending a message, and here is that message: "Carry the news ... Boogaloo dudes ('stand up, come on')." You could put an entire choral choir behind this and it would never get any more majestic than that. Extra-credit inspirational verse: "Television man is crazy / Saying we're juvenile delinquent wrecks / Oh, man, I need TV when I've got T. Rex?" (2010)

My Kid Could Paint That (**Amir Bar-Lev, 2007**)

As filmmaker Amir Bar-Lev can be heard mentioning at one point, this started out as a documentary "about modern art," by which I think he mostly meant the American work that spun out of New York after World War II, starting with abstract expressionism and continuing on through post-Warhol pop art, much of which eventually came to command grotesquely bloated prices. Bar-Lev focuses on the work of Marla Olmstead of Binghamton, New York, who made a splash in the art world circa 2005 as a 4-year-old with her vivid abstract canvases. Bar-Lev sketches out the story of how her work came to attention first in a Binghamton coffeeshop, where the owner thought it would be funny to hang her paintings. When people wanted to buy them, that started the ball rolling. Eventually Marla's work ended up in a local gallery, and then to a showing and reviewed in New York City. At that point, the freakish nature of the story—*preschooler as brilliant abstract expressionist*—took over.

Midway through the filming of this documentary, the hysteria reaches the point where a *60 Minutes* piece airs about Marla. An astute media observer here notes that these kinds of stories, once they take on a life of their own, sooner or later become about the controversy they raise, even if they have to invent new twists. In this case it was exactly that *60 Minutes* story, which questioned whether or not

Marla is the one producing, or at least completing, the work credited to her. And so the undermining seed is planted, and this film limps home attempting to solve the arguably off-the-point but deeply puzzling mystery. The questions it raises are not easy. Do you like abstract art? Why? Do you like it less if it is produced by a kid? Why? Do you like it less if it is produced by her father? Why? Does your opinion about an artwork change after you learn personal details of an artist's life? Why? Is it impossible to form a judgment about art if you don't have information about the artist? Why? And so forth.

I think a lot of the paintings credited to Marla are great. And when the various art critics and lovers of her work start bringing the analysis, it's hard not to be even more impressed. At one point the elements of a painting are lovingly discussed by an enthusiastic owner, and make a good argument for how impressive the work is. At the same time, I have to admit that the mystery can't help but give me some pause. If the father is actually the artist, why doesn't he take credit? If Marla is actually the artist, why can't her production of it be captured on film? In fact, one of her paintings *is* produced on film, but now the problem is embedded at deeper levels: somehow that painting doesn't seem up to the quality of her other work. But is that true, or has it become a problem of perception, of a personal bias created by what we know or think we know? The work that can be seen at Marla's website, created since this documentary, seems to me even better than what's on view in the documentary, which is encouraging. For now, we may have to accept that this movie and Marla's (and/or her father's) work seem to be one of those points where we find "reality" utterly pixelated—compare the situation in another movie with an art mystery, *Who the #$&% Is Jackson Pollock?* (2010)

N

The letter N is a simple and solid consonant, as plain as the brown earth, representing basically only one sound and a sound that no other letter approximates or mimics. Well, oh, wait a second. There is also the "ng" formation, a kind of vocalized choking noise emulating the sounds G and N might make if they were having sex. Oh, wait, yes, note: this also applies with K, as in "thunk." Which is the sound my head makes on my desktop every time I attempt these catalogs. Because I just remembered the little tricks N gets up to with K, G, and who knows what other letters, I can't think about it now I'm in a bit of a bad mood. I'm speaking, of course, of the so-called silent letter. Know what I mean, gnat? Can we think about this for a second? The silent letter—the *silent* letter? Aren't we supposed to be talking about speech here?! What are these silent letters doing all over the place?! It makes me feel so negative. The primary sound of N is made with a vocalized pushing of the tongue to the roof of the mouth. It is similar to M, a tender grunt made with closed lips. The vocalizing enables either to be elongated at will, viz., "hmm," a feat that B, D, and other vocalized consonants can't do. But M and N are easily distinguished—one involves a compression of the lips, and the other the tongue as described above. Alphabet makers must have seen some similarity, if they put them next to one another and made their shapes so similar, even including the parallel hump shapes of the lowercases, which I neglected to mention before. The letter N is the first letter in the second half of the alphabet—and it's a long way home from here, baby. Sometimes, like a sandwich made with apostrophes, it represents "and" all on its own, e.g., "well, get in that kitchen / Make some noise with the pots 'n' pans." But the letter N may be most famous now for its general air of rejection: no, non, nyet, nope, negatory, N/A, said nope, nuh-uh, no way, naw I don't think so, and so forth. Compare Y. Children express negation by chanting "na-na-na" at one another. Later, as adults, they will do the same by calling one another nihilists. In scientific and mathematical formulation n is the ultimate cipher, a focal point of expression, that which we solve for. I read an article once about shopping for computers and it advised looking for the best deals at the "n - 1" level of technology, where n represented the present state of the art and "n - 1" the state of the art just before that. Some very good deals on machines there still, if you understand the market. But do I understand the market these days? I think I would have to say N. (2015)

Randy Newman, "I Want You to Hurt Like I Do" (1988)
Some of those early Randy Newman albums seem to me a bit over-rated, but it all balances out because I think some of those from the '80s are underrated—notably *Trouble in Paradise* and *Land of Dreams*, the latter of which provides a home for this song. A lot of Randy Newman's best stuff tends to get over by slapping a wiseass smirk in front of outrageously ignorant declarations, usually about racism and its analogues, set carefully into musically lulling settings (Newman takes his place in a family of movie composers). His partisans fob the excesses off on capital-I irony. It's seems a lot of passive-aggressive energy to me, to get to the point, but it still works much of the time, not least because Newman himself remains so careful about what he does. He's got a lot of courage and a lot of wit too. That's a good combination and this is where he puts it over with few

peers. At first it seems like the usual for Newman, with the singer's self-reported reprehensible behavior, the way he treats his family and loved ones and shirks his responsibilities, most painfully his children. But it's rousing when you realize how truthful he is, from beginning to end, and how Newman has found perhaps the perfect mouthpiece to put it over—a cynical performer much like himself. There's actually nothing funny about it. It's tragic. It's mean. It's brutal. The only thing that gives irony any purchase at all is the idea that someone like the singer describes himself could come up with this single great prize of insight—*I want you to hurt like I do.* (2012)

Nirvana, "Come as You Are" (April 18, 1992, #32)

No, this is not the song that tore down the wall and liberated a generation. That was "Smells Like Teen Spirit," which you can remember by its vastly more iconic title. But I think that this, the second go at the top 40 and also from the *Nevermind* album, is the better song. It has the gloomy moodiness Cobain is famous for, much of it compressed into the canny, lilting melody he has concocted, which enables just the bass and a simple drum pattern and his voice to carry a lot of it, certainly all the way to the chorus, where things are suitably filled out with escalating tensions and big guitar chords and hard-hit drums. What is he going on about? Something about a gun? Memory? "Memoria"? There are many syllables in the verses, almost chanted—"Come as you are, as you were / As I want you to be / As a friend, as a friend / As on old enemy"—but it's also kind of hard to make out the words as he's singing. It is the point with so many Nirvana songs, the voice straining against the notes straining against the words and the resulting frictions, followed by release. This is one of the finest they ever did. It just soars, floats off like a hot-air balloon and twirls in kodachrome daylight, and it's so beautiful for a moment it's almost overwhelming. (2010)

Lazirvana (Nirvana laser light show)

It's not easy to get all the way behind something wherein the experience is purely enhanced by smoking pot. But the Pacific Science

Center's latest laser light show, *Lazirvana*, is exactly that. Well, all right, it's probably for Nirvana fans only. And I didn't smoke any pot beforehand. But the fact is that this show is more entertaining than anyone could have had a right to expect. There's something soothing and right about lying on your back in the dark, watching bright lights and listening to some of your favorite music.

Based on a fairly canny selection of tracks from the Nirvana catalog, *Lazirvana* turns what would normally promise to be just the usual cut-and-dried case of pulsating spirographics animation into something far more enjoyable, which of course is not to be confused with profound. It doesn't hurt either that the volume for this show is set to LOUD and that most of the shapes are abstract (a sad stick figure in the opening of "Come As You Are" was embarrassing and awkward—I was glad there was little more of that).

All that you would expect were present—"Smells Like Teen Spirit," "Heart-Shaped Box," and "All Apologies" front and center—but the material draws also from less familiar sources, and includes "Sliver," "Plateau," and more nice touches.

For the most part, the graphics are the usual pastiche of morphing geometry but some worked particularly well. "Teen Spirit" and a couple others boasted multilevel 3D animation, and when all the stops were pulled, as on "Scentless Apprentice," there was a certain, um, overwhelming majestic transcendence to the whole thing. You wanted to stand up and cheer. Except it was so nice and comfortable on the floor. Make a point of getting there early. You do want a spot on the floor for this one. (1997)

Nirvana, "Moist Vagina" (1993)
Not just one of Kurt Cobain's most personal songs, but in fact one of the most personal songs by anyone ever. This is a category where "greatest" does not always equate to comfortable listening

experience. See Hank Williams's "Angel of Death," John Lennon's "Mother," Big Star's "Nightime," or Marianne Faithfull's "Why D'ya Do It." In the case of "Moist Vagina," it doesn't matter to me that it doesn't make sense. It doesn't have to. He is using language in another way. Or he is using another language. Whatever he means to be saying, he can't get it out in any simple or straightforward way. There's too much shame, choking him off, making the words disappear. But he doesn't need to do much more. The radioactive language does a lot of the work here—the title, most obviously. Try talking to anyone about this song. It's impossible. It's worse than "Rape Me." People snicker. They blush. They get annoyed, or mad. They act as if they've seen a turd on the clean floor, a big one, a fresh one. Just speaking the title in conversation connects you instantly with the profound and unsettling shame. These clinical, detached words. The awkwardness, the tentativeness of the "story," lights the way to a kind of bruised innocence everyone knows. The ferocious litany of taboos burns into you, and the effect is harsh. Something haunts this song—something small and afraid. You just don't know what. "She had a moist vagina. I something ... of her anus. I prefer her to wear the other. Marijuana. Marijuana. Marijuana." "Marijuana" is repeated something like 15 times towards the end of the song. And then, as finale, a vocal croak that goes as far as breath can take it, proving once again that Kurt Cobain had a voice that will live forever, and he was willing to do whatever he felt like with it. Of course this was a B-side. If Wal-Mart isn't going to carry "Rape Me," which got changed to something lame, I forget what, then no way in hell are they letting anything like this near it. It came with the "All Apologies" single, which I bought for this song, as much as I was annoyed by its title. Once I got past that, the rest was easy. (2005)

No (Pablo Larrain, 2012)

Not bad, not bad. I thought Chilean director Pablo Larrain's *Tony Manero* was more interesting, if not necessarily the better movie. This story of the 1988 Pinochet referendum in Chile comes with all kinds of built-in advantages, not least the upbeat story. Gale Garcia Bernal, aka Latin America's Jean-Pierre Leaud, is a welcome presence as always. The plotline, involving two people in one ad agency working on opposing sides of a political battle, is not only ridiculous, but also "not true." And other points of importance have also been exposed as "not true," including the real-life existence of the main character, Rene Saavedra (Bernal). Well, nobody's perfect. Truthiness on display, at multiple levels. (2014)

O

Oh there have to be so many ways to go with this, right? — having arrived at the fourth vowel and 15th letter of the alphabet. Coordination of the following. Considerations for the poetic "O," to which I admit I am partial, as in "O joy" (although, on conventional grounds, I really don't mind typing the H, except, you know, oh what the blasted hell is it doing there). Maybe the poetic O now bears a burden of irony, but also, straight up, it's *poetic*. O lovely locution. O bring it on. Considerations for the orgasm, naturally. The orgasm face, to wit—the "oh face" (or is that "O face," because it's more poetical?). Considerations for Om, which rises from the belly and extends vibrations-wise into the universe. Speaking of the universe, O is among the most universal of the vowels, right? Certainly in the long version. The short version is a little more problematical, swapping around, with A, various mysterious intonations I confess I don't always hear (sometimes, both A and O, combined with U, or W, or A with itself), as in "stop," "halt," "caught," "awful," "foul," and/or "aardvark." But let that go. It's English, Jake. In O we do find one of the most beautiful letters in the perfect shape of the circle. The mystic circle. The only thing more perfect is the sphere, which O kind of approximates too. In contrast, since I brought it up, there is the masculinist upright bar of the I, and all attendant problems with ego fixation (as noted elsewhere). But among the letters there is otherwise truly no tri- angle, no square, no rectangle. Ironically, in some fonts the O be- comes a square. That's a chortle, but more often it is the D taking the shape if any letter does. But what do I know about typefaces? I scribble in notebooks. Still, the letter O, the letter I probably, and what else? U? Here we are now at the primal levels. Does that per- haps account for why O is tucked so relatively deep into the alpha- bet, all the way to the back in the second half? What is *that* about? Furthermore, stepping back for a little light perspective, take that third tray of letters from the alphabet the way I learned it—L, M, N, O, and P. I think there might have been a rock band called LMNOP and it's really fun to say too, or sing, as in the "ABC Song." You could almost spell out the word "lemon" if you could get that O up in front of the N. And throw in the E. Well, you know what I mean. Making lemons out of lemonade, right? Well, that's just O for you. Everywhere you want to be. (2015)

Danny O'Keefe, "Good Time Charlie's Got the Blues" (Sept. 23, 1972, #9)
Spokane native Danny O'Keefe must have always known he had a winner with this song. He recorded it in 1967, though that version was never released, and then he gave it away to a band called the Bards, from Moses Lake, Washington. Then he recorded it again for his first album, and then he recorded it one more time for his second album, and that's the version that finally made the airwaves. It came out at going-back-to-school time for me in my senior year of high school, and I loved to hear it come sidling in on the radio as I drove around. So acutely aware of the passage of time, the Faulknerian unceasingness of it, so full of sadness. "You know my heart keeps tellin' me," the singer bleats, "you're not a kid at 33." No, you're not a kid at 33, I know that feeling too now, but I didn't feel that much like a kid at 17 either, so I identified. Its burden is the well-worn burden of convention and expectation. The singer is not where he is supposed to be in life, he knows that nearly as well as he knows that

where he's supposed to be is not where he wants to be. That endless dilemma, because also he doesn't exactly know where he wants to be. On the road, pickin' a guitar, sitting soft at a sunset—those are the things he wants, although unfortunately "Everybody's gone away / Said they're movin' to LA." And furthermore, the hard truths of life just now really seem to be settling in: "Some gotta win, some gotta lose." A pause to let that sink in. "Good Time Charlie's got the blues." It's almost funny, if you think of it as ruminating third-person braggadocio, but the mood of the song throws sand all over that and everything, except further delicious wistful sadness. (2014)

Roy Orbison, "In Dreams" (Feb. 23, 1963, #7)
This is probably here for one reason only: its uncanny use by David Lynch in his 1986 movie, *Blue Velvet*. Roy Orbison has plenty of good songs, for any of which the case can be made over this—"Crying," "Only the Lonely," "Running Scared." Yeah, yeah. And I love them too. But I can never forget the way I saw this ("A candy-colored clown they call the sandman") utterly reinvented. At the same time it's a perfectly typical, and typically effective, Roy Orbison outing, full of tender feelings of loss, yearning, and pain that somehow only his operatic warble gets over with just the right mixture of uncertainty and confidence. The dreams he happens to occupy may not be the same as Frank Booth's, last seen gasping into his face mask. But they are equally as futile, verging on a kind of romance of emptiness without crossing the line into out-and-out nihilism, obscured rather by willfully blind hope, and thus far more affecting. That, in short, is the Roy Orbison specialty. And watch how he does it: skating atop a musical arrangement that pits a little band against a big orchestra and builds the tension inexorably as it goes, he tells the tale. In dreams he walks with her. In dreams he talks with her. They're together in dreams. In dreams. But just before the dawn— well, you know how this ends. Come on. It's a Roy Orbison song. He remembers that she said good-bye. (2010)

Susan Orlean, *The Orchid Thief* (1998)

In general terms, you're never going to go far wrong picking up a nonfiction book by a *New Yorker* writer, and sure enough, Susan Orlean's meditations on her travels through Florida and the life of its plant life was pretty slick. It made me think about orchids more than I ever have, and it taught me a few things I hadn't known (for some reason I had the impression they were all odorless). I think I liked it best when she got into some history of Florida real estate scams. I responded on a general level to the collector bug infecting so many of the people she meets and describes, including the star of the show, John Laroche. I don't know much about orchids but I am familiar with the collector mentality—and it did make me want to know more about orchids. A few times it sent me rushing to the Internet to look up pictures, which are oddly missing in this book. There shouldn't just be pictures in this book, there should be old-fashioned color plates. Orlean's book and those Internet pictures didn't even close the gap enough for me—I realized, with some frustration, that I wanted good high-definition color photos *and* someone I could interact with and put questions to. Even better than pictures, actual plants, with someone to point out their features. A one- to two-hour presentation with full multimedia and, preferably, live plants. With extensive time for questions and answers and digressions. A guided tour. Orlean's book awakened the interest, at least for as long as it took me to read it. I suspect it won't go much further than that, but still, that's pretty good for a guy with the opposite of a green thumb and a book with no pictures. I came to it because of the furshlugginer *Adaptation.* movie, of course, and the effect was to make me realize again what a slight and indulgent movie it is. I suppose saying it does a disservice to the book or writer is missing the point, because Orlean probably made more money and found more fame and opportunity this way than if the movie had been the least bit sincere, let alone faithful. I know, I know, in that case it would at best be in reruns by now on some nature cable-TV channel. But that's the version I want to see! (Note to self: DVR.) (2012)

Gilbert O'Sullivan, "Alone Again (Naturally)"
(July 1, 1972, #1, 6 wks.)
Irish skiffle-influenced singer/songwriter Gilbert O'Sullivan (not to be confused with Gilbert & Sullivan, it says here) basically ruled the AM radio waves in the summer of 1972 with this nagging ditty that almost instantly crawled under my skin. Aftershocks could still be felt in 1999 with its use in the movie *The Virgin Suicides* and it still retains power today, with its drippy sing-songy wallow in self-pity and its extraordinary capacity to provoke delicious sadness. File under "guilty pleasure"—but I also note it had a six-week stay at #1, a much longer run than usual for the '60s and '70s. So, in liking it, I was hardly alone ("again, naturally"). It's utterly forthright, if cloyingly precious, in declaring its despondency: "I promise myself to treat myself / And visit a nearby tower / And climbing to the top / Throw myself off." Crying time starts in the third verse, all groundwork laid, when the singer describes, first, his mother's bewilderment at his father's death, and then, shortly after, her own death. "I cried and cried all day," he announces. Well, who wouldn't? I hadn't heard this in the longest time and in my memory it also featured the death of a pet, a cat I thought, but that doesn't seem to be here, nor anything like it in O'Sullivan's two other, vastly inferior chart appearances ("Clair" and "Get Down"). So I must have imagined it. Take a listen to this, if you don't remember it, and you'll understand why anyone might recall it including a dead beloved kitten. And so, right here, this is the end of the line for me with Gilbert O'Sullivan, which leaves him, of course... (2010)

P

With P, it's personal. After all, if I had happened to find myself among the landed aristocracy P would be all over my handkerchiefs, luggage, and pillowcases. So I have to like it by default, or seek further therapy. It's true that the letter itself bears unfortunate intimations of evacuation—#1, pee, #2, poop—even using it by name, e.g., "did you eat asparagus, your P smells funny." Never mind for the moment about those combinations with H or the silent mode, as in "physics" and "psychologists. The primary sound P makes is a comical charming delight, the hollow burst of a champagne cork. It encapsulates the pop moment with uncanny perfection, for those of us who love pop—P really brings the onomatopoeia here, the insouciant way that pop music, pop art, and the pop whatnot erupt into existence, explosively, hit the vocal for a beat, and slam the door shut again just like that. Is there anything more pop than the word "pop" itself? (At the same time, this could be part of the unfortunate association with droppings.) Speaking of pop and P, however, you should be careful when you use P with a microphone. Strangely, although the P mouth noise seems so natural to me, who bears it in his name, it is not used at all in the Arabic language—and in light of that, perhaps not surprisingly, it is also not actually used that much in English, ranking at #19 in frequency of usage. A question: How is all this related to the

garden vegetable I eat with a knife, done it all my life? The perspi-
cacious truth is out there (we hope). That reminds me that princes
and princesses everywhere have a certain obvious fondness for P,
except for the one who complained about the garden vegetable under her super plush 20 mattresses and 20 feather-beds. Jesus, lady,
get a life. Then there is the matter of minding one's Ps and Qs.
What *is* meant by that curious phrase? Speculation includes that it
stands for "pints" and "quarts," thus "please control your drinking."
Another possible acronym is "prime quality." Also "please," with the
Q serving as some awkward approximation of either "thank you" or
"excuse me," which in general makes me think the theory is arrant
nonsense—probably they all are. And I am off on fool's errands
again. But now I've abandoned my own Ps and Qs by speaking in
such a way. Down in the lowercase register, you have to wonder what
b, d, p, and perhaps q think about one another in their crazy funhouse mirror gyrations of line and ball. Here's another question,
this time about cause and effect: Are the earlier letters in the alphabet inherently more interesting, or are we more interested in them
because they come first? Because I have to tell you, in the end, it
looks like P just might be something of a drab and uninteresting
fellow after all. There's P all over this place. Ew. (2015)

Graham Parker & the Rumour, *Stick to Me* **(1977)**
It's going too far to say this represents a lost album, but it's still an
interesting story. With some buzz at their backs from the first two
albums of the year before, Graham Parker and the Rumour toured
a bunch and then retreated to the studio to record the third album
before embarking on more touring. Weeks of work went into it,
from the descriptions—string sections, a high concept for a long
psychedelic soul song, and all the usual angsty blood, sweat, and
tears. I suspect there's more to getting an album in the can than
most people (me included) generally know. All finished, something turned out to be wrong with the master tape, and suddenly
it was all lost. They had literally one week before they were set to

197

travel again. They went back to the studio. Nick Lowe presided over the board and the band pounded through the set, treating it necessarily more like live performance than whatever it was they had worked out before. For me, only dimly aware of the story, it was the first Graham Parker album I heard and it lit me up. Once I knew the *Stick to Me* story I could hear the rushed quality of it. "The Heat in Harlem," the stab at psychedelic soul, clearly suffers most. I don't know that it ever had enough in it to compete with "Time Has Come Today" but I wish I could hear the original to judge. Otherwise I think the circumstances may have actually served the session well, contributing to what makes it so good. The music is irresistible, spry and quick to its points, with an impatient edge, restless, prowling and moving and hitting sweet spots on practically every track. I like the way it retreats to the Muscle Shoals soul moves they have so fully absorbed. I like the way it entertains romantic American migratory history ("Soul on Ice," "The New York Shuffle," "The Heat in Harlem," "The Raid")—the desire to identify with some heroic American vision is so ingenuous it's ultimately winning. And I will say this about "The Heat in Harlem"—it only fails for me when I start to think about it too much. Otherwise it's all of a piece from when I was first infatuated with the album. It had me at the needle drop and the roaring title song, which takes off like a jet and drags everything else behind it, supersonic style. Both sides good. (2012)

Edmund Pearson, *Studies in Murder* (1924)
By my calculations, Edmund Lester Pearson was 12 and living in Newburyport, Massachusetts, less than 100 miles away, at the time of the murders in Fall River for which Lizzie Borden stood trial. The murders obviously made an impression on him. They are not only the subject of the longest and most detailed piece in this first collection of crime accounts by the meticulous librarian, but are mentioned in the other pieces here as well—and come up in his other collections for that matter (many of which are unfortunately long out of print and not readily available). Indeed, they were the subject once again

of his last book. As with the Scotsman William Roughead, of the late 19th century, the New Englander Pearson is a gifted amateur criminologist with a knack for thoroughness, relentlessly uncovering the relevant documents, reading them closely, and then telling the tales of the cases in polite, straightforward fashion, arguably glossing over some of the unpleasantness but never shying away from communicating the realities. It's the kind of thing, this bowing to the tender sensibilities of the reader, that most crime journalists of the past 50 years or so don't bother with any longer—in fact, the shocking and the lurid is pretty much what they always play to. Pearson picks his cases carefully, with an eye for those that remain most mystifying, either in terms of the whodunit itself or, more interestingly, in terms of the motivations that produced or could have justified them, the mystery of the human soul. He proceeds with a deceptively soothing, studious tone that examines everything in reach. The Borden murders would appear to stand as Pearson's primal American crime. It's not hard to see that Lizzie Borden, in her early 30s at the time, has to be considered the most likely suspect, though she was acquitted by a jury and remained in Fall River until her death in her 60s. It's not even hard to see, at least on some basic level that accepts such a degree of fury against her parents in the first place, what may have motivated her. What is most unsettling, however, and what seems to affect Pearson most about it, though he never quite expresses it so explicitly, is how perfectly forces of the universe seem to align and conspire in order to make the case against her such a difficult one. Though it is clear she must have done it, all the evidence is vague and circumstantial, eternally strangely allusive and indeterminate for such a savage crime, committed on a lovely summer midday in a house full of people coming and going. (2010)

A Personal Journey With Martin Scorsese Through American Movies
(**Martin Scorsese / Michael Henry Wilson, 1995**)
I'm not always sure what others mean by "essay-film," but I know my own sense of it favors both an individual point of view, and movie

clips—projects like *Los Angeles Plays Itself* and this long love letter from
Martin Scorsese, his salute to the movies of America in the middle of
the last century. As such, it is necessarily deep-dipped in the medium
itself. It was made in collaboration with the British Film Institute and
originally aired on UK television in 1995 (making its way to the US
some three years later). Scorsese is the host, with lots of voiceover
explication. Organized by digressive rumination, it comes armed
with—and this is the important part—copious film clips. You are
usually looking at scenes from movies, occasionally broken up by ar-
chival interview clips with key figures of film such as Clint Eastwood,
John Ford, Fritz Lang, Gregory Peck, Nicholas Ray, Douglas Sirk, and
Billy Wilder. It is the medium *on* the medium.

I was flabbergasted to find out how much I did not know when
I first saw *Personal Journey* several years ago, how much was simply
unfamiliar. Yet even in those cases I was not prepared for all the
great insight that Scorsese brings. *The Band Wagon, Cabiria, Footlight
Parade, 42nd Street, The Furies, Leave Her to Heaven, The Left-Handed
Gun, Murder by Contract, My Dream Is Yours, The Naked Spur, The
Regeneration, The Roaring Twenties, The Robe, The Tall T*—some of
them were vaguely familiar as titles. I furiously wrote down every
one and immediately ported them to my Netflix queue—those that
are available anyway. A good many are not. (I suspect I'm not the
only one trying such an exercise, because many fall into Netflix's
"very long wait" category.)

The documentary is organized like a text, divided into three
parts, each with its own set of chapters. Part 1 has sections on "The
Director's Dilemma," looking at the competing forces of commercial consideration and artistic integrity that confront film directors,
and "The Director as Storyteller," where Scorsese breaks down the
developments of his favorite genres (Westerns, gangster films, and
musicals), each of which gets a chapter. In Parts 2 and 3, he traces
broader developments: basic origins, the coming of sound, then

color, and then widescreen. In "The Director as Smuggler," which continues into Part 3, he explores trafficking in the socially taboo, including an impressively lucid discussion of film noir. Last, in "The Director as Iconoclast," he presents a kind of alternative canon, where the rules were broken, filmmakers made to pay a stiff price, and new standards created. Here you find discussion of films that surprise and don't surprise: *Bonnie and Clyde, Broken Blossoms, Citizen Kane, Faces, The Great Dictator, Lolita, The Man With the Golden Arm, A Streetcar Named Desire, Sweet Smell of Success.*

At the same time, all along, Scorsese offers a fundamental education on film, discussing the business of making them and going in depth into what makes it a unique art form, at one point listing and showing wonderful examples of basic film syntax: close-ups, irises, dissolves, masking, dolly shots, tracking shots, cross-cutting. "I've always felt that visual literacy is just as important as verbal literacy," he says (in chorus with every film director ever). It's often a treat just to hear him explain things. I will say I had some misgivings that in his discussions of *The Birth of a Nation* and Elia Kazan he is silent on the controversies surrounding them. It did not surprise me with Kazan, of course. He's been clear on that elsewhere. Still, call me PC if you must, I think the vile aspects of *The Birth of a Nation* should be affirmed in any discussion of it. It's a movie I respect, and enjoy seeing, and despise in equal measures.

Another point that suggests how good Scorsese is in *Personal Journey*: Scorsese's avowed favorite film genres, into which he travels so deeply, are probably my own least favorite. Scorsese compares Westerns, musicals, and gangster pictures to jazz, as inherently and uniquely American art forms, pointing out the appeal of the enduring American frontier myth of the West, the burgeoning metropolises of the East with their constant flows of immigrants who must survive in a society that systematically marginalizes them, and Broadway. His narrative here makes films I know I don't like look vibrant and interesting—*Murder by Contract, The Left-Handed Gun, The Searchers*—and he makes me want to look at them again. Often it turns out I still don't like them. But I admit I like the way they play in this documentary.

Scorsese's whole approach is at once so ambitious and so illuminating that I'm happy just watching him break it all down and following along where he rambles, wherever he wants to go. At nearly four hours it's way too short. He almost casually grapples with giant issues, and the insights can come thick and fast and from all directions as he clarifies things. He doesn't shy away from difficult and complex issues such as violence either. In that particular case, he turns to Fritz Lang to make the point. Wearing an eye-patch and monocle, sucking on a hand-rolled cigarette, speaking in rumbling tones with a thick German accent and ruined face, Lang lays it out straight: "Violence has become in my opinion a definite point in the script. It has a dramaturgical reason to be there. You see, I don't think that people believe in the devil, with the horns and the forked tail. And therefore they don't believe in punishment after they are dead. So my question was ... what are people *fearing*? ... And that is physical pain. And physical pain comes from violence. And that, I think, is today the only fact which people really fear, and therefore it has become a definite part of life, and naturally also of scripts." (2014)

Pet Shop Boys, "Liberation" (1993)
I like the wukka-wukka guitar that textures and drives this. I like the scenario in the lyrics of love finally acknowledged and accepted, and I like that it happens on a car ride late at night, involving the simple expedient of holding hands. And I love the way the orchestral sounds swell right at the moments when the emotional intensity is greatest, which includes the opening, a rapid dive into swirling waters. In the end, it doesn't need much of Neil Tennant's sly irony—virtually none, in fact—nor does it need much of Chris Lowe's production muscle either. It's just a nice and simple song with a nice and simple message. It

might even be evidence that either or both of these Pet Shop Boys may well be prone to my own greatest weakness, crippling sentimentalism, played so straight here that it's practically opaque about any other intentions or aims. "The night, the stars / A light shone through the dark.... Your love is liberation, liberation." It might even be characterized as "sincere," if one is inclined to take the position and risk the ridicule (better keep the scare quotes anyway). (2011)

Picnic at Hanging Rock (Peter Weir, 1975)

Yeah, I love this one. Last time through noticed how it uses the *Psycho* strategy of an early-disappearing leading woman in another way. Instead of a fallen woman, the focus is a trio of innocents—albeit unwitting imperialists, if you want to look at it that way. And they are gone from the movie nearly as soon. And there's no psychiatrist to explain it at the end either. Almost perfectly mysterious. (2013)

Pogues, *If I Should Fall From Grace With God* (1988)

From Shane MacGowan's croaking essays just at hitting the note to all the painfully trendy problems of presenting as an "Irish punk" outfit in the late '80s, about the only thing the Pogues might have had going for them was a strategy of setting expectations low. Maybe that's why this knocked me sprawling. No trick is missed: the title track briskly sets forth the terms and rocks good and hard while they're at it. "Metropolis" is an instrumental that puts James Bond in the drunk tank. "Thousands Are Sailing" is genuinely stirring. And "Worms" is the perfect note of nihilism on which to end. The turn by the much missed Kirsty MacColl on "Fairytale of New York" is a nice touch, but it's MacGowan that makes you want to bawl. Corny, sure—but still, you're crying, and it's Christmas. He has all of that ability and a lot more and it's all here. (2007)

Robert Polito, *Savage Art* (1995)

The thing I like best about Robert Polito's biography of Jim Thompson is the light it sheds on Thompson's work. What I consider the best—*A Hell of a Woman*, say—is not necessarily as celebrated as some others, and one in particular: *The Killer Inside Me*. Granted, *Savage Art* is a biography, and Polito's critical assessments have to be extracted. But until this I had flailed away at reading Thompson without direction, and was often disappointed. Thompson's catalog runs to 30 or better titles, and there are some stinkers in the mess. I know because I read two of them—*The Alcoholics* and *The Criminals*, bought for their titles obviously. I was thus happy to see Polito dismiss them quickly, which had the effect of making me more inclined to believe him generally. He's also a good writer in his own right. Thompson lived a singularly depressing life, but Polito keeps things moving along, with lots of interesting detail. I wasn't surprised but was still interested to learn that Thompson was a binge writer, locking himself away for intense bursts of work. His best often has that magical quality of first drafts that somehow come out just right (see also: Sherwood Anderson, Philip K. Dick). It's so rare and unusual, it's something to appreciate in and of itself (for all his reputation for that kind of thing, for example, I think Jack Kerouac managed it only once, with *The Subterraneans*). Polito has also proved his critical bona fides with the two great Library of America volumes, *Crime Novels: American Noir*. Jim Thompson is obviously right in his wheelhouse. Thompson himself is about what you would expect him to be from reading the novels, a leathery old drunk with a marked edge of desperation. A faintly Bukowski type of character, alcoholic and impoverished for much of his life. All that anxiety in the novels had to come from somewhere, and Polito neatly catalogs it from start to finish. I thought the saddest part of Thompson's life, the way Polito tells it, was that Thompson always felt strongly that his work was not recognized for what it is, Stanley Kubrick's late interest notwithstanding. Thompson always held out hope—how could he not? At this point, I'm not sure you can overstate his position to the second half of the 20th century, in terms of the disquieting preoccupations with human depravity that wear a crime fiction

mask. Polito and this book steered me to most of my current favorites by Thompson. (2013)

Iggy Pop, "Five Foot One" (1979)
With horns and the band tight as can be and Iggy's various improvs
(working or not) carefully preserved in the pristine rock amber
of James Williamson's precise, dusky production, Iggy's 1979 *New
Values* album works splendidly a lot of the time. The title song avails
of this aesthetic and other songs here as well: "Tell Me a Story,"
"Girls," "I'm Bored," "Billy Is a Runaway." But nowhere is the sound
more put together than on "Five Foot One," a five-minute display of
wanton modulated chamber-rock. Everything from the heartbeat
bass to the tidy drumkit to the rolling waves of the horn charts and
electric guitars and Iggy's goofs off all of it feels studied, and thus
vaguely abstracted and distanced, but compensating with a humor
that is lusty and alive, and a band that rocks expertly. No one but
Iggy Pop is capable of such stunts. The scenario here is funny, a
griping carny with a short-guy complex who is hot for some. "With a
bottle of aspirin and a sackful of jokes / I wish I could go home with
all the big folks," he declares outright. "I wish life could be Swedish
magazines." At that point the song has opened up wide and working on open cylinders like a mighty machine or intricate household
appliance. You can dance if you want to. "I won't grow any more
any more any more," he finally concedes as the noise envelops him.
(2011)

See also: Iggy & the Stooges, Stooges.

Elvis Presley, "Make the World Go Away" (1970)
No part of Elvis Presley's career is a gray area (or every part is), but
1970 comes close. Still basking in the glow of his late-1968 comeback, before he had mostly slipped into rote biz again as he had a
decade before, 1970 was the year Presley recorded one of his most
singular albums, *Elvis Country (I'm 10,000 Years Old)*, a concept work

that attempts to embrace and weave together all country under his banner: bluegrass, honky tonk, rockabilly, etc. "Make the World Go Away," which closes out the original album (since decked out in reissues with multiple additional tracks), is likely intended as the countrypolitan statement. A Hank Cochran song, it has been a hit twice—by Timi Yuro in 1963 and by Eddy Arnold in 1965, the latter of which is probably the best-known version. It was also recorded by Ray Price (the first to do so, in 1963), the Osmonds, Roger Whittaker, Mickey Gilley, Engelbert Humperdinck, Tom Jones, and many others. It would have to be the strings mainly that make it countrypolitan, but it's also the Presley vocal style of the period— compare "Suspicious Minds," "Kentucky Rain," "In the Ghetto." He sounds hoarse, tired, and depressed. I don't say that like it's a bad thing. It's highly effective. The sadness of all these songs is their chief virtue, and I wouldn't be a bit surprised if Presley, the consummate professional, were playing deliberately to the dimming fatigue. "Get it off - get it off my shoulders," he whimpers in "Make the World Go Away," speaking for all of us I guess at one point or another. The sentiment is just right, the mood of the song suited exactly to the performance, as Elvis Presley simply lays claim to ownership of one more pop song others are known for. (2014)

Elvis Presley, *The Sun Sessions* **(1954-1955)**
The most important album of Elvis Presley's career, not to mention arguably in rock 'n' roll history, is actually a pastiche of Sun singles and outtakes, recorded in 1954 and 1955 but not put together as an album until the mid-'70s. Since then, various takes have gone in and come out, the cover art has changed once or twice or more, and it's been remastered nearly as often, following whims of the times. But oh who cares? In the end, all definitions fade and are inadequate to the material here. Recorded before Elvis was even 21, backed by a couple of talented good ol' boys on guitar and bass, drawing on resources imported direct from the primal human experience, I can't imagine what these songs must have sounded like

to the people who made regional hits of them in the mid-'50s US South. It's fresh, it's catchy, it's appealing, and it's still tempting to reiterate the claims that have become cliches: "the big bang of rock 'n' roll," etc. But listen, these three guys and particularly the singer (with Sun's Sam Phillips at the board) go about their business with astonishing efficiency, neatly stitching together fragments of country and blues in a way no one quite had before, and somehow they changed everything. (2007)

Prince, *Controversy* (1981)
Prince's follow-up to *Dirty Mind* is pretty much where I got on board the project, along with the Time's second release, the comedy album *What Time Is It? Controversy* doesn't add much to the turf staked out in the previous album, but digs in and makes clear he's in it to win it, whatever in the hell "it" was. The title song, in fact, sounds remarkably in form like the title song for *Dirty Mind*, but with the expedient addition of an unexpurgated Lord's Prayer at the bridge, intoned with all due solemnity over a pulsing beat powered by funk guitar. The track that impressed me most and brought me full into the fold was "Sexuality," a pinpoint-perfect exercise that revs up and works out like a finely tuned machine. I learned the throwaways by heart, and came to believe that once you have the timing to them down, to the point that your voice is indistinguishable from Prince's as you chant along, that you become, for those few moments, Prince himself: "We live in a world overrun by tourists. Tourists—89 flowers on their back. Inventors of the Accu-jack. They look at life through a pocket camera. What? No flash again? They're all a bunch of double drags who teach their kids that love is bad. Half of the staff of their brain is on vacation." And, later, this lovely admonishing mot: "What's to be expected is three minus three. Absolutely nothing." (A similar effect obtains for me with Everything But the Girl and Buddy Holly, if not quite yet the Velvet Underground.) This album comes in closer to 40 minutes than 30, but with the same number of songs as the last, which meant only

that Prince was starting to let himself stretch out, a foreshadowing of what was to come in many ways—I'm trying to avoid the word "indulgent" here. *Controversy* is anything but even across its offerings. I could do without "Do Me Baby," "Ronnie, Talk to Russia," "Annie Christian," or "Jack U Off," and already that's half the tracks. Then again, "Ronnie, Talk to Russia" and "Annie Christian" (and "Controversy") demonstrated a bracing willingness not just to flout convention but to plain attack it, in a style that *seemed*, anyway, to find its sources in the hippie ethos of the '60s. *Who was this guy?* was the general question. (2011)

Francine Prose, *Reading Like a Writer* (2006)
As a general rule I try to avoid self-help books of all kinds, especially for writers, although the latter now and then become shiny distracting objects I find coming home with me from somewhere. This one is different. It's more of a self-help book for readers than for writers. That's something I can get behind—I need the pointers! Francine Prose is in a comfort zone when she talks about reading, breaking it down first by "Words," "Sentences," and "Paragraphs"— and even they come after "Close Reading," the first chapter and essentially statement of purpose, which may contain the single most useful prescriptive strategy for reading I know: "[Begin] at the beginning," she counsels, "lingering over every word, every phrase, every image, considering how it enhance[s] and contribute[s] to the story as a whole." That's her approach to teaching (she says she and a class can get through up to 10 pages of a narrative in a day), but it's also her approach to reading—and mine too now, within the limits of my patience (which, alas, remains too often too quickly tried). This is when reading can become the most rewarding—going slow, slow, slow. It reminds me of the old piece of advice about the best way to understand a poem: memorize it. Then it is in your head and accessible to ruminating thought and connection. I like Prose's taste too, presented as a quick list in that first chapter: "Chekhov, Joyce, Austen, George Eliot, Kafka, Tolstoy, Flannery

O'Connor, Katherine Mansfield, Nabokov, Heinrich von Kleist, Raymond Carver, Jane Bowles, James Baldwin, Alice Munro, Mavis Gallant." Lots of usual suspects there, but also new directions for me as well, and more within the book, which is packed with great examples and great writing. In fact, the section at the end she calls "Books to Be Read Immediately" (there is no list of books to be read later) has made itself one of those go-to places I like to keep around and consult frequently—among other things it has already brought me back to Jane Austen, and routed me more directly to Flannery O'Connor and Paul Bowles. Prose (yes, her real name) is a lucent writer and I learned a lot from this book. (2012)

Psycho **(Alfred Hitchcock, 1960)**
Alfred Hitchcock's full-tilt stab at horror must have come as something of a surprise to those who had grown used to the technicolor antics and all-star capers of those sparkling Hitchcock Hollywood productions in the '50s, whatever weird trails they might have gone down, such as *Vertigo*. But *Psycho* remains a classic horror show to this day, one of the pictures that is most associated with Hitchcock and one by which he may be best remembered. It came at the tail end of arguably his greatest run, after *Vertigo* and *North by Northwest*, and it heralded the dawn of the kandy-kolored tangerine dream decade that was to follow with the grit and harsh contrasts of a movie that was black and white on multiple levels to its core.

It takes a number of chances, most notably in the single-minded way it goes for the look and feel of a tawdry low-budget shocker as well as in the relatively brief screen time given to its leading woman, Janet Leigh. In many ways, and in spite of its feature length, it operates as a particularly meticulous installment of his TV show, complete with story twists and surprises and a clumsy everything's-all-right- rationalism-of-science coda, delivered in the reassuring avuncular tones of a professional psychiatrist.

The best parts of *Psycho*, no question, all feature Janet Leigh, and once she's done in, in the famous shower scene, the life of this movie tends to drain away as inexorably as the chocolate syrup used for blood in that scene, lingering on a brilliant and brilliantly cold shot of Leigh's dead face pressed into the bathroom floor, eyes wide open and unblinking (next stop, by historical perspective: the '60s). Until that point *Psycho* is as lean and ruthless in its brutal arithmetic as anything Hitchcock or indeed most other filmmakers have ever done.

Like this: The opening shot of the Phoenix skyline slowly, slowly swirls in on and finally enters from the outside a cheap hotel room where a midday tryst between Marion Crane (Janet Leigh) and Sam Loomis (John Gavin), her jut-jawed lunk of a boyfriend, is being concluded. Marion is a good girl, you know that because she's prowling around the hotel room in white underwear, and talking sincerely about marrying Sam. But still, note, it's her underwear she is prowling around in. Sam is recently divorced, we finally learn, but living under a heavy yoke of alimony—he's like Guy Haines in *Strangers on a Train*. "They also pay who meet in hotel rooms," Marion murmurs, trying to make the case that she has already taken on the better-or-worse chores of a marriage, as ready for the commitment (and pleasures) as anyone could be. When Sam scoffs that she can lick the stamps when he sends his alimony payments, Marion says, "I'll lick the stamps."

Later, back at work, she finds herself on the wrong end of a leering flirtation with an older man (Frank Albertson) flaunting a pile of cash, and even whose comments on the weather are somehow lascivious: "Hot as fresh milk!" On an impulse she finds a way to rob him. Back in her home, packing to get out of town, she's prowling around now in black underwear, because now she's a bad girl, even if her crime is for love. And thus begins the greatest low-speed chase sequence for 35 years, until O.J. tried to beat it to Mexico. Once again a score by Bernard Herrmann is called on to perform yeoman's work in making Marion's flight scenes work so well.

By the time Marion spots the Bates Motel sign swimming out of nighttime rain it's likely plain to any and all that she is a doomed woman—no friends, no help, guilt heavy on her single woman's brow. These are facts about her that Norman Bates (played by a youthful and unsettling Anthony Perkins, who has perhaps never been better) figures out quickly. Her false name on the register, her isolation, her shifting stories of her circumstances, and finally her all but unambiguous acknowledgment of her guilt—she is quickly marked out as an ideal victim for a serial killer.

Perkins is so great because he's at once so boyishly charming and yet so weirdly malevolent that he is almost perfectly creepy, establishing himself as one of the great screen villains, surrounded by his stuffed birds and with his peephole into Marion's room (Marion *Crane's* room), where we can watch nearly as eagerly as he does as Janet Leigh's clothes come off and she wraps herself in a sexy robe before heading into the bathroom to take her final shower.

For all his charm, Bates has an evident edge gnawing at him, which never lets viewers relax in his presence, as when he responds to Marion's suggestion that he consider institutionalizing his mother, who is obviously troubled. He bristles, furious. "What do you know about caring?" he says. "People always mean well. The cluck their thick tongues, and shake their heads, and suggest, oh so very delicately..." It's not a comfortable moment, sequestered at that moment in Bates's parlor behind the office, eating a sandwich and milk while he watches her sardonically.

The appearance of Perkins also heralds the arrival of the film's unexpected humor, which is icy, cutting, and can be very funny, one of its greatest and most enduring features, yet always careful, again, never to give away too many of the film's secrets. Some of the best jokes are not understood until later viewings, as when Bates, apologizing for the awkward position created by the fight that Marion has overheard him have with his mother, says, "My mother—what is the phrase?—she isn't quite herself today."

If the first half of *Psycho* stands as the greatest episode of Hitchcock's TV show ever made, the second half for the most part is more typical of its humdrum output, as Marion's sister Lila (Vera Miles), a private detective (Martin Balsam), and Sam all put their heads together to try to solve the mystery of what happened to Marion. And solve it they do, of course, as with any TV show plot. And then, as a kind of dessert for the gourmand, the psychiatrist (Simon Oakland) struts forth to illuminate mysteries of serial murder. For me the best way to take this last scene is as another of Hitchcock's jokes, and in that light it's not a bad one, though unfortunately as much as anything one at the expense of the squares watching. I suppose they don't deserve any better, but it's as cold as anything else here. (2011)

Q

The letter Q stands in as the crown royalty queen class of the alphabet. Is there any other letter so nauseatingly cute, so entirely useless? It is eccentric similar to the way the knight chess piece moves, which at least can be turned to the purpose of the game. Practically everything Q does could be done just as well by K and W in combination, or K all by itself ("out of Irak!"). Furthermore, Q has the temerity to impose a truly ridiculous requirement, which is that it will not appear in public, at least in the English language, without accompaniment of its Batman-Robin sidekick U, no doubt as bare-legged as the Boy Wonder himself. "Wherever go I," says this silly letter in the haughty tones of the peerage (meaning itself, Q, not the letter I), "there goes U." And why is this? Does anyone know? Does anyone even ask? On the other hand, consider the rakish beauty of the circle intersected by the coy slash. In lowercase, the sly variation on both p and g is elegant as silk. Here I am, suddenly charmed by Q! Quick, I need a drinq. Various American marketers over the years have demonstrated that the phonetic replacement somehow just isn't kwite convincing, or even that kwik to parse. And of course Q looms somewhat more useful in other languages, where it may be a form of the throat-clearing found in the German "ch" (generally absent as a mouth noise from English). Around here it's quickly apparent that it's quite an affectation, no question. At least we respect that about it, using it so sparingly that it ranks #25 in the alphabet for frequency of use, ahead of only Z. I want to say that even Z belongs ahead of Q for that matter, because of its undeniably unique mouth noise sound, but you can't have everything, and we'll get to that. Q does have some utility representing the word "question" (as in "a Q and A story"), signifying a transcribed interview. It was also the name of one of the worst characters ever to appear in the Star Trek franchise (though I would hazard that Lwaxana Troi still remains single worst by orders of magnitude). Maybe that's why I don't like Q. Because, let's be clear, I don't. But I think it's more likely a matter of the ridiculous unnecessary work it brings to the enterprise of the English language. Again, it might be interesting to get the perspective of children and ESL students, whatever their thoughts are on this monumentally useless letter. Why don't we just remove it—25 is a much better number than 26. In the long run, generations from now, the figure of Q would just become an exotic meaningless shape like a bunch of those Cyrillic letters or whatnot. At least say you'll think about it. (2015)

Queens of the Stone Age, *Rated R* (2000)
The last truly great show I saw was Queens of the Stone Age on the last Saturday night of an October, touring on this. I met my friends late, or we all dribbled in. People were wearing masks and costumes. The opening band was OK. Waiting for the headliner, with the floor steadily filling as people moved forward and jock-eyed for position, I got into an argument with a friend who told me he was going to vote for George W. Bush. I couldn't even begin to imagine. After 10 or 15 minutes of it a mutual friend stepped in and judiciously endorsed Dubya's Social Security privatization scheme. Back then, Republicans still talked about "privatization" because it still tested well. First guy: Furthermore, Al Gore is too socialist. My whole world turned upside down. The millennium—I realized it was upon me. Then the Queens came on and opened

with the bawling "Nicotine, valium, vicodin, marijuana, ecstasy and alcohol"; the aroma of baking opened up around us on all sides with hippie-style sharing of wares. The roar emanating stage-wise pounded as seductive as it was bruising. All you had to do was feel it. Dancing desperately to the beguiling, insistent throb immediately became the order of the night, high and a little drunk and deeply disturbed. The joy felt visceral and deep-red, as if one had just survived a disaster, something in the desert. Something that came from the desert. (2007)

R

It's clear no letter of the alphabet is more approved by pirates, but R has much more going for it as well. It's ranked #8 overall for frequency of use—#4 among consonants, after only T, N, and S. In English it is primarily a growling noise, with the tongue flipped back in the mouth to texture the vocalization (an "alveolar approximant," in the argot of linguistics). But in other languages, such as Spanish, it takes on a rolling, purring, motorized sound called trilling, which I have never been able to make, just as I never learned to stick two fingers in my mouth and make a piercing whistle. I don't see these as flaws, particularly as I don't speak Spanish, but yes, the potential for problems is there. R is tucked pretty far down there, as the 18th letter of the alphabet—it's 18, I just don't know what to say. Now that we are so deep into the alphabet, do individual letters even have distinct personalities anymore? That is our course of inquiry, you see, and the obvious answer is yes, of course they do. But the workhorses that make up the majority of letters in this tray of the alphabet as I learned it, namely Q, R, S, T, and U, are mostly too busy representin' and performing extremely important stitching-together language work, notably R, S, and T (and with the notable exception of Q, as previously discussed). U is a vowel—as with pitchers on baseball teams, the numbers favor the impact of vowels as single units over the everyday players that are the consonants. Vowels have to be considered separately. The baili-wick of R includes a primitive one-upmanship function of making everything better—bigger, faster, more wonderfuller—just by show-ing up at the ends of adjectives (with E and doubling consonants as needed). If you think that's great I'll tell you it's greater, and I'll be growling too, because that's the way R rolls. R is always going to be one step ahead of you, at least until S and T combine to stop the greater quarrel, and make it the definitive greatest. Working with verbs, R makes nouns with admirable work ethics: doer, thinker, farmer, and (the greatest of them all) writer. In mathematics, R rep-resents the set of all so-called real numbers ("real numbers"—never mind). R also works part-time as a warning to parents (and red flag to adolescents) about certain movies. I have always respected R as a utility player in the alphabet, such are its many faceless powers—how can you not? But as a handwritten letter, printed or cursive, capitalized or lowercase, it is somehow always a nuisance to make and never quite looks the way it should. For the sake of R's dignity, it's a good thing there's typing.

Ramones, *Ramones* (1976)
We all know there should be prominent statues in public places and speeches every year in honor of the Ramones. It's impossible to overstate the vitality and pleasure of this music, *still*, the more so when heard as an album, like the blast of a live set, all 14 shards at once and in sequence. It is a rush of oxygen to the brain. This is truly the ground zero of a wide swath that followed and still implic-itly follows it. It cost $6,400 to record. The song count-off emerges as badge of pride and identity. The songs are short—six under two minutes, the longest is 2:35. And while the Ramones didn't invent the "the" style of band name they sure helped bring it back. The band lived in the middle of a huge city, wore shades, sneakers, blue jeans, and black leather. This was their world: too much TV, too many trashy B-movies, drugs, comic books, dysfunctional families, sketchy street scenes, and, of course, hangin' around with nothin'

to do. The unholy alliance of '60s garage and Brill Building pop, the basic Ramones musical aesthetic strategy, was a revelation at the time and is still. Simply for so imposingly inventing itself as if all at once, this album will always be on the short list of the band's best. For me, it's the beginning of a long, delicious, fun-filled ride across many years and many albums. It stands within the Ramones catalog as a most emphatic "1-2-3-4." (2012)

Rashomon (**Akira Kurosawa, 1950**)
Akira Kurosawa's breakthrough art-house hit introduced him to Western audiences as something of an ambitious and self-serious (not to say pretentious) filmmaker. *Rashomon* has its analogues in Ingmar Bergman's *The Seventh Seal* and Jean-Luc Godard's *Breathless*, both of which came a few years later, as compact black-and-white non-English-speaking pictures that lend themselves afterward to lively discussion over coffee, french fries, and cigarettes, and which incidentally tended to over-define their creators. They are a bit obvious.

Nevertheless, I remain fond of *Rashomon*, even as I most often get the sense in latter-day reviews that many are unexcited about it now, arguing that at this point the picture is more famous for being famous. David Thomson, in the 2002 edition of his *New Biographical Dictionary of Film*, says that its "debate on truth is trite." But I like it—for the artful way it is shot, for its music, for its players, and yes, even for its debate on truth.

The simplest synopsis is that it's the story of a crime told from three different points of view, each of which tends to emphasize elements that favor the teller. An aristocrat (Masayuki Mori)—a samurai, in fact, as this is a historical picture—and his wife (Machiko Kyo) are attacked in the woods by the notorious bandit Tajomaru (Toshiro Mifune in his usual hysterics), who sexually assaults the wife. Later, a woodsman (Takashi Shimura, great as always) discovers the body and evidence of the crime. A trial follows. There's a good deal more complexity to it than that, however—and a good deal more simplicity too. More than anything, it's impressively stripped down in the way it proceeds, unfolding like a puzzle. The various versions remain stubbornly nested within one another in ways that are not easy to parse.

The frame of the story is set in time shortly after the trial, and at the ruined Rashomon gate of Kyoto. The woodsman and a priest are caught in a downpour (the usual excellent rain from Kurosawa) and taking shelter there. They are joined by a bandit who presses them to tell the story of the trial, about which both are obviously distraught. The woodsman obliges him—and thus, the first point to understand is that all of the three versions are essentially funneled through the woodsman, who it will turn out has an agenda, and a version, of his own.

Kurosawa cleverly distracts us from that by plunging directly into the story, cutting from the downpour at the gate to a more peaceful scene dappled by sunlight. A famously impressive tracking shot ensues as the woodsman is shown walking through the woods, accompanied by low-key music with a stirring marching tempo on the soundtrack. These tangles of foliage and the sun glaring through are there every time the picture resets again to the central narrative, as if continually underlining how even the brightest daylight is inevitably obscured by fecund life itself. Kazuo Miyagawa's camera, at times aimed right at the sun, seems to be constantly on the move, focused yet busy, in what it shows us and how—an effect also owing to Kurosawa's editing.

That is contrasted by the stark near-emptiness of the trial scenes with the principals placed about the frame like so many potted plants, and the interrogator whose voice we never hear and who is evidently represented only by the camera. Into this clean, square, regular box, demarcated by high-contrast shadow and light, foreground and background, the confusing tangle of the story is placed layer by layer: the encounter between the bandit and the married couple; the encounter between the bandit and the samurai; the encounter between the bandit and the wife; and the aftermath between the samurai and his wife.

That story is told over and over again, yet its details shift constantly. Aspects of the different stories are compatible, but no story entirely supports any other. Each of the main actors, along with the woodsman, is shown as attractive and unattractive, admirable and despicable, animated by honorable and by low motivations. Craven, upright, treacherous, transcendent, shameful, life-affirming, venal, principled. So it goes. The complexity of sorting it out becomes, at about the one-hour mark, a bit of a knot. Then, back at the gate in the downpour, the bandit goads the woodsman into giving one more version, ostensibly his unvarnished own, and yet somehow the least believable of them all.

In the end we know little more than the essential facts of the incident that we learned in the first place: the samurai is dead, the wife's dagger is missing, and the bandit claims credit for the death. Some things here that you might not think could work actually do, and pretty well. My favorite is the medium who delivers the samurai's side of the story from beyond the grave. I love how it's accepted that this is as valid a way as any of extracting testimony regarding the facts of a case. Even more than that, I love the weird otherworldliness of it, the wild carryings-on of the medium (within that sterile setting of the court), the flailing and the rattles and feathers and various trappings of her craft, and the strange tenor of the voice that speaks through her after she has made her contact with the samurai. It's bold and theatrical.

Perhaps because there's no good way to end such a determinedly confounding enigma, it does not end well, finishing on a ham-handed metaphor that only serves to bring the artificiality of the preceding exercise into sharper relief. That is unfortunate. But until the point of the distractingly pointless discovery made at the Rashomon gate, and all its tiny ramifications too quickly elaborated, Kurosawa's picture remains worth a look—all motion and image and shifting nuance; not a minute too long or too short and with virtually nothing out of place. (2011)

Lou Reed and John Cale, *Songs for Drella* **(1990)**
This is a bit of a solemn project, a memorial album for Andy Warhol that Lou Reed and John Cale collaborated on after many years of estrangement, coming together in memory of their mentor and friend, and blowing apart again almost immediately after. Perhaps because of lingering strains between them—or perhaps for some other reason entirely—the result is closer in feel to John Lennon's and Yoko Ono's *Double Fantasy* album than any kind of Velvets redux. Both artists are credited coequally for all 15 songs here but the styles veer about quite wildly, settling in two distinct places, one that sounds like John Cale and the other like Lou Reed. If the lead vocal is giving away the "real songwriter" here, then it's Reed by 10 to five. It's never actually that simple, of course, and *Songs for Drella* also does work as the Velvets redux everybody wanted. But that is more because the sense of Andy Warhol is so potent here, taking off from the manifold images of him that Reed, Cale, and we as listeners carry around with us. They explore his biography, as in the opening "Smalltown," or in "Slip Away (A Warning)," which remembers the aftermath of his shooting. They play with his aesthetics and background milieu on "Trouble With Classicists" and "Images." Mostly they heap love on him. You can feel it. This is a side of that scene that I never knew so well before. The degree of affection for Warhol that is on every song here, however melancholy, guilty, or defensive, is remarkable. It's impossible to miss, the one thing I always get it. They liked Warhol. They resented him. They became exasperated by him. But more than anything they admired and loved him fiercely. They are humbled and proud to have been associated with him, and grateful. All that comes through the weird tensions and cross-currents that are nearly as palpable here. It's all

good music, for all these reasons and more, but I think Reed has the advantage over Cale (which he evidently pressed, with twice as many songs). This is the year after Reed's mini-comeback *New York*, one of his better periods. He's all over his controlled noisy guitar squall thing here, and when he goes into his *Coney Island Baby* adorable pouty confessional style at the very end, in the song "Hello It's Me," he gets the last word and uses it to nearly steal the show. But I think the whole album is just prime really, an interesting collaboration and a great bunch of songs and a testament, tender and very moving at its best. (2012)

Reggae Philharmonic Orchestra, *The Reggae Philharmonic Orchestra* **(1988)**
Here's another one I picked out of a slush pile in a newspaper office. It makes the unusual mistake of leading with its worst track, an ill-advised cover of Cab Calloway's "Minnie the Moocher." I'm hard put to think of very many other albums that have done that. *Born in the U.S.A.*, and what else? On the other hand, it was shrewd enough to follow that with the best track, "Love and Hate," which is so good they included a second version (labeled an instrumental but with vocals). The Reggae Philharmonic Orchestra has some ties to Steel Pulse but most of its players are so obscure they don't yet merit Wikipedia notes even. It's called an orchestra evidently because string players such as solo violinists and cello players are featured prominently, and also likely because the orchestral (or faux orchestral) sweetening is layered on with swooning abandon. It's reggae to the extent of the general structure and texture of the beats, which nonetheless tend to be well submerged in the mixes. The players, as shown on the cover, also appear to wear dreads, and if that doesn't make something reggae I don't know what. As a vinyl product I relied mostly on its first side, which includes "Love and Hate" and then a few others nearly as good. The second side included another weird cover, "As Time Goes By" (which at least is better than the Calloway), along with an instrumental version of same, and also the

second "Love and Hate." So it's reasonably skimpy business here, 10 songs, two repeated, and thus I suppose little surprise that they never hit big, or even little. But "Love and Hate" was one of those songs I adored and frequently included on mixtapes, and remain willing to stump for hard. Which raises the question: WHEN DOES THE COMEBACK TOUR START? (2011)

Regurgitator, *tu-plang* (1996)
The first album by Australian band Regurgitator came in the mail the last time anyone was bothering to send me free albums—1996 sounds about right. I flipped for it in a big way—it was a curiosity and the band was a mystery, with intriguing cover art, eccentric information in small font only in the booklet, and this music. It went into high rotation for a couple of months. Hard to figure out who they were, or what this was. Now the Internet knows more about Regurgitator, and I see they've had a whole career and are reasonably popular. In fact, this album went to #3 Down Under and even yielded a top 40 hit in "Kong Foo Sing," which may indeed be the best song here. In fairness, nothing seems to have dented any other English-speaking or European or any other charts anywhere, beyond New Zealand. Insert usual "that's a shame," because there are plenty of reasons to like this, starting with the determined career suicide gesture of opening your debut album with a song called "I Sucked a Lot of Cock to Get Where I Am." That pushed me anyway toward a disposition in its favor, and they delivered with these feverish mash-ups of hip-hop, drum-and-bass attack, screwy PiL vocals, heavy bottoms, surf-rock flourishes, and gratuitous obscenity as it pleased them. It's Stranglers-style mood pieces for people in bad moods. It's surprisingly listenable, and surprising in any number of ways, with vicious hooks, a wealth of ways to use the studio, and unusual instruments. It's capable of a good deal of very pure heaviosity and even willful menace, which probably would have scared me a little when I was about 14, if I'd happened to wake up to it in the middle of the night and it was playing on the radio. But

since I was already 40 by the time I actually heard it, I registered the vein and kept moving. It's a little prize, and I was happy to find it remains so. (2013)

Replacements, *Let It Be* (1984)
Most consider this far and away the best Replacements album, which is interesting given the Kiss cover, the instantly outdated "Answering Machine," and throwaways like "Gary's Got a Boner" and "Tommy Gets His Tonsils Out." But what's good here is not merely good but magnitudes of superlatives: amazing, awesome, unparalleled, hairs at the back of your neck, your favorite way to put it. "Unsatisfied" takes a respectable shot at anthem for a generation. "Androgynous" is as fresh as a minute ago and 6,000 years in the making. "We're Comin' Out," "I Will Dare," "Sixteen Blue"—for that matter, "Answering Machine"—all of them. Timeless. Searing. Moving. Dramatic. Real. Don't let the shambolics fool you. (2006)

See also: Hüsker Dü/ Replacements, Minneapolis

Rolling Stones, "Jumpin' Jack Flash" (June 15, 1968, #3)
There are times I'm pretty sure it's the greatest rock 'n' roll song ever made. Other times it's only overplayed and trite—the penalty for loving a song too much and too well perhaps, though it remains resilient enough to stage pulsating comebacks every few years, usually following another look at Martin Scorsese's amazing *Mean Streets*—or, best of all, when it takes me by surprise in the wilds of life. I'm sure part of the reason I like "Jumpin' Jack Flash" so well is that it came from the *Beggars Banquet* sessions. Why "Jumpin' Jack Flash" was not released on the album is anybody's guess, as far as I know. I'm willing to take the mythologizing route at this point and make the extravagant claims: It's too *big* to be contained on an album. It *is* an album. Unto itself. It rewired our brains and forced us to redefine the very concept of what an album is, etc. Yes, I know. But there is a tremendous amount packed into this three

and a half minutes. That impossible trebly crashing guitar, that stomping back beat, the way it finds a space that logically belongs to somebody else a long time ago and puts its stamp all over it. Older than rock 'n' roll—older than the 20th century. But work the focus and there it is again: the Stones, Mick Jagger a-leaping about the place, cranking out the mocking, jeering, irresistible sounds of bitter envy and revelry. For better and for worse. And in sickness and in health too, for that matter. In other words, and to get right to the point, "Jumpin' Jack Flash is a gas gas gas." (2014)

Roman Polanski: Wanted and Desired (**Marina Zenovich, 2008**)
This HBO documentary preceded by little more than a year the revival of interest in Roman Polanski's criminal case, which started with his arrest in Switzerland in 2009. It appeared possible that he might be extradited to the US. I never noticed it going by, but I saw Phil Dellio included it on his list early in 2010 of the best films of the 2000s. Between that and all the furor I knew it was one I wanted to see. And it is indeed worth seeing. Among other virtues, for me, it includes information I hadn't known before about the legal and ethical improprieties of the presiding judge on the case in the '70s, Laurence Rittenband (who died in 1993). More generally, it struck me as fair, not only about the crime itself, which it doesn't minimize, but also about all the events that swirled around it and the people involved. It doesn't excuse Polanski, but it provides a useful context.

This is one of those cases, of course, in which people tend to line up on opposite sides and take their pleasure throwing blunt objects at one another in the service of discourse (see also O.J. Simpson, Jonbenet Ramsey, Monica Lewinsky, second Iraq War, or, more recently, Casey Anthony). So I want to tread carefully. There's no question that Polanski committed a crime, no question that his defenders often say such silly things that they are, on balance, actively harmful to Polanski's cause, e.g., Whoopi Goldberg's assertion that she knows it wasn't a "rape-rape." It's also a useful thought experiment to ask what if it had been the filmmaker's daughter, or anyone's, who had been the victim in this case.

But, in fact—another revelation for me in this endlessly interesting documentary, and case—we do happen to know how the victim and her family reacted. They agreed with the legal system on the whole, which plea-bargained the charges down to the most minor (unlawful sexual intercourse); most of the evaluating authorities then recommended probation. Samantha Gailey (now Geimer), Polanski's victim, appears here in an interview and says as much. In her early 40s in the interview, married and with children, and having won a civil suit against Polanski in the '90s, she appears convincingly at peace about the whole thing—if anything, the evident lingering resentments are directed toward the rapacious media coverage.

That's the most critical piece here to me. This documentary quietly makes a persuasive case that the media coverage amounts virtually to an unindicted co-conspirator. One of the reasons Judge Rittenband evidently came to behave so bizarrely, and illegally, in his oversight of the case and the trial was exactly because of the pressure that the media coverage was exerting by ginning up such easy outrage. I'm not immune to such outrage myself. I was angry like most others about the O.J. Simpson verdict, and I still believe those feelings were not exactly misplaced—that he probably committed the crime and certainly, as his subsequent life has affirmed, that he deserved to be imprisoned. But this is dangerous territory. I was also nearly as outraged as everyone else was a year later about the behavior of Jonbenet Ramsey's parents in the aftermath of their daughter's strange and mysterious death. But that has turned out to be a case where "everyone," fueled by irresponsible nonstop cable-news coverage, had it exactly wrong. Cases such as Jonbenet Ramsey, Bill Clinton, or Michael Jackson, black and white to so many, are to me instead more and more cotton battings of gray.

There are too many intangibles, and too many unknowns, to be able to judge.

Thus, simply as a matter of coping—and the O.J. Simpson case notwithstanding—I tend to favor now the judgments of juries and those closely involved with any given case. Because I remain intrigued by true-crime stories, it's practically the only way I can manage to stay out of the trap of outrage overload. I try particularly hard, though I do understand the inherent entertainment value on some level, to avoid the maelstroms of media coverage when I see them, which is one reason I have been indifferent to the Casey Anthony trial, beyond its interest as a puzzling case. It's not that hard to recognize the madness coming in—the face of Nancy Grace is very often involved and that alone is usually a pretty good clue that hysteria distortion has set in.

There's an interesting show on the Investigation Discovery channel now, *I (Almost) Got Away With It*. The premise is criminals escaping jail or prison and how they survive and evade recapture. The most recent season has tended to devolve down to lowlifes who rarely manage to stay out longer than a few months, and it's often become nearly as unpleasant to watch as any of those weekend MSNBC prison things (which are simply too much). But the first season featured cases with nuance and interesting gray areas, implicitly raising difficult questions about punishment and rehabilitation, including stories of people who stayed out for decades, essentially going straight and living productive and useful lives before they were finally captured. (Sara Jane Olson likely remains the best example of the moral ins and outs of these kinds of cases, and it's another one where the discourse tends to be bellicose and polarized.)

So with Polanski, yes, I admit to my biases. I love his work. I have compassion for him based on the events of his biography. I'm glad he was able to make the movies he's made since he fled the US—I think some of them rank with his best and most important. The stain of his crime has been on him since virtually the day he committed it and it will be remembered as part of his legacy even after his death. He will never escape it. Those who believe he should have been thrown into a hole may (or may not) find some comfort in this documentary, which makes his crimes and punishments quite clear. It's just as clear that only a minority of people directly involved in the case at the time believed he deserved such harsh punishment. And the people calling for his blood were often the ones behaving most unconscionably. (2011)

Rome, Open City (**Roberto Rossellini, 1945**)
The low budget works, but that's partly because it's not often you get wartime Rome as your backdrop. In a way, that makes it not low budget at all. (2013)

Linda Ronstadt, "Someone to Lay Down Beside Me" (1976)
It's a Karla Bonoff song, and she's actually recorded a nice version of it herself, but the Linda Ronstadt is the one that got enough radio airplay to catch my attention, somehow only late at night as I recall, so here we are. I only needed to hear it once. It felt like dying inside, like one of those dreams where you're caught naked somewhere you're not supposed to be. It's one obviously for all the lonely people, and if I'm giving away too much about myself with this, I'm also pretty sure everybody out there knows what this song feels like in some way, has felt it sometime, at some Dark Night of the Soul level. The yearning ache alone in bed in the middle of the night. The planet is overcrowded, everybody on TV is coupled up and happy, so are most of the fantasy people walking around in songs and movies, and many of your friends, and all the rest are having dramatic breakups and quickly moving on to next partners. This song, in its arguable self-pitying solipsism and self-centered baby boomer ingratitude, speaks for the rest of us. (2011)

William Roughead, *Classic Crimes* **(1913-1937)**
William Roughead and Edmund Lester Pearson began corresponding in the '20s and by the evidence enjoyed a long, close, and cordial

friendship, each recognizing the other as something of a spiritual broth-er. Born only 10 years apart, both had their own careers—Roughead as a lawyer in Scotland, Pearson as a librarian in Washington, D.C., Massachusetts, and New York City. But they devoted all the rest of their time to the details of crime cases. Pearson has his touchstone obsession with the Lizzie Borden case, whereas Roughead tended to be more catholic and wide-ranging in his appreciations, pushing back further into history, and not confining himself only to murder. Both are ex-cellent, wry, and charming writers; fans of Roughead have included Henry James, Toni Morrison, and Franklin Roosevelt. This collection of Roughead's work published by the *New York Review of Books* gath-ers up a dozen cases across the scope of his career—as he referred to them, "adventures in criminal biography." It's a solid collection. His work presently can be maddening in the duplications scattered across his out-of-print volumes (and which tend to command disappointingly high prices anyway). This collection includes the details of the case of Deacon Brodie, which inspired Robert Louis Stevenson's *Strange Case of Dr. Jekyll and Mr. Hyde*, of Madeleine Smith, a "trial of the century" nom-inee in the 19th century, and of Burke and Hare, early 19th-century se-rial killers in Scotland who enterprisingly and systematically harvested corpses for medical students, a lucrative trade then. The motivations and the crimes are sadly timeless; very little reported so breathlessly nowadays is anything that has not already happened one way or an-other for centuries and probably millennia, and usually for the same reasons. As with Pearson, Roughead tends in some ways toward the ponderous, and occasionally can even become a bit of a scold, which I suspect is all just a way of maintaining distance from the mayhem in which he otherwise happily wallows. You are well-advised to keep a good dictionary on hand when reading him as his vocabulary, drawing on many Scottish idioms now largely lost, is as rich as it is apt. (2011)

Leon Russell, "Me and Baby Jane" (1972)
Sometimes it feels like Leon Russell has been lost to history since even before the '70s ended, dwelling forever there with his makeup

and top hat and hair as one of the clownish features of the times, with maybe Leo Sayer, Minnie Riperton, or Carl Douglas. But I have never been able to get a handful of his songs out of my head, most of them circa 1972 and the album *Carney*—"Magic Mirror," "Tight Rope," and a few others, but more than any this woeful hymn to a love affair ruined forever by heroin and death. At the time I was hearing it on the radio (how it got there I don't know) it never failed to get me by the throat. The croak of Russell's voice, now and then missing notes, the softly marching tempo at the chorus, and the signature rich tones of his piano playing. It uses the drug lifestyle just right—though no doubt one reason it never made the hit parade. It never glorifies but never judges or condemns or blames either, and barely shrinks from anything. Just a brief memory of "the needle in her vein" to etch the picture in. I'm not sure exactly how Leon Russell does what he does—sometimes I'm not even sure what it is he's doing exactly—but "Me and Baby Jane" is the best example of him doing it: swooningly sad, ripe to the point of bursting, yet somehow softly understated, always tender, and above all completely beautiful. (2011)

Russian Ark **(Aleksandr Sokurov, 2002)**
As much as anything it is the technical achievement of *Russian Ark* that impresses, so that's a good place to start. It's striking—one continuous single take on a steadicam, lasting over 90 minutes, and on top of that an epic costume drama with a cast of thousands. Think of all the famous long takes you know—in *Touch of Evil, Goodfellas, The Player,* and/or *Gravity*—and multiply exponentially. As a mathematical formula, it may be expressed as [*Touch of Evil* x 9] to the power of *Barry Lyndon*. *Russian Ark* is no easy breeze, and it falls too easily and quickly into the look and feel of a pretentious and aimless art film. That technical achievement is remarkably subtle, certainly for someone like me who often has to have long takes pointed out, and otherwise the movie features not one but two central characters who appear to be time travelers

or perhaps shape shifters of some kind, or perhaps ghosts (one is never seen—he is represented by the camera point of view). They spend the movie prowling the corridors and galleries of the Hermitage Museum in St. Petersburg, Russia, swapping barbs and a general air of sadness as scenes from 300 years of Russian history materialize and play around them. Put it this way. You're unlikely to get much out of it if you don't know at least something about Russian history and probably if you aren't willing to look at it more than once. I know that's a damning review so I hasten to add: It is worth the energies. But anyone can understand why a person might not be inclined that way.

Indeed, I'm not always sure the grand experiment proves out. By going so far to one extreme of cinema, it incidentally ratchets up the theatricality. Occasional mistakes in timing or inappropriate aware-ness of the camera, for example, would normally call for another take to iron out, right? That luxury was not afforded director, co-writer, and co-star Aleksandr Sokurov with such self-imposed constraints as this, and so in many moments *Russian Ark* has more the quivering live feel of a stage production, which diminishes it some. Add to that a dense literary overlay, with a narrative high concept of science fic-tion ghost story and the eternal husbanding of Russian culture, and you have a project that is insanely ambitious and potentially doomed in countless ways.

But the fact is its many small flaws come to seem minor as the pic-ture unfolds its many, many impressive treasures—literal and figura-tive. The artwork and interiors of the Hermitage carry the day when nothing else does. In the end I think the single take is appropriate enough, if only for the interesting counterpoint and symmetry it pro-vides to one of Soviet Russia's acknowledged masters of cinema, Sergei Eisenstein—the pioneer of montage and other cinematic arts of the cut. There is not a single cut in *Russian Ark*, of course—no montage whatsoever. None. But I don't read that as a rejection of Eisenstein's aesthetic, however, but more another element to add to what is really this picture's central preoccupation: the vastness of Russian culture, which in turn is a reflection of the vastness of Russia itself.

Russia is not just the place where montage was invented, Sokurov's decision implies—it is a place whose culture is capable of embracing all of cinema. And art. And life. And death and time too. The not-so-friendly ghost that we see, a Frenchman played masterfully by Sergei Dreiden, credited as "The Stranger" but known by the ghost of the camera as "The European," is caustic about Russia, dismissing it witheringly as a motley of European copycats and wannabes. The ghost of the camera, a Russian credited at IMDb.com as "The Time Traveller" (Sokurov, who is not credited in the picture for this role), glumly attempts to rebut him. In the terms of this narrative, the other appears to be all that each of these two ghosts has, and the Time Traveller is the first to recognize the wisdom in not alienating his only companion.

Meanwhile, the costume drama, the great artwork on every wall, and various historical scenes play out and swirl around us, moving through some 33 or more chambers of the museum complex, including a grand finish in the Winter Palace. There are other ghosts too. There is the cruel Peter the Great. There is the great patron Catherine II, and there she is again, later, running away from the camera in an extraordinarily beautiful outdoor scene. (It is the cold gray weather of an afternoon in late December. The footsteps of people crunch in the snow.) There is the pomp and bluster of a diplomatic function involving a Persian envoy. There are soldiers performing formal marching maneuvers. And there is the spectacular ballroom scene in the Winter Palace at the end, complete with full orchestra and hundreds of graceful dancing couples.

It's not hard—and it's somewhat tempting, certainly on first view—to dismiss *Russian Ark* as a stunt, a kind of documentary in real time of production design, and a bit of a showoff at that. But there are many layers to this. The first distinct sound we hear is a ship's horn and the last image we see is of the sea. The "ark" conceit, a vessel that is alive and vital with a cargo of essential Russian culture and sailing the oceans of time, is worked out meticulously. The formidable Hermitage Museum and its vast collection—only a fraction of which is glimpsed here—provide a setting that is nigh perfect. And cinematographer Tilman Buttner deserves all the credit in the world for pulling off a physically demanding task and keeping it remarkably poised and beautiful. (2014)

S

S is for serpent, which it looks like and which it sounds like. But don't hold that against it. It has nothing to do with sin other than fronting for the word. It doesn't actually want you to eat an apple. It's far too busy demonstrating the Calvinist work ethic as one of the busiest letters in the alphabet—#7 most frequently used, which somewhat belies its rather lowly position as the 19th of 26 letters. Consider its many duties. Perhaps it's best known as The Pluralizer, converting one noun to many nouns by the simple expedient of showing up, sometimes, for the ladies and the laddies, with helper letter E and doubling consonants as needed. With S, there's always room for more. A friend becomes friends, a cat becomes cats. Put S at the end of many verbs and they are activated, moving forcefully into the eternal present. You already know you can run, eat, learn, but *runs, eats, learns* is for when you are actually doing it, a pinpoint focus on pure activity. For the most part, S maintains its integrity, but as with so many letters in this English alphabet it is occasionally lured from the straight and narrow. It is essentially a sibilant, a subtle sound made with the tongue at the back of the upper teeth, and a sharp exhalation. It is a remarkably penetrating noise as anyone can tell you who has sat in a darkened theater with people randomly hissing about things they don't like. Pair S with H, however, and the sibilance is still there but now caused by the jaw mostly closing the mouth against the exhalation to please be quiet please, another sound sadly heard too often in theaters nowadays, along with its cause, people randomly having conversations—plural. S is so pleased with itself about this land grab with H that it also molests the letter U at will for the same effect, as in "sugar" and "sure." This does not occur without surcease, which makes it annoying. It's small potatoes, of course, compared to the gyrations of some other letters we could name. Otherwise, S struggles for a personality. Inevitably it is a computer programming language. Someday each letter of the alphabet will have its own programming language and mergers will be allowed only if they spell words found in the Scrabble dictionary. One thing you can say about S is that it certainly has a lovely sinuous shape, printed or cursive, and damn the serpentine association. Just as there is no I in team there is no S in evil (though here its blunt force strength as The Pluralizer unfortunately works against it). Ultimately, that very fungibility of S saves it. It is so perfectly utilitarian. You can add it to the end of maybe 75% of the words in the English language and arrive at something with a perfectly new and useful meaning. S does have the unfortunate propensity of so many consonants to pair off with itself: pass, lassitude, gross, mission ... wait, what was that noise my mouth just made? Oh crafty S with your many ways!

Safe (Todd Haynes, 1995)

Safe is maddeningly good at being hard to pin down, but that's also the source of its greatest weakness, which is a tendency to look like it's making broad plays for ironic laughs, particularly in its second half, with an all too easy target in the self-actualization preoccupations and clichés of its late-'80s Southern California setting. This is unfortunate because the movie is much more often deadly serious about articulating what I might as well call a spiritual malaise. Here it is referred to as "environmental illness," the term of art in the period of the film for an evident immune-system condition that still hasn't been scientifically validated, but has traveled under many names: chemical sensitivity, 20th century syndrome, sick building syndrome, and, currently, multiple chemical sensitivity.

I believe I know this disease and apparently so do director / writer Todd Haynes and Julianne Moore, who plays the victim here, Carol White, in an amazing turn. This disease is there in all the scenes of Los Angeles freeway traffic, at dusk, at night, in the day, crawling along in haze. It's there in the nightmares of gray-tone parking garages. It's there in the power-line towers and batches of parallel lines draped and running in skeins overhead. It's there in the interiors of the fine San Fernando Valley homes, stuffed with treated fabrics, cleaning chemicals, molded plastics, and body odors. And it's there in one of the picture's canniest elements, its sound design, which simply records the ambient noise that surrounds us constantly: the drone of planes overhead, the whine of vacuum cleaners, the washes of traffic's white noise, the radios and televisions playing in the background of so many interiors, including AM talk radio in one memorable scene inside a car.

Safe opens like a mystery, inside the front seat of a luxury car (we see the hood emblem) traveling down streets of a gated community at dusk. We don't see anyone, inside or outside the car, just driveways, palm trees, distant houses, parked cars, and the purplish street. Ed Tomney's music is all oppressively saturated keyboard chords. It feels ominous and strange immediately, as in the early auto interior sequences of *Mulholland Dr.* and in *Vertigo*. In fact, *Safe* could nearly as easily have taken the shape of a horror picture, a variation on Cronenberg-style body horror themes. In many way it is exactly that.

Practically the first time we see Carol it is from above, with her husband on top of her, making love. She is removed from it, yet solicitous, affectionate and sensitive as he squirms for his orgasm, kissing him gently when he is finished, but disengaged. Moore's performance, as someone tightly wound and folded into herself, is dazzling. On the one hand she fits into the routine of the bored rich women on their cycles of self-help books, aerobics classes, lunches with girlfriends, and abusive husbands (Xander Berkeley as Carol's husband Greg is good, all sublimated rage and frustration on his second marriage). But Carol is different from them, more tentative and alienated. She doesn't seem entirely alive somehow. When she feels stress she drinks milk, a small detail but unsettling.

Haynes is working close to the lines here. Sometimes he goes over them. But other times he stays this side of them, tempting impulses to excess, but reining them in. For example, in many ways the purest syntax of the self-actualization movements is found in the promotional videos, with their New Age music, stock footage images of beaches and waterfalls, and soothing voiceovers. Haynes's versions are spot-on, just cheesy enough to make you want to groan, just soothing enough to help you identify with Carol's finding hope in them. Is it funny or is it serious? The question remains open.

The first half of *Safe* is a masterpiece in its own right. It builds tension grindingly, taking on elements of *The Exorcist* or *The Brood* in the many clinical settings, the awful tenor of developments and the sense one is hurtling into oblivion. Scenes such as her desperate attempt to get away from Los Angeles traffic fumes by driving into a parking garage, or the baby shower where she has an asthmatic attack, or even just one perfectly realized nosebleed, ratchet the tension. It's hard to understand what is happening, but something is. Those scenes are never funny. When she has to be hospitalized after she steps into a dry-cleaning establishment that is being fumigated, it's evident something is genuinely wrong.

But then comes the second half of *Safe*, with the Wrenwood retreat and the guru and other characters that populate it. Here, things like a close encounter with a semi-trailer truck during a nature walk, or a Joan Baez type of folk singer, push hard on the credibility. It's funny to think that anyone would put a retreat for people suffering from environmental illness near a highway (the noise of passing traffic is a constant feature of the camp exteriors), but it's funny in a way that takes one out of the movie's primary spell too.

There are still good things, notably the performances of Peter Friedman as the unctuous camp guru, Kate McGregor-Stewart as his nun-like helpmeet, and especially Jessica Harper as one of the patients. Even James LeGros, as his usual amiable creepy idiot, gets a nice turn. And you know what? When Eleanor Graham steps up to sing after the camp group has closed an evening gathering with their benediction—"We are one with the power that created us. We are safe, and all is well in our world"—that gentle little warble really works.

The question remains: Is it real, or is it a joke? This is where I think the attempts at humor are most unfortunate, because they stack the deck unfairly against the one thing that has been so carefully constructed here, which is the validity of Carol's problem, and how vividly *Safe* renders it, even guides us into connecting with it. Anyone who has spent too much time in bad freeway traffic and parking garages will not have to go far to get this on a visceral level. The rest of you can have a good laugh, maybe. (2012)

Alice Sebold, *The Lovely Bones* **(2002)**
Do biographical details of an author's life matter? Even before I came to understand that Alice Sebold is herself the survivor of a violent crime—the subject of her first published book, a memoir, *Lucky*—I had been vaguely troubled or put off by something in this scrupulously worked out novel, Sebold's first. The premise struck me initially as almost breathtakingly audacious, the story narrated from beyond the grave by Susie Salmon, a 14-year-old girl who, in the first chapter, is captured, raped, murdered, and dismembered by a serial sexual predator living in her suburban neighborhood. At a suitably ghostly

distance she observes the grief of her family and friends as they attempt to come to terms with what to them is only her unexplained
disappearance. They are reasonably certain she wouldn't have run
away, that she has probably been killed, but nothing is certain, or
ever will be for them again. Though Sebold includes some fanciful
ideas about heaven and the afterlife, not all of which work, mostly
she stays close to the ground, focused on the anguish of Susie's family and, more incidentally, that of Susie's spirit, which is helpless to
comfort them. The tale thus careens uncertainly between a ghost
story, a true crime case study, and a kind of Kubler-Ross self-help
session on grief. It tries to get the benefit of all and in the end cheats
itself of everything. The idea that seems at first so fresh and original
soon becomes mired down in the ungainly mechanics of lumbering
a plot forward. Of course the family will get over it, even if it splits
them apart; they have no other choice. And, inevitably, there will be
a manhunt. Sebold's burden of what to do about her killer tends to
sprawl suffocatingly over everything—letting him get away becomes
all too quickly freighted with the frustrated baggage of victimology
and vengeance, and yet bringing him to some kind of justice, particularly from the point of view of the transcendently spiritualized narrator, is if anything even more problematic, a problem that Sebold
does not solve. By playing with the fire of such powerful material,
Sebold only succeeds in creating a new cliché, one now on display
in a new true-crime show on the Investigation Discovery channel,
Stolen Voices, Buried Secrets—the voiceover-from-beyond-the-grave bit.
Better, I think, that Sebold had gone the route of a superior show on
that same channel, *Disappeared*, and focused on the bewilderment of
those left behind who simply don't know, and *can't* know, rather than
telegraphing everything. This would also have had the virtue of enabling her to leave heaven out of it altogether. (2011)

Neil Sedaka, "Laughter in the Rain" (Nov. 16, 1974, #1)
Neil Sedaka took up his position at the Brill Building in the early
'60s with a charming teenybop act and a quiverful of tunes that

often lodged dangerously in one's head: "Calendar Girl," "Happy Birthday, Sweet Sixteen," "Next Door to an Angel," like that. He dropped out of sight then, reemerging with a comeback bid in the mid-'70s that turned ultimately into an unpleasant lounge play, along the way massacring one of his best hits, "Breaking Up Is Hard to Do," slowing it to an unbearable crawl and acting too hard as if he meant it and we'd care if he did. Wrong twice, chum. Early into that comeback, however, he must have been hungry or something because this song (and its flip, "The Immigrant Song," written in sympathy for John Lennon, and also another song he gave to the Captain & Tennille, "Love Will Keep Us Together") redeemed all for me for a year or two. Wistful, poignant, unafraid to go for the heart-throat with aching strings and a soaring chorus, it's an emotional inversion and mirror image on some impenetrable level to the Everly Brothers' "Crying in the Rain." Personally, I have always found people infinitely more attractive in the rain, and the images here of walking hand in hand with the one he loves, without an umbrella soaked to the skin, hearing laughter, just go right through me (even if he says it's on a country road when it *should* be on a downtown street). Am I embarrassed to like this as much as I do? Yes, perhaps. (2010)

Sex Pistols, "Anarchy in the U.K." (1977)
This is so obvious and, in a way, self-serving that I'm almost embarrassed to put it on a list of my favorites. But long before it was the hallmark of a cultural earthquake / tidal wave that changed everything, etc., blahhh, it was this funny-weird song that a friend turned up on a 45 single. A 45 single! That by itself seemed strange enough at the time. Then it turned out to be this. Sure, there's a lot of scary sensation to it, big swaggering words like "anarchy" and "Antichrist" and all that unholy cackling from Johnny Rotten (nom de whatever for John Lydon), plus he's not such a great singer, or anyway misses a lot of notes. But it's as much pure pop for now people as anything by Nick Lowe and his Stiff brethren, and that's

how I took it. I just loved it. Somebody put it on a tape for me, and I dubbed it from there onto all kinds of tapes for other people. I still think it's a pretty swell song, with a big raw wailing guitar sound and martial marching tempos, and all the carrying on from Lydon. There's something thrilling about it. "There's so many ways to get what you want!" "It's the only way to be!" And, of course, the line that resonates most across the ages: "I wanna destroy!" Each and every one with an exclamation point embedded in the grain of the vocals and the emphatic kick of the band. I was perfectly prepared to accept this as the future of rock 'n' roll. I'm still not sure it wasn't, although by the time I was reading about them regularly in fan magazines they were pretty much over. They weren't exactly dead, they still aren't (and that includes poor old Sid). But they were over—an interesting state of affairs that this song utterly embodies, tensions and all. (2011)

Shangri-Las, "I Can Never Go Home Anymore" (Nov. 20, 1965, #6) The Shangri-Las, composed of two sets of sisters out of Queens, New York, are probably best known and remembered for their biggest hit, 1964's "Leader of the Pack," a novelty that doesn't wear particularly well after 45-plus years, even though the camp flounce can still seem charming (e.g., "Yes, we see!"). I think a couple of other songs actually represent them much, much better: the sultry "Remember (Walkin' in the Sand)" first, which is approximately 110% pure raw teen sex. And this overripe, all too potent morality tale, tarted up like a little opera compressed into just over three minutes. Packed to the gills with extravagant flourishes and asides, none misses its mark, and all hit very hard. The story is an eternal one, bold and simple, told in the first person by the girl: the girl loves the boy, the girl's mother forbids the love, the girl runs away, the mother takes sick and dies. And now, [title]. The small points tell: the sheer dynamics that shuttle between soft and harsh. The hushed, urgent entreaty at the start: "Listen / Does this sound familiar?" The strings and backing vocals that layer through and swell like frosting in a slice of cake, counterpointing the narrative. The way the vocal dips toward the mic on, "I was sure I was right." The lullaby that comes from nowhere and drives it home. The haunting cry of "Mama!" And the killing choke at the end. Those unprepared for the wallop here can find themselves taken apart by this song— it's happened to me. There's a case to be made that this is not only the finest moment ever of a good many for producer and songwriter Shadow Morton, but also the greatest "teen opera" of all time, Phil Spector notwithstanding. (2010)

William Shatner, "That's Me Trying" (2004)
I know that this and the album it comes from, *Has Been*, are mostly intended as a grand joke. And it's a pretty good joke, I'll hold my hand up there, riffing off Shatner's stock in trade here at the end of his career, the fatally insincere buffoon in his dotage, lost in the consequences of a lifetime of refusing responsibility. But there's something that tugs very hard at the heartstrings, embedded deeply in the details of the lyrics written by Nick Hornby. The singer tracks down his disaffected daughter by looking up her address in "the phone book at the library," and comments, "Weird, that you've been living maybe two miles away for the best part of 20 years." A lifetime of loss is compressed into that. He can't remember how old she is, or who was president when she was born. And he's not about to change—"But I don't wanna talk about any of that bad stuff, why I missed out on your wedding and your high school graduation"—except in teeny, impossibly tentative, and too-little-too-late ways: "I'd like to explain, but I ... can't." The chorus is a dagger to the heart, free-floating and aching: "Years of silence / Not enough / Who could blame us / Giving up?" I think it's arguable that Hornby and Ben Folds, the musical brains behind the project, have more to do with what makes this work than Shatner. Yet even as Shatner's hammy improvs clutter it up (is there any doubt he's responsible for the "daughter dad action" throwaway that very nearly torpedoes the whole thing?), I'm not

sure anyone else could have pulled it off. Shatner occupies the role perfectly, as the bumbling foolish Dad you can't help hating and loving both. Sometimes the only thing you can do is hang your head at the sheer pitifulness of it. (2011)

Shrek (**Andrew Adamson / Vicky Jenson, 2001**)
What surprised me most about a revisit to *Shrek* is how dated it has become. Full disclosure: though I saw *Shrek* when it was new, I have not since taken advantage of any of the subsequent franchise, which includes three sequels, five video games, various TV spinoffs, a comic book, and a Broadway musical. I make my complaints also acknowledging that many of the picture's strengths are still there: taking a page out of *The Princess Bride*, it's as knowing as ever about its sources, operates at both adult and kid levels, and tells its story with clarity, uncluttered by distraction. It's just complex enough to be interesting, and it is witty more often than gross (and even when it is gross, it is tame by today's standards).

One of the most obvious ways *Shrek* shows its age is also the one to be expected, which is the state of the art of the animation. I recall that the CGI here was considered one of its strong points on release, but now it just looks 12 years old—12 years that encompass a whole lot of innovation and development in the industry. Though it was conceived at one point in 3D, *Shrek* now seems to present-day animation somewhat as Hanna-Barbera of '70s TV was to it. But I don't make the finest distinctions among animation. The dated qualities of the *Shrek* CGI were enough for me to notice, but not enough to annoy. I would call Jay Ward one of my favorite animators and he's nothing if not primitive ("illustrated radio," as Chuck Jones once dismissed it), so partly that's a matter of my own aesthetic.

But another quality that dates *Shrek* is a bit more of an obstacle for me. That's the music, which seems to me so wrong as to be painful, cringe-inducing in its own right. It's mired in late-'90s alt-rock cliché, which is already conceptually jarring even as texture here. It's made even more so when one gets down to specifics: two songs by Smash Mouth, including one, "All Star," that serves as theme, plus the Eels, Joan Jett (on her third or fourth rise), and Self. There's even John Cale warbling out a cover of a Leonard Cohen song, "Hallelujah," which I admit I was mighty happy to hear, but it was still a distraction from the picture.

Babe and *The Matrix* (of course) are referenced here. Cameron Diaz is the voice for Princess Fiona. I don't have anything against Diaz, but she's by and large way overmatched—cast, I suspect, as much as anything because she was an "it" girl of the moment, riding high from turns in *Fear and Loathing in Las Vegas, There's Something About Mary, Being John Malkovich* (remarkably drabbed down), and *Charlie's Angels*. To me, she is another aspect of *Shrek* that seems stuck *back there*. But the voice casting otherwise is one of the picture's great features. John Lithgow is fine swallowing the microphone as the big-chinned but fatally short Lord Farquaad. Mike Myers is great as Shrek, the big ugly green ogre with a Scottish accent who must rescue a princess in order to win back the privacy that he craves. Eddie Murphy as Donkey is the star of this show, slipping easily into all manner of shtick in his familiar stand-up style. He is inspired, funny all the way through. Only one example: a discussion between Shrek and Donkey about the inner nature of ogres. Shrek says it is layered like an onion. This causes Donkey to go off on a riff about parfaits. "You know, not everybody likes onions," he says. "Parfait's gotta be the most delicious thing on the whole damn planet."

Shrek is also a great parody of Disney features—it comes of a great love of them. *Shrek* is programmatically the inversion of Disney, its heroes an ugly ogre, an ass, and a princess who (depending as always on the beholder) mysteriously shuttles between "beautiful" and "ugly." It makes explicit references to *Peter Pan, Snow White and the Seven Dwarfs*, and the 1991 *Beauty and the Beast*. The *Snow White* lift is notably good at turning tables. Princess Fiona, up early in the morning, finds a bluebird and sings to it, finally hitting a note that explodes the bird so she can steal the eggs.

Shrek is pretty funny all the way through. The fairy tale narrative arc works, ending on a big showy finish with a Monkees cover by Smash Mouth, "I'm a Believer." Bad music again, I know, yes, cringe cringe. But on the whole the movie works so that such things become almost forgivable. (2013)

Silicon Teens, *Music for Parties* (1980)
The Silicon Teens takes the drift of the Monkees and the Archies to a logical conclusion, teaming up four people—Darryl, Jacki, Paul, and Diane, by name—who not only are not musicians, nor even human, but *in fact do not exist at all.* Which explains the lack of last names for one thing. In fact, it is a larky one-off goof project by Daniel Miller, one man alone with his thoughts in a studio, which he did shortly before starting up the Mute label, whose acts included Depeche Mode, Erasure, and Yazoo. When you think about all those things you won't be surprised to find out what *Music for Parties* is. Bouncy-ball synthpop covers of classic rock 'n' roll and/or top 40 pop standards, plus a handful of originals with vaguely sinister overtones. So let's see here: "Memphis," "Doo Wah Diddy Diddy," "You Really Got Me," "Judy in Disguise," "Sweet Little Sixteen," do you see what I am talking about yet? It really blipped in and out fast in 1980. I found out about it when a friend pulled it out of the library of a radio station. I don't remember ever reading much about it. But I loved it immediately and intensely for a few weeks. Eventually I forgot about it until I ran across a download, and wow, flipped for it all over again. The act's biggest claim to fame has its origins on this, their only album, in the cover of "Red River Rock," which caught the attention of John Hughes, who ordered up a rerecorded version for the opening titles of 1987's *Planes, Trains, and Automobiles.* I like it a lot. I'd also like to commend one of the

originals, the instrumental "State of Shock (pt. 2)." There is not a "State of Shock (pt. 1)" on the album. It seems to me that this is as it should be. It's real outer space spy movie stuff, with lovely tones and textures to some of the bouncy-ball parts of it. Well, all parts of it are the bouncy-ball parts if you know what I mean, but it really gets itself going on a head of steam, and builds from there. It's so easy to be infatuated with this and then forget it utterly for decades. So give it a listen now. You can thank me in 2044, if you remember. (2012)

Carly Simon, "That's the Way I've Always Heard it Should Be" (June 5, 1971, #10)
Carly Simon's first hit is far and away her best, not least because it manages to escape the soundalike formula she struck on with her next, "Anticipation," which subsequently led to her biggest, "You're So Vain" and on to further meadows. It's a formula I like. In fact, I count Carly Simon as my personal favorite woman pop singer of the '70s, at least in the category of guilty pleasure—she's analogous for me to Petula Clark in the '60s and Sheena Easton in the '80s. But "That's the Way" is beyond all that even—yes, I see your point, it's more proto-Adult Contemporary, not just in its soft, wispy textures, lulling piano, whispering vocal, aching strings, but also in another sense altogether, in its themes, both adult and almost painfully contemporary upper-middle-class: "My friends from college are all married now / They have their houses and their lawns." This might be coming from the same general geographical vicinity as "Be My Baby" but it's a continent apart in terms of class, sitting in a paneled room reading Cheever. Yet there is also something entirely universal going on here. The cold and distant family, the isolation of the singer confronting the next step of her life, the fearful prospect, marriage, which even in the midst of the burgeoning feminism of the day remained an inevitability, certainly a step the singer feels compelled to take without questioning, except for this brief cry for help. She can't articulate why shes doing it any better than anyone else in this song

can articulate anything ("My father sits at night with no lights on / His cigarette glows in the dark"). It's terrifying, yet familiar. I was in high school when it was on the radio, I had not even had a girlfriend yet, and still the sadness and the terror of this deceptively quiet plaint could devastate me. It still can. (2010)

Frank Sinatra, *The Sinatra Christmas Album* (1963)
I came to know this in the late '70s, when I was working night-shifts in a nursing home. The dayroom for the station I tended was decked out for the holidays in a kind of sad and shabby fashion that's not hard to imagine, with stuff from thrift stores. The album was part of the little collection of records gathered there and in the darkest deeps of the night that December, along about the two o'clock or three o'clock hours, I used to wander down to the dayroom and turn on the colored lights and play it on the suitcase record player someone had brought in. I sat there in one of the rickety rocking chairs, playing it soft and rocking and thinking about things like my future and my past and where everything was headed. It was deliciously sad start to finish, notably the woeful "I'll Be Home for Christmas" and "The Christmas Waltz," with Sinatra's sad little "Merry Christmas!" at the end of it. If I was in the mood, sometimes I flipped it over and played the church songs. More often I just played the first side once or twice, or three times. All those associations are buried in it for me still, even sitting in front of my computer all this time later playing it on iTunes. Sometimes, with everything, it's so complex and so beautiful all at once that it's almost too much. I think that's the kind of thing Christmas does to you more than Sinatra, but there's also an art to his way of channeling that too. (2012)

Sister Sledge, "Lost in Music" (1979)
The Chic brothers, Nile Rodgers and Bernard Edwards, never strayed far from a predictable set of lyrical concerns, which is only one of the reasons I love them as much as I do: living well, dressing nice, and

dancing. Usually giddy happy, sometimes a little down, always strong. That about covers it. One subset dedicated itself narrowly to the pleasures of music itself—the 1983 "In Love With Music" by the flagship Chic is a good example. But this is the best, from Sister Sledge, one of Chic's greatest side projects, on the *We Are Family* album. It feels like a statement of purpose, a virtual manifesto. All the usual elements are in place: bass and funky guitar chops locked in groove, as the powerful and sweet undertow, with the keyboards and strings establishing a swirling, soaring context, and then the glorious harmonies and interplay of the Sledge sisters, who sound hypnotized, helpless before the power of the music in which they say they are lost—and in which they are obviously fully engaged. It's inspiring in its single-mindedness: "We're lost in music / Feel so alive / I quit my 9 to 5," goes the chorus. The verses get down to details, elaborating on the life of performing and throwing everything away for it: "Some people ask me / What are you gonna be / Why don't you go get a job, uh-uh / All that I could say / I won't give up my music / Not me, not now, no way, no how, oh...oh..." There's even a throwaway reference to "Suspicious Minds" ("caught in a trap")—who knows what the hell it's doing there. To me it's more evidence of the abandon, underlining the point because they can. Because they saw the opportunity and did. Lost in music. (2011)

Skogie & the Flaming Pachucos, Minneapolis, ca. 1973
The memory of seeing Skogie & the Flaming Pachucos lives on now as perhaps more than it was, but on the other hand it's hard to overstate: more or less my first rock club experience. I had been to concerts before—it was still the era of concerts, good and bad: Jethro Tull, Yes, Miles Davis, Weather Report, so on so forth. This was something else entirely—something that rattled something inside me awake, although it still took a few years before I really got out of bed. It was the only time I saw them, at some kind of all-ages place in Minneapolis. I cannot for the life of me remember where or exactly when this was—maybe the spring of '73? I think I was still in high school, but nearly done. It was dark and crowded. I was

in the back of the room and it was hard to even see the stage. I was uncomfortable and a little scared by how close and packed it was and I regretted being there and was exasperated with myself for succumbing once again to peer pressure. That all changed when the band came out and started. Even though I could still barely see them through the shoulders of taller people in front of me, and I was still uncomfortable with the packed room, the throbbing din of it was amazing. The sound was so big it swallowed you. They were some kind of retro garage-band outfit, built their act out of a shrewd blend of covers and originals, and were aware of glam and the Stooges and New York Dolls. They were electrifying, loud, hilarious, rocking, fun. It was such a singularly amazing experience that I didn't even grasp the reality of it until years later, when rock clubs came around in the punk era and I started to have the experience again, and have pursued it repeatedly since, and was still finding it more than 25 years later, at a Queens of the Stone Age show in Seattle's Capitol Hill. Later I would find out that Skogie's real name was Rick Moore. He moved to Los Angeles and was the first husband of actress Demi Guynes, who kept his name. He was a charismatic front man, a wild kinetic guy working off the music. I had no context for it. I wish I could see them again. (2003)

Patti Smith, *Horses* (1975)
As exalted as it is earthbound, and on so many levels, Patti Smith's great debut, along with a performance I witnessed of her and her remarkable band early in 1976, ushered me into a whole new world of rock 'n' roll at a moment in my life when I needed it badly. This was an important album for me. I want to point out just three examples of its profound dichotomies and the lovely ways she works and plays with her material.

First, the cover shot by her friend, the photographer Robert Mapplethorpe, is a simple enough black and white shot of the New Jersey native posed against a wall with a jacket slung over her shoulder, looking for all the world like some yobby thug stepping from the shadows of some bleak London subculture. Look more closely, however, and you see that Mapplethorpe carefully set up the shot to create a play of light and shadow just behind her that gives her angel wings.

The title, next, is a simple common noun evocative of western movies and literature, young girls, agriculture, jousting, rodeos, and other homely matters mostly mundane in their times and places. Yet the horse, of course, is also a potent and deeply embedded symbol that cuts across European, Native American, Arabian, and Eastern cultures. In the wilds of the Internet, the website Zimbio told me that the horse symbolizes "success, freedom, travel, strength, power, nobility, wisdom and loyalty. It is also a symbol of life and death, grace and beauty." Patti Smith harks to much of that one way or another in her remarkable 9:26 "Land" suite on *Horses*, additionally working in an inscrutable scenario of teen rape, a cover of Cannibal & the Headhunters' 1965 hit "Land of 1,000 Dances" (covered also by Wilson Pickett, in 1966), and a cameo appearance by the sea (which, remember, composes not just 71% of the earth's surface but 71% of our body by composition as well), resorting to bringing the thing up to full speed as needed by chanting, "Horses ... horses ... horses."

Last in this quickie survey, the album opens with a cover of the old mid-'60s garage-rock chestnut, "Gloria." But this is not just any old cover of the song that launched one million teen dance parties, as Smith's opening figure—which does not appear in the Van Morrison original—makes abundantly clear: "Jesus died for somebody's sins, but not mine." This G-L-O-R-I-A has much less to do with somebody in a beehive hairdo snapping gum and a lot more to do with "in excelsis Deo" and the affairs of a church. I'm still not sure which church that is, given the opening remarks, but there was a time when I was convinced it was the one true church, and I desperately wanted to join. (2011)

Scott Smith, *A Simple Plan* (1993)

I came to this for a few reasons, starting with being so impressed
when I took another look at the Sam Raimi movie based on it
(whose screenplay Scott Smith wrote). It won some praise from
Stephen King. Then, going through Cormac McCarthy's *No
Country for Old Men* soon after seeing *A Simple Plan*, I realized how
similar their premises were. When I got to a scene where the principal in *A Simple Plan*, Hank Mitchell, was flipping a coin in order
to make one of his many heinous decisions, the parallels cut pretty
close. McCarthy is the better writer, of course, with more gravitas
and reputation, and he's also better able to expand the story to
bigger themes. Smith's novel gets pretty loopy pretty fast—I'm of
the school (if such a school exists) that Smith made a better job of
the second pass, with the screenplay. Still, as the King imprimatur
would indicate, the book operates successfully as a horror thriller.
Mitchell, the first-person narrator, makes for an intriguing monster—rationalizing, self-pitying, with his feet on the ground. Jim
Thompson territory, a little, particularly when he gets to the actual killing. In the end I had Mitchell pegged as all but remorse-
less serial killer, but Smith doesn't go there in his coda, which is
just as well. That would be unbelievable, and there's a good case
anyway that Mitchell is just sunk into the psychological state of in-
sensibility known in poker as "pot-committed." The baby Amanda
was a nice touch—the baby who soaks up all the bad vibes and
becomes an unpleasant element in her own right. Hank's brother
Jacob, played by Billy Bob Thornton in the movie, works better in
the book's version as an obese and forever-consuming sad sack (although Thornton creates a different, equally memorable character with one of his best performances in the movie version). Smith
also works the money aspect well. Four million dollars is a lot of
money, and in the end I had nearly as hard a time as any character
here letting go of it, plagued by endless worrying of the problem.
Couldn't you try this? Couldn't you try that? I also happened to be
convinced when they first found it that they should turn it in and

walk away, and not just because I'd seen the movie twice. But once the rationalizing and especially the bad deeds were underway, I was pretty much right in there with them every step of the way. Interesting how shrewd it is that way, working the levers of greed. (2012)

Phoebe Snow, "Take Your Children Home" (1974)
In which I disclose both methodology and a base sentimentality that motivates me: One reason I never made it as a journalist was lack of an ability to stay on top of things and fix on what is interesting to a wide or general (or even niche and specific) audience, which is mostly a matter of keeping up, which probably just means I'm lazy or a crank or both. But there you go. Instead of swimming the zeitgeist, I have to make long lists way far in advance and plod through them in order. Phoebe Snow's lovely "Take Your Children Home" made it to the list because in 2009 it became the unofficial theme song of the death of my cat Floyd—the song paralyzed me with sadness when shuffle suddenly began insisting on it shortly after he died unexpectedly. Phoebe Snow's death came in 2011, the last grace note in her own sad story of children found, lost, taken home. And now my time to write about this song has come in the same week that my cat Esme has died—Floyd's sister, who outlived him by more than four years to make it to 16 years old. My constant companion, and best friend in many ways. "Death has no mercy," as the Grateful Dead put it, and I feel that acutely in this moment. But I feel grace at work too, putting this song in my way. It's more playful than I'm letting on, with these circumstances—it's more a shambolic meditation on carousing at heart, but I hear (or project) such a world of wisdom into the title phrase, rooted in the here and now yet facing the eternal. "Take your children home, I am one." Death as a matter of going home. So even as this song makes me appallingly sad ("children" being so vulnerable by definition), it comforts me too. I like to think that Floyd and Esme are both safe at home now, where I took them. (2013)

Sonic Youth, "The Diamond Sea" (1995)

I love "The Diamond Sea" possibly more than any other Sonic Youth. It clocks in at 19:36, modulating from a lovely wistful tune to roaring sheets of noise and back again several times. It may be the best evidence of how thoughtful they were in terms of constructing their noise—not just noise for the sake of noise, random blasts of ear pierce, but noise set carefully into context, for a purpose. In this case, an homage to Kurt Cobain. It was anyway a perfect soundtrack for crossing a gray lake on gray mornings to work. It made me sad, and happy, and when the noise started I turned it up. It is beautiful, as is the melody, into and out of which the noise morphs. (2005)

Sonic Youth, "Shadow of a Doubt" (1986)

This eternally mysterious sound sculpture is focused on incidentals of two Alfred Hitchcock movies—named after one, with plot points from the other, *Strangers on a Train*, woven into the whisper-chant from Kim Gordon. In my YouTube travels I found a nice homemade video made out of this song and scenes from *Twin Peaks: Fire Walk With Me*. It is an inspired mashup, like the song, potent with black and blue and gray imagery and currents. Here the Sonic Youth trademark strange tunings are distilled to purest forms, jewel-hard and gleaming. Compare "Providence" on *Daydream Nation*. As musique concrète the open spaces are similar but the sense of a narrative is stronger in "Providence"—something is lost and must be found. In "Shadow of a Doubt" there is only the sense that a narrative might exist. Or narrative itself—the sense that *narrative* might exist. "I swear I didn't mean it / I swear it wasn't meant to be / Must a been a dream ... He said / 'You take me and I'll be you' / 'You kill him and I'll kill her' / Kiss me." This is a way of looking at things that is like what one finds in the David Lynch movie, dreams and fragments and an idea that *narrative might exist*, as the prequel is retrospective to the TV series. This may be one reason why the video mashup works so well. To close the loop, you also find this way of looking at things in some Alfred Hitchcock pictures, notably *Vertigo* and *Shadow of a Doubt*, which don't so much eschew narrative as grow absent-minded about its existence, distracted by ... something. And Sonic Youth wraps it all up in a beautiful strange noise that lingers to effect. (2012)

Sonny & Cher, "I Got You Babe" (July 31, 1965, #1, 3 wks.)
YES, I say. Sonny & Cher's goopy first hit retains its charms, in spite of the ultimate fate of these fur-vested standard-bearers of one version of the '60s, the one that worshiped at the feet of Phil Spector immediately before the tidal wave of Animals, Beatles, Kinks, and Stones washed them deep into the hinterlands of inconsequence. I suppose my favoring it has something to do with its being one of the first singles I actually purchased (along with "Help!" by the Beatles and "Save Your Heart for Me" by Gary Lewis & the Playboys). "I Got You Babe" enters and departs with the tempo of a gassy ape, or maybe it's the oboe that makes me think that. It's a simple, plaintive, and dare I say innocent declaration of love, which arrives even as summer closes down and it's time to go back to school. Just two nutty kids alone and left to fend for themselves in a desperate world, never mind that one (Sonny) is 11 years older than the other, which makes him a bit less convincing as a nutty kid. But forget that and dig the message (even now there is something about Sonny Bono that irresistibly invites potshots; it was the hallmark of Cher's stand-up on their TV variety show and, for his part, Sonny addressed it in his solo follow-up to this, "Laugh at Me"). Erm, where was I? Oh yes, dig the message: "They say we're young and we don't know, won't find out until we grow" (sung very sweetly). "Well I don't know if all that's true, 'cos you got me, and baby I got you" (sung very poorly). In short: "Don't let them say your hair's too long." Cut. Freeze. Fade. Indelible. (2010)

The Sopranos **(HBO TV series, 1999-2007)**
At some point I realized I was spotty on everything so I started from the beginning and slow-walked this in, once I knew it was really

finally finished in 2007. Partly I didn't want it to be over and partly, as a result of times with and without cable, I had missed most of the very long last season and significant parts of others and I wanted to see it all in order. *The Sopranos* always had a lot of problems to contend with—perhaps most notably, being yet another Italian mafia gangsters story, with all the natural aimlessness, mechanical swells, and central character invulnerabilities of series television. It had some tendency toward art-film pretensions too, arguably. Middlebrow entertainment for the NPR middle class, OK, maybe. Yet I think all that was overcome by its many virtues. It's a great sprawling story with great sprawling characters and complexity, with much of substance about good and evil and human frailty, an amazing cast headed by the amazing James Gandolfini, and for a bonus almost always great surprises on the soundtrack. Every episode made me tense and ill even as it went straight to the familiar heart of the American Dream as we know it today, over and over again. Maybe the biggest surprise? Especially in the first two seasons, it has one of the absolute best depictions of psychotherapy anywhere, ever—the kind you and I get, when our health insurance covers it. (2014)

Britney Spears, ...*Baby One More Time* (1999)
Oh man, I had some low expectations coming back to this—well, "coming back." I liked the songs when they were on the radio. But when I finally picked up a cheap used copy of the album it didn't seem to me to amount to much more than the hits, and the hits didn't sound so good anymore. So I filed it. I had always felt a little like someone claiming to enjoy *Playboy* for the thoughtful and hard-hitting articles anyway whenever I tried to talk about the virtues of Britney Spears—her good fortune of a sweet and sultry voice which she can play like an instrument, the infectious layers of glittering production, and some basic understanding of the principles of pop music and hooks and so forth, not to mention an erratic but unmistakable sense on her part for soul singing. As her

public persona developed into chronic celebrity problems it grew too tiresome and I thought I had put it behind me. In fact, I'm not even sure why I included it on the list of albums I am still working from, at the time intended for much shorter write-ups. I think I wondered how my audience then would respond to something so blatantly mainstream. Anyway, holy buckets, it sounds way better than I remember. It's still the hits I tend to favor; the stellar track this time is definitely "Sometimes" (#21 in 1999), which might be the most obvious Spice Girls knockoff here. It's sweet and hot and all kind of sad and uncertain about a love relationship, and swells up big on the chorus, lush and full of presence. The kind of thing you can't always put in words, you know? So I usually turn it up a little for that one. Then a song called "Soda Pop" follows, so winsomely sweet as to be nauseating. It's part of what chased me away from the album in the first place. But then that's followed by "Born to Make You Happy," which is not a hit but good, with her bruised vocals playing nicely off a chanting background line. In a certain mood, which the album is at pains to set by that point, it's tolerable enough—if you feel mired in by saccharine dreck, hang on. There's bound to be better, or maybe the dreck will clarify into the more and more pleasing passages I seem to hear in this every time now. To be sure, there are silly exercises here, such as "E-Mail My Heart," which pains me just to type. But then there's a decent Sonny & Cher cover (and I like the pick). I'd say there are at least four or five good to great songs here. (2012)

Spirited Away (Hayao Miyazaki, 2001)
In our 21st-century world of revitalized animated features, impresario Hayao Miyazaki and Studio Ghibli have arguably risen to the top of the heap (with Pixar not far back), and Spirited Away has earned a consensus distinction as being the best of the best of them. Spirited Away is indeed a fine adventure yarn, with a winning heroine, inventiveness by the pound, and a moment of overwhelming emotional clarity when the true nature of one of its most important characters

is revealed—a truly inspired, even cunning revelation, which is fully appreciated only by paying the picture another visit in order to better grasp the nuances and intricacies in light of it.

At which point, for me, a funny thing happened. I was left more underwhelmed than I had been prepared for. It has felt hollow and a little too long on subsequent viewings. Objectively, the movie is everything it was the first time—looks good, moves well, nice rhythm of surprises, with a spunky heroine you can't help rooting for against unsettling, tough, and mysterious foes. It's weird enough that I liked it—but conventional enough that I didn't love it. That helped me remember my main ongoing problem with the fantasy genre (where I don't even like Lewis Carroll, the most obvious source for this): it tends to require too much memorizing. And, in turn, that reminded me of my problems with so-called YA (young adult) literature, which has enjoyed a huge vogue in the past 20 years.

Let me start with a digression. Last year, working with two friends on a countdown project of favorite movies, which we presented on Facebook, one commenter never failed to register objections to anything even the least bit fantastic—science fiction, David Lynch, most horror, and anything with animation were discussed by him in dire terms of dwindling cultural values. While I have some sympathies with the view—I could do with a lot fewer comic book movies clogging up the multiplexes myself, for one—no aesthetic that rules out *Close Encounters of the Third Kind*, *Videodrome*, or *Grave of the Fireflies* is going to work for me.

That said, however, I am suspicious of the popularity of YA literature. It's not the literature itself, which, what I've read, is rarely objectionable, often quite entertaining, and tends to have excellent values. My concerns are more about the OAs (old adults) who make a fetish of it. And I want to be careful what I'm saying here as I don't begrudge or object to anyone finding entertainment or elucidation in anything they want. I love Jack Webb, the *Star Trek* franchise, and Lifetime movies, so I know I have quirks too, and we are all allowed by my lights. But there's something sad to me about grown adults so immersed in adolescent culture. (And never mind all this comes from a middle-aged someone who operates a blog dedicated coequally to rock 'n' roll in its various mythic proportions.)

When I have dipped into these things, such as the Harry Potter series, I often come away impressed, thinking how much I would have liked them myself as an adolescent. (My own YA favorites were Edward Eager, who I consider near the equal in his way of J.K. Rowling, Norton Juster, who probably isn't, and "Carolyn Keene," a team of anonymous back benchers who certainly are not.) But here's the thing. Even as YA literature roams at will across genres, often dwelling at once in fantasy, science fiction, and even horror realms, one thing it never does is stray far from a certain stubborn optimism about the human condition. That is why it exists. It is administered like nutrition the way baby food is to infants, an important element in overcoming tendencies toward some analogue of "failure to thrive." Infants need the physical nutrition. Adolescents need the spiritual nutrition of believing it's all worth it and that sincere effort within an ethical frame is rewarded, and reward enough in itself—when, as adults, we know that no such thing is true at all in this world. Dealing with *that* is the most interesting aspect of FA (fully adult) literature for me, and it's nowhere to be found, by design, in YA. (A rock 'n' roll equivalent of YA literature, in defense of that middle-aged someone I mentioned above, might be *The Rocky Horror Picture Show*, which is explicitly *not* dangerous, all trappings notwithstanding.)

As much as anything, that's my problem with *Spirited Away*. The most interesting issues it raises—such as that adults tend naturally, and horrifyingly, in the direction of gluttony, which includes our heroine's parents too—are mostly ducked. It does not avoid at all the issues of environmentalism that it raises, which is where it comes tantalizingly close to a fully realized critical vision, but it is too coy by half, too often addressing the issues it raises too indirectly, or without proper emphasis, e.g., in regard to Haku's revelation, *WTF there are apartment buildings there now?!* The filthy river spirit, for another example, which is mistaken for a "stink" spirit, is indeed filled to a shocking degree with disgusting industrial waste, but it is never explicitly named as a river spirit until well past that crucial scene. (This all from the English language version; it's possible things differ in the Japanese.)

Much is made of the development of our heroine, Chihiro, over the course of the movie and the adventure, but I don't see it. She looked and sounded like a slightly bored and know-it-all teen before, and she looks and sounds like that after. The context of our experience of her adventure may make her seem more mature, a kind of grayscale optical illusion. But I don't see any evidence she was that immature before, when after all she is in the middle of a traumatizing move, or conversely is so much more mature after.

And now that the official damning is over I guess I can make with the faint praise. Because the fact is I am sure I am judging it with inappropriate standards—this and so many animated features require allowance for lack of psychological complexity and then they open up like fireworks. *Spirited Away* can be dazzling, lively, spooky, and creative. It locates itself in an otherworldly bathhouse for the spirits, which feels more like a brothel in a manufacturing facility, with a crazy menagerie that includes primitive-cartoon soot-ball creatures, a No-Face spirit in a black robe and quasi-Guy-Fawkes mask, a six-armed boiler man, a strange giant baby, disembodied heads, identical twin witches (where have I heard that one before?), trains that glide across water, and more.

Never mind that it shades off into incoherence in the second half of the adventure; it works itself up to a really sweet moment on the climax, literally soaring as it pulls that off, swelling on Joe Hisaichi's transparent use of the John Williams / Disney playbook of Big Moment Movie Music. Who am I to buck what the crowds demand? No one, that's who. In that moment, *Spirited Away* works just like gang-busters. (2012)

Splendor in the Grass (**Elia Kazan, 1961**)
It's interesting how many big hothouse American productions of the late '50s and early '60s were focused on crack-ups of various kinds, often headed up by Method acolytes such as James Dean, Marlon Brando, and Paul Newman. Here Natalie Wood, only about 22 but already ubiquitous from years as a child performer, gets the nervous breakdown honors and she does all right, though it's not really in her range. If *Pillow Talk* is a comedy of the sexual revolution, I guess this must be one of its tragedies. The mental institution was my clue. (2014)

Split Enz, *Dizrythmia* (**1977**)
I don't remember now how I ended up with the early Split Enz albums, before their New Wave breakthrough of 1980. Some clerk at a record store must have told me to buy them. The first, *Mental Notes*, I recall as something of a wan Roxy Music knockoff. This, their third, was more to my taste, more of a pop album, dotted by horns, keyboard strings, and lusty guitar licks, aided and abetted no doubt by producer Geoff Emerick, late of the Beatles, Badfinger, America, etc., etc. Neil Finn had joined the band and makes his first LP appearance here; brother Tim was a founding member and indeed involved in writing nearly all the songs, wholly or in part, along with Eddie Rayner, who has co-credit on four of the nine tracks. Only one song even approaches anything like stellar status, but they are nonetheless workmanlike about the way they hammer together hooks and melodies in the service of earworm fare that often continues to echo through cerebral cortexes hours and days later. That's what the Finns do, basically. Two here were even hits

Down Under: "My Mistake" and "Bold as Brass," and it's not hard to imagine them playing on the radio. A couple of others, at six-minutes-plus each, recall the band's collective Roxy Music infatuation, and not without charms. The knockout song for me is "Charlie," which is also a bit long at 5:31. But it's lovely all through, with a loping bass figure, a vocal left to twist in space on various breaks, and memorably lush cascading piano flourishes. It's a real show-stopper, forever calling attention to itself by the ache it produces. Tim Finn and Rayner were reportedly disappointed with the vocal, but Emerick argued for keeping it and ultimately prevailed. I would like to personally thank him for that. Interestingly (or not), as a vinyl album this is one that played better for me "upside down"—that is, while I usually tended to play both sides when I listened to it, as I did with many albums, in this case (and a few others) I preferred to listen to the second side first. Somehow that sequencing worked better for me. I'm not sure how I came to these decisions, or even what compelled me in the first place to try them. (2011)

Bruce Springsteen, "Downbound Train" (1984)
More confessions of a one-time Bruce Springsteen snob: Here's the song that turned me around on him, the reason I favor *Born in the U.S.A.* of all his albums (also the sequence of which this is part, from "Cover Me" through to "I'm on Fire"). I know it's the triumphal ascendance point of his career, which can be annoying to the faithful. It's harder to feel special for one thing when you are sharing the object of your adoration with whole stadiumsful of people showing up late. And there are some signs here already perhaps of the problems that were ahead, the frustrating admixture of bloat and vacuousness in there with all the good stuff. But one of the things I like most about Bruce Springsteen is that he has an ability to look around and feel sad, genuinely sad. "Downbound Train," which feels like a lost alternate-universe fragment of a chapter from *The Grapes of Wrath,* might be the best example of that I know. He's talking about injustice in as lucid and straightforward a manner

as could be. He's not looking away from anything. He's working in a carwash. It grounds the high points of his other songs, delivers their joys better, knowing that all the extremes are acknowledged and felt. This is how I think Bruce Springsteen does it. He is carrying a heavy load in this song—presumably that's why it's a train. And I love the way the burden flattens the words in his mouth into rounded vowels and sliding growls. On the lines "Now I swing a sledgehammer on a railroad gang / Knocking down them cross ties, working in the rain," he is practically just moaning and honking. It's good that people make lyrics available on the Internet, although thinking about it now every sense of those words is there in the vocal—the sense of working, and futility. See also "Wichita Lineman" by Glen Campbell. (2013)

Bruce Springsteen, "Independence Day" (1980)
If Bruce Springsteen won me over by osmosis, across a period of many years, I can still remember the moment when I clicked over to being admirer and fan, which came with this song. It was when I was moving from Minneapolis to Seattle, dragging a U-Haul trailer behind an iffy Dodge station wagon, foolishly going out of my way to visit a small town in South Dakota that had represented the Midwest to me since I was 8 years old. I thought I was taking advantage of a chance to visit it once more. I didn't realize until this song happened to start that I was actually detouring to say goodbye to the Midwest and the first half of my life, at which point I burst into a few minutes of hard, wracking tears. It would be easy enough to quibble with the fuzzy aspect of the lyrics here, the inexpertly rendered and incoherent scene between a father and son. It doesn't matter. It's the sound of it, the doleful mourning quality, the way he sings, "Just say goodbye it's Independence Day," focusing it so explicitly on the word and the idea of "independence." It's one of the truest expressions of "independence" I know, going past the usual screechy good humor associated with patriotism and the 4th of July and all that—the hubbub Dick Cheney said we would be

greeted with in Iraq in 2003, for example. Mel Gibson bellowing "Freedom!" in *Braveheart*. "Dependence," as any monarchist can tell you, does have its comforts. An independence day is a mixed thing, that's the reality. It is also a loss, and thrusts one into a future without certainty. (2012)

Robert Louis Stevenson, *Strange Case of Dr. Jekyll and Mr. Hyde* (1886)
I'm not real high on this one, for reasons perhaps good and bad both. I never formed any appreciation of Robert Louis Stevenson. That's a big part of it. Even as a kid I was left cold by *Treasure Island*. And that probably would have been that for me but for Stephen King's *Danse Macabre*, which included *Jekyll and Hyde* on short lists of essentials, along with *Dracula, Frankenstein*, etc. But alas. There is an interesting idea in Stevenson's *Jekyll and Hyde*, with its proto-Cronenberg scenarios of cooking chemicals and altered flesh—body horror. By happenstance, there's also an unsettling undertow of inchoate Freudian theory, with the battle between the ego (Jekyll) and the id (Hyde)—even the names are weirdly parallel, though decades early. There is a good opening scene, with Hyde making a remarkable first appearance trampling a little girl. It's all quite moody—London fog, dirty dark streets, the pestilential city, so on so forth. But the writing often seems disjointed, rambling, off the point or actively hiding the point. An envelope to be opened only on the death of one character contains an envelope to be opened only on the death of another. Really? There are altogether too many sealed envelopes, legal documents, street directions, letters, and notes in this short novel. I don't mind epistolary (I adore *Les Liaisons Dangereuses*), but at the same time, to my parochial modern ear, the narrative strategy has something of a higher bar to clear. One interesting point, in this arguably debased era of the Hulk, is that Dr. Jekyll is much the more robust, healthier, and *larger* of the two. Hyde is a bit of a homunculus. Otherwise his description is minimal except in terms of its effects on others, who of course

are revolted and repulsed to a one. Stevenson also shows many of them mystified as to why Hyde has this effect on them, which is a nice detail, as though the revulsion were instinctual, taking place at instinctive levels below consciousness. I like that. But too much of this to my taste is about solving the mystery of the legal estate(s) of Jekyll and Hyde. There's something wild going on here and we're looking at dry documents. (2014)

Rod Stewart, *Gasoline Alley* (1970)
OK all right no getting around it, we're going to have to caveat Rod Stewart to death right here right now. First, on the general critical storm and Rod Stewart's supposed fall from Olympian heights of the awthentic: I really don't get it. I happen to like "Da Ya Think I'm Sexy" (and not just for the spelling of "do") more than other loud critical knights of the realm would have it. At the same time, Rod Stewart is closer to the end than the front of a long line of standard-bearers I intend to get to one fine day, well behind Ella Fitzgerald, Dinah Washington, Billy Eckstine, Ray Charles, James Brown, yeah yeah Sinatra, etc., etc., and as a matter of fact even behind Linda Ronstadt. (For perspective, however, he's ahead of Bing Crosby, Perry Como, and Eddie Fisher.) Long story short: I haven't got to that stuff yet and may never. And then the Faces—or is it just "Faces"? Classic rock pure enough, they remain among the enduring mysteries for me. The loud critical knights of the realm seem to rank *most* of their releases as indispensable and/or essential but to date practically all of it has escaped me, with or without Rod Stewart. Except for "Itchycoo Park"—which for that matter I have the impression the knights don't care for. And *finally*, as much as I like so much about the follow-up *Every Picture Tells a Story*, it appears to have finally unfortunately lost its appeal to me permanently, particularly the flagship "Maggie May," thanks to the weapon of FM radio bludgeon. As with "Stairway to Heaven" and *Led Zeppelin IV* I may never enjoy hearing any of it again. My loss, I know. And so, with all that said and my apologies for going on about it, *Gasoline*

Alley is a perfectly splendid album. Everything about it, everything, is just about perfect. (2007)

Whit Stillman. See *Damsels in Distress, The Last Days of Disco.*

Stooges, *Fun House* (1970)

I was vaguely aware of the Stooges in high school, but my general understanding at the time, from hippie contemporaries, was that it was very bad and scary music that only demented people would be interested in. Already the legends of Iggy suffering injuries in performance were circulating. Naturally I accepted the solemn word of mouth. So I did not actually catch up to the Stooges proper until many years later, in the late '70s, backtracking from an infatuation with Iggy Pop caught in the reflection of David Bowie. At first I thought *The Stooges* was the better album of the two (with *Raw Power* crowding both hard) because the sound seemed simpler and more direct and because the year song ("1969" vs. "1970") was stronger and more anthemic. I came to find out how wrong I was about this assessment during a crucial period in the early '80s.

To be clear, and to get right to the point, *Fun House* was an album—ultimately *the* album—for drinking. Try it yourself—or not. All disclaimers apply. It starts with "Down on the Street," which wastes no time in pounding with authority. How did I ever think the first album was the more direct? Indeed, the song is locked in ferociously, and immediately, over which the squalling vocals and squalling guitar of Iggy Stooge and Ron Asheton in tandem and alone get to work, roaming like creatures at play. The guitar (filtered, fuzzed-up, wah-wah'd) is notably unearthly in its blend of feedback squeal, pealing notes, and noisy chords. It's a stone ball.

No time to waste, on to "Loose," and by now you should be. In other words, word to the wise, start your drinking early. You need to get a sense of the timing for this, and you will. Because you want to

INDEX

be right for "Loose," which occupies a territory that few other rock songs can. It surges and churns and drives, but Iggy is riding it on the vocal like the famous photo of him foot-stepping across the hands of adoring fans. Fun house, amusement park, carnival ride, spinning, whirling, diving, looping, sawing, burring. Fuck, yeah. What a vocal. The art of head-bobbing is also easily picked up here—the very word "loose," as called out and used repeatedly, provides a good place to grab on and hold tight. It's a big ride.

"T.V. Eye"—that's the single, haha. No, it should have been ("Down on the Street" and "1970" actually were). It's the blessed Stooges din we've been living in for two songs now, but with a brooding paranoia like a TV show and an overriding concept too. Something about ... we are the dupes of TV, and furthermore, the TV is looking back. Lunatic lines, obviously, but shouldn't matter because the intensity is just so all of a piece. Now Iggy Stooge capers and leaps about the microphone like a mad imp, until the band transforms into a juggernaut that hunts down his screaming ass. This is told both directly and in terms of the way the song is written and recorded, going into something of a fugue state, which then devolves back to the guitar, solo, literally solo, riffing, and so eventually back into the Stooges amusement park we have now stayed with for three songs, and huzzah.

The last song on the side, "Dirt," is also the longest, and here is where the deepest drunken trances occurred, with the spooky way the vocal unspools, and the punishing guitar and drum trap bash and moody nagging bass line. You sort of fly into this one from the rush of the three before it, and here is actually a good place even for "the whirlies" to hit, if you can get down with that and have the stomach for it. (I no longer do, by the way, so all reports here are from memory, and furthermore, this is not exactly recommended.) The listener at this point may go free-floating off into a place of great space and no gravity, whirling, slowly, in almost a state of pre-birth—a profound experience. "Do you feel it? / Do you feel it when you touch me? / Said do you feel it when you touch me?" What's that he says? I could swear it's "cut."

Well, you get the picture I hope. The other side is good too, with "1970" and a title song and finally a free jazz exercise called "L.A. Blues" (complete with tenor saxophone, also heard on the rest of the side). But *Fun House* for me was always mainly a one-sided album: "Down on the Street" (3:42), "Loose" (3:33), "T.V. Eye" (4:17), and "Dirt" (7:00). Repeat as needed. It is a thrill ride and a mighty crusher. (2014)

See also: Iggy Pop, Iggy & the Stooges.

La Strada **(Federico Fellini, 1954)**
"La strada" is Italian for "the road" and that is probably as good a way in as any to this great Fellini picture. Three years before Jack Kerouac and a decade past Bob Hope and Bing Crosby—and well in front of *The Road Warrior*—this steps in with yet another variation on the look, feel, and traditions, now well worn, of the road story. Some of the most powerful moments in *La Strada* are set in motion simply by transition shots showing the principals on the move again across the postwar landscape of Italy, in their ramshackle transport of motorcycle, sidecar, and covered wagon.

La Strada is frequently classified as neorealism—as much as anything for its exteriors and the desolate postwar mise en scene, not to mention that it's Italian when neorealism ruled Italian cinema—but it proceeds much more like an improbable dream. It plunges straightway into its disorienting narrative, introducing two-bit circus strongman Zampano (Anthony Quinn), who is in the process of buying the child-like and otherworldly Gelsomina (Giulietta Masina) from her mother. He has also just informed them that another daughter he had purchased previously, Gelsomina's sister Rosa, is now dead; evidently he can't even say where she is buried. Within minutes Zampano and Gelsomina are on the road.

Gelsomina is charmingly eager to embark on the adventure, excited about becoming a panhandling street performer, which seems glamorous to her—and, indeed, looks like a lot of fun. She clearly adores the privilege of calling herself an artist. Her spirit is warm and immediate, the one touchstone it's always safe to retreat to in this movie. Paradoxically her persistent good nature also makes it easier to deal with Zampano's abuse of her, which begins almost right away.

Along the way they encounter a high-spirited acrobat known as the Fool (Richard Basehart), who teases both of them, often in humiliating ways. He is also possessed of one of the most annoying giggles ever recorded on film. They are three cards drawn from a tarot deck, and in many ways their fates are sealed when they meet. It's another reason it's virtually impossible to assess *La Strada* in terms of neorealism. The movie is often fantastical—in the stunts the characters perform, in the carnival-like entertainments, in the people they meet and things they see, and in the sheer bigger-than-life exuberance leaking on all sides.

One of the most contradictory aspects of the whole thing, in fact, is how sad the story is, yet so joyful in the telling. The saddest parts— and there is much of that, both subtle and overt—tend to happen at a distance, or even mostly off-stage (save one horrific scene that is linchpin to the finish), while the surface basks in the sunshine of the strangely beautiful. There is thus some cognitive dissonance going on, as it is so charming to watch even as it deals calculatedly with cruelty and loss.

Being an American of a certain age, it's strange for me to see Anthony Quinn and Richard Basehart in such a setting, but the real star of the show is Giulietta Masina anyway. Her performances are often compared to Charlie Chaplin and that's easy enough to see. I see even a little more Harpo Marx in this role, but same difference—Fellini is using her in part as a way to draw on one of the deepest sources of the cinema, the silent comic (with its own roots before the movies of course in the clown)—an element that again pulls against the essential tragedy of this story, leaving us in some confusion between the lighthearted and silly with the base selfishness of human motive, and eventually personal doom.

Another countervailing force: There's a musical theme by Nino Rota here that Fellini uses very nicely (it sounds much like one Rota wrote for Francis Ford Coppola's *Godfather* movies). It's stated first by the Fool, playing it on a toy violin, and then by Gelsomina on the trumpet, in an almost impossibly beautiful moment during a visit to a convent. Finally Zampano hears a woman singing it toward the end of the picture, and from her he finds out the ultimate fate of Gelsomina, a sad and mean finish whose story shatters him.

There are so many great pieces to this picture. Gelsomina is an innocent and very nearly incompetent, making her treatment even more unsettling. Of course she falls in love with Zampano; her satisfaction when Zampano introduces her to others as his wife is manifest, charming, and heartbreaking. When she decides later that Zampano's miserable treatment of her is actually evidence that he loves her, it hurts to see. Zampano is just no good and no good is going to come of staying with him. He may have feelings for her but he's selfish, and a brute, and he will not change. Gelsomina's mistake is to stay with him, and she realizes that eventually, though too late.

Maybe my head is still too full of Stanley Kubrick's and Steven Spielberg's *A.I.* after spending so much time with it recently, but I think I'm seeing a coarse and depraved Pinocchio story buried in the details of *La Strada* and the directions it takes. In this case, the pup-pet-master Zampano has created not a simulacrum of a boy, but of a wife. He trains Gelsomina in performance skills, and in wife skills, by beating her regularly, and philandering. Gelsomina does everything she can to live up to his ideals and to make their life together a real-ity. She becomes a better entertainer, and more subservient partner, though never close to great at either. In the end she pays dearly for her efforts—but in the end, in the final scene at a nighttime beach, it's arguable that she is the one who has triumphed, becoming the one real wife Zampano ever has, years after she has gone. (2012)

Strat-O-Matic Baseball, 1985-1993
In the winter and spring around the time I turned 30 my friend Jerry introduced me to Strat-O-Matic Baseball, a board game. This was very convenient. I was feeling as restless as I had in my life and something like the comforting illusion of the permanency of base-ball tradition lured me. The real thing seemed a lumbering affair and none of the players or teams, stars and champions of the time— the Detroit Tigers, San Diego Padres, Mario Soto, Dale Murphy, Dan Quisenberry, and all the rest—much interested me, and that whole year of 1984 was more or less lost on me, though at least I en-joyed a September with the Minnesota Twins in the pennant race.

These were drinking days for me. In terms of volume, it was prob-ably the heyday of my drinking. It came upon me gradually, starting when I was newly married and attempting to launch a writing ca-reer. I was just beginning to sell reviews and features to local news-papers and smaller, more marginal magazines, all of them seemingly in thrall to the terminally hip or to their advertisers or, the worst of them, to both. I was tickled of course to be getting checks in the mail for my work. But they were on the order of $40.

I soon discovered the chicken wing circuit—promotional PR events with or without food, entertainment, and/or drinks. Frequently

"FREE!!!" These events were staged for a variety of reasons: to promote a new artist or the release of an album, book, or video, to celebrate openings of shows or businesses, to kick off various promotional efforts, to publicize services of an agency, as staff parties in media outlets, and who knows what else. December was a bonanza, with its slate of Christmas parties, but there were events every week of the year.

My freelance journalist friends and I graded them according to what they offered. No food and no-host bar was a laugher—why even bother, unless you had to for some reason. More common were the vegetable tray events, which were all right to start with. Better still were the chicken-wing events, meaning that hot food was available, served out of those square silver warmer trays. Best of all, of course: free drink events. That crashing noise you heard was us rushing to get there.

I also began to school myself in the happy hour deals around Minneapolis, out of which like the finest dumpsters a person could eat cheaply and relatively well, if perfect health and perhaps even dignity too were not a major concern. All that good food, served for a couple of hours every day starting around 5 p.m. (as often as not sitting in more of those square silver warmer trays), could be had for the mere price of one or two beers. And those beers were a total pleasure to gulp down with friends anyway, feeling generally pretty good that you could skate by so providentially—or depressed that you'd been reduced to such measures, depending on the day.

The Strat-O-Matic brand began with a baseball board game created by a man named Harold Richman, who was barely 21. He sold it out of his parent's home in 1961. The first games didn't include all the players from that season but by 1963 the basic game that I played with Jerry in 1985 had been set. In 1972 an advanced version was produced, which is preferred by the true aficionados, and in the mid-'80s computer versions began to be released. Along the way, Strat-O-Matic also developed similar games for football, basketball, hockey, and others.

The play of the baseball game is simple, but seemed rich and infinitely varied to me. A typical game lasts about 40 minutes. Three dice are used, one red and two white. The number on the red die indicates whether to consult the pitcher's card or the batter's card: 1-2-3 belonged to batters, 4-5-6 to pitchers. The combined numbers of the white dice, 2-12, provided scenarios listed on those cards: groundouts, popouts, strikeouts, singles, doubles, homeruns, and so forth. Other charts enabled stealing, sacrifices, playing the infield in, even injuries and rainouts, and more. Each player card was based on the statistics of an individual player from an individual season. Teams came with 20 cards each, and an additional pool of utility-player cards were also available every year.

Dice baseball was not entirely a new fascination. When I was about 14 I had found directions somewhere for a game with primitively simple rules based on two dice: 2-triple, 3-double, 4-single, 5-out, 6-out, 7-double play, and so on. I organized a league of two divisions with four teams each and tried to make a pennant race of it in a season that lasted I don't remember how many games—many, perhaps even 162. With nothing whatsoever to differentiate the teams other than random luck, I was saddened to see the law of averages inexorably subsume all, and toward the end the first-place teams were separated from the last by only a matter of two or three games. It looked like it was headed for a massive jam-up tie but it wasn't exciting. I gave it up and never finished.

So when Jerry, a fiercely devoted fan of the St. Louis Cardinals, pulled out his 1981 Strat-O-Matic set one night when I was visiting, I immediately started to see the possibilities. There were so many that I became positively feverish. We started by improvising a brackets-style playoff with most of the 1981 teams. We drafted teams and set up seeds and then met every week to play the whole thing through. It took several weeks and was exciting and fun. Jerry was bitter when the Cardinals fell out midway. My beloved Minnesota Twins, no surprise, flushed out even earlier. Eventually Jerry piloted the Milwaukee Brewers to a championship. It was a fun ritual, meeting at his apartment in suburban Richfield, Minnesota, and making or ordering pizza, as we hunched over his coffee table and saw it through, dice roll by dice roll. We talked about it a lot on the phone during the rest of the week.

The 1981 set was the wrong one to have, Jerry and I both agreed on that. That had been a strike season, with a significant number of games lost, followed by one of those bizarre schemes to jury-rig a postseason. I happily took responsibility for purchasing the 1984 set and did so as soon as it became available in stores, sometime around late March or early April of 1985. Then Jerry and I organized a season and divided the loot. Jerry took National League teams and I took American League, as befitted our orientations. "There goes another novel," Jerry liked to joke about our plans.

That first season was scheduled to run 35 games. Though I groaned about it (1927 hardliner that I tend to be), I agreed to divisional play and a five-game league championship playoff. The custodian of each league was assigned first pick of the team to manage through the playoff. And then the sweet cherry of a seven-game World Series. It was a beautiful plan. But already I was leaning away from the social aspects of the game, which are well and truly enjoyable, and getting more into the solitaire game, whose sole appeal (a tremendous one) is that it makes you loom large as Einstein's horror, an omniscient omnipotent God gleefully throwing dice. I was happiest at that time when I could settle down alone at the kitchen table in solitude, with drink of my choice and the game pieces and charts spread around me.

My excitement even affected my dice rolling. Where Jerry would fondle the three dice and then gently let them drop warm from his hand, I had to pick them up and throw them away quickly and hard. At key points of games inevitably I found myself digging around under furniture for them. Finally I resorted to using the box lid itself, overturning it in front of me on the table and throwing the dice into the far corner of it, as in my mind it took on the aspect of an outdoor stadium viewed from above at an odd angle. The weird bounces and ricochets taken by the dice were even reminiscent of when as a kid I hurled a rubber ball against a stoop, scooping up the random returns, grounders, pops, line drives, and flies, and inventing a game out of it.

Jerry never lived up to his side of that bargain, which is nothing against him. He was always more interested in the social play, the competition, and baseball itself, then just getting underway for the year again. He was in no way prepared to keep up with my obsessional play, as I churned through dozens of games each week. He was also, I think, miffed about a decision I had made with my wife that spring to move from Minneapolis. He was a good friend—we had many good friends—but in May the die was cast, so to speak. We made the decision to quit our jobs and move to Seattle, and now plans to accomplish it were underway. We were looking at a 2,000-mile move to a city where we knew virtually no one and had no jobs and no place to stay. I became more preoccupied with tearing out and packing the foundations of my life, but even so I found time to drink and continue playing dice baseball through July.

Then the move itself was full upon us, and we were finding out about U-Haul rentals and putting together a garage sale and a final blast going-away party and figuring out what to do with all our stuff and trying to find time to say good-bye to everyone. For several weeks every time we saw anyone we wondered if it was the last we'd see them. Many times it was. In early August, with a feeling of impending cataclysm overtaking me, I sadly played a last night of games and then packed away the Strat-O-Matic box, double-taping it to keep its many pieces and cards and the papers recording statistics safe and in one place, wondering if I would ever have the opportunity to play again.

$$\mathcal{Q}$$

Of course I did, soon after we were set up in a tiny studio apartment in Seattle in September. A built-in breakfast nook in the kitchen provided a great space and I quickly finished out that first season. Not surprisingly, the Detroit Tigers won the pennant, with the Toronto Blue Jays trailing as the closest competition. Then, fully solitaire now and with few pretensions of finding others to play with, I set up an even more ambitious season, which I dutifully dubbed "Season II." It included 16 teams divided into two leagues. One league was for historical teams such as the 1927 New York Yankees and the 1965 Minnesota Twins, while a draft in the other league enabled teams that finished in the rear the season before to obtain Hall of Famers, whose cards I had just ordered.

As a result, the Seattle Mariners opened Season II with Al Simmons, Ernie Banks, and Walter Johnson on their roster. With all that extra firepower, they prefigured a future unimaginably far away and won it all, defeating the 1954 Cleveland Indians in the World Series in six games. Al Simmons took the triple crown and Walter Johnson was far and away the best pitcher in the league, with a perfect record of 7-0 and ERA of 1.43 (trailed by Bill "Who?" Laskey of the San Francisco Giants, with 2.30). I went on to play four more full seasons, enlarging the schedule to 70 games starting with Season V.

At the time of this writing I have been stalled for years at about two-thirds of the way through Season VII. I haven't played a game for months, nor played them regularly in years.

For a long time, particularly 1986 and 1987, dice baseball was what I cared most about. I joked, when I got a job shortly after moving to Seattle, about finding a way to play the game at work. I knew that was impossible, but I found that I could often slip away at lunch and come home and fit a single game in, as long as nothing bizarre such as lengthy extra innings or a complex series of injuries happened. Obviously, when those things did happen, it only meant that I came back to work from lunch late, and somewhat rueful perhaps.

Friday nights specifically were devoted to orgies of games, when I would play a half dozen or more of them, the events of each blurring into the next toward the end of the night. I typically geared up for them with the suitable accouterments: beer, bourbon, always; marijuana when I could; cocaine when it fell my way (rarely). The more substance I consumed, the more substance the games seemed to take on. Maybe that's the way it works with anything? Incredible things would happen: ninth-inning rallies, unexpected shutouts, shocking victories and defeats, no-hitters, stunning homeruns. Nothing stopped me. I kept my bourbon in a tumbler, a bottle of beer beside it and my little pipe too. I sucked and I drew and I made marks with my pencil and I picked up the three dice again and threw them at the box lid. Or, between games, I tallied statistics, toted up and figured out the standings and various league leaders. The numbers, as I produced and entered them, were often profoundly satisfying. I had an eerie sense of some of those big numbers coming up off the paper as I wrote them down, coming off the paper and through the pencil and into my fingertips and up my arm, so that it was almost as if someone else were writing them down and I was merely observing them posted.

I can't, of course, conclude a piece about dice baseball without commending to you Robert Coover's 1968 novel, *The Universal Baseball Association, Inc., J. Henry Waugh, Prop.*, which is startlingly true to life. Coover just had to have been here too. It is in most ways a sad, isolated, and lonely existence, one that continually erodes genuine human contact, as covered in the novel. But it's one filled as well with moments of intense gratification. Compiling statistics and playing games are absorbing, time-consuming tasks that don't easily brook interruption. But a time finally came when there was simply no one with whom I could talk or share stories or anecdotes. My wife was gone. Jerry was long gone. Even the booze was behind me. There was only me and the dice and the pieces of paper and the information, and suddenly it didn't seem to mean very much anymore.

And yet in a way those late '80s times stand still as the glory days of dice baseball in my mind. There was the season that the Dodgers surprised everyone, the season that featured a showdown between the New York Mets and the 1927 Yankees, the season when the Red Sox didn't lose the World Series (albeit with Mickey Mantle undoing the curse of the Babe in center). There was the continuing disappointment of Hank Aaron and the surprising resiliency of Bill Laskey, the sadness at the passing of the Seattle Mariners and, more than once, of the Minnesota Twins. And always, forever, the dominating power of the 1927 Yankees. Yes, those were the glory days, with the drink at my side and the darkness outside pouring through the window behind me and the dice flung ecstatically to corners of the apartment. So many dramatic moments, so many memories. But this is just about where I start to get really boring. (1999)

Streetwise (**Martin Bell, 1984**)
Seattle may have earned a reputation as a bastion of laidback West Coast style, but this documentary of the mid-'80s has a different story to tell, chronicling the daily grind of runaways surviving on

the city streets. The average age of the figures populating this grim yet beautiful meditation: probably about 14. Most of them left the certain horrors of their domestic origins for the uncertain horrors they confront here. These kids, who come across as preternaturally old even as they inhabit the emaciated garb of youth, wearing the faces of children, casually discuss robbing, dumpster diving, hitch-hiking, "faggots," johns, and tricks ("dates") with one another and with the camera. They fend for themselves and occasionally find champions who attempt to fend for them too. But it's a loser's game and they know it as surely as those of us peering in at them from beyond the screens.

Perhaps the most heartbreaking image that recurs all through is when we see any of the young girls we have come to know slightly, whose words may still echo in our minds, leaning into the window of a car stopped at the curb and then opening the door and climbing in. But the interactions with their parents are heartbreaking too. One mother is a waitress who barely survives herself and obviously has no ability to control or even much influence her daughter's behavior, though she cares and tries in her way. At one point, with her daughter attempting to carry on an easygoing, bantering conversation of small talk with her from another room in their home, there is a long silence followed by the mother finally responding, "Be quiet now, honey, I'm trying to drink." There is also a story about a father and his son, Dewayne, which may be the saddest one of all that we actually witness. They speak via telephone handsets on opposite sides of the glass window of a prison visiting chamber; the imprisoned father reminds Dewayne he has only three more years to go before his release, admonishing him to be good.

To find out the fates of these children nearly 30 years on is only to confirm the death of all irony within the confines of this sad, circumscribed place: suicide, AIDS, nine children and counting, gone straight, stabbed in a street incident. One of them became a victim of

Gary Ridgway, the Green River Killer, in 1987. Her name is Roberta Joseph Hayes, and even though she plays a small part here she has the best shot for immortality because of her association with a famous serial killer. She is the one who will always be talked about first. (2010)

Donna Summer, "Love to Love You Baby" (Dec. 20, 1975, #2)
Before I ever found the camp values in this, let alone the musical, it seemed to me first of all shocking, raw, almost pornographic, and I couldn't believe it was on the radio, particularly the long version, which clocks in at just under 17 minutes. "Can't believe it's on the radio" is one of my favorite genres of music, so naturally I was instantly intrigued. I remember visiting a friend at the time who had just moved into a basement apartment somewhere off Lyndale and Franklin in Minneapolis, all fitted out with bars on the windows, which ran along the ceiling edges. It was a studio apartment that came with a space heater in the fireplace, which glowed orange, with fake blocks of charred wood. That was rather strange for an apartment at the time. We hoofed up to a nearby liquor store and bought beer with most of the last of our money. It was winter and there was snow on the ground. It had been about a year so there was some catching up to do. At one point this song went on, the long album side. Hearing now what I was hearing then it's hard for me to figure out, beyond I guess the sexualized moaning and groaning, what was so shocking. A lot about it is conventional, formally structured, rigid in its way, almost overly so, and most of it is not particularly sexualized. But it still felt sleazy and supercool at once, even as we were giggling nervously, lights down and candles burning. That's when I noticed that the apartment windows along the ceilings showcased bright blue and red neon lights from outside, further obfuscating normal bounds with the orange glow from the fireplace, as Donna Summer and her various technicians smoothly modulated through their paces, like a big float in a small town parade. (2010)

T

Alphabetically, T falls at #20, but in terms of frequency of usage, it is #2, trailing only E. Among other things, that makes T the #1 consonant. But don't get too excited—as with Jack Nicklaus and Tiger Woods, T is unlikely to overtake E any time soon. E represents 12.7% of all letters used whereas T is nearly four points behind, at 9.0%. After that the bunching is tight: A, 8.2% ... O, 7.5% ... I, 7.0% ... N, 6.7% ... S, 6.3%, and so forth. Still, at #2, T has a grip on its destiny. As a thought experiment, I wonder how things would change if the definite article, "the," were changed to "xqz," made up of the three least-used letters. I suppose we'll never know because it has the drawbacks of appearing unpronounceable and also makes no etymological sense. We would never get used to it. Imagine encountering this sentence in a story: "Hey," said xqz handyman, "will you grab me xqz pliers over there, please." No. It would never do. For the most part, T operates as the so-called "voiceless alveolar stop," the noise made with the tip of the tongue against the region of the mouth back of the upper teeth. It doesn't seem to me exactly the most natural sound to make with a mouth, not like M or R or S (let alone H, a sound that adults make at the rate of 16 to 20 times per minute). This might explain why T arrives so late in the alphabet—it is dead last in Hebrew, for example. When H sidles up next to T, it's time to start lisping. Why is T given this assignment? I don't have time to go into that or into Thomas or thyme either. Sometimes when T and I appear together, they act like S and H (not to mention I and T): "purgation," "ratio," "Croatia." Nobody got time for that. For that matter, the whole TH mouth noise adventure is something of a peculiarity, unknown altogether, for example, in German, French, Persian, Japanese, and Mandarin. For those of us with a penchant for the square (not mutually exclusive with one for the curve!), T is one of the finest shapes to be found in the alphabet. So pleasing in fact that the T-square, an instrument or tool that enables drawing or testing right angles, was named for it. It stands on a single point, bearing its horizontal crossbar with equanimity and poise. In its lowercase form it takes on the look of the Christian cross and/or fishhooks, but it's still a pretty good-looking letter, simple, sturdy, evocative, eternally enduring, or suggesting such things. T is yet another one of those little letter narcissists that likes to double up and pal around with itself, doppelganger style. T is hardly the only letter that does so, but it shows an especial effrontery by doing so in the word "letter" itself. Tsk, tsk.

Tad, *God's Balls* (1989)
Tad's debut album for Sub Pop, arguably the apotheosis of everything that grunge ever intended or could hope to be, has been out of print for ages—and went out of print actually not that many years after its release. Which ought to be an actionable offense. All that talk about grunge as the fusion of metal and punk-rock is realized so completely here, it's evident in the song titles themselves—"Behemoth," "Pork Chop," "Helot," "Sex God Missy," "Boiler Room," "Satan's Chainsaw," so on and so forth—as well as in the cover art, offering a simple black and white portrait of bruiser Tad Doyle, ready to brawl, framed on either side by his rhythm section henchmen. This is music you feel in your bowels. At moments it sounds like the center of a war zone heard from a tank rolling down a city street at night: terrifying, galvanizing, utterly and completely alive

and thrilling. I mean that in the best possible way. It is a bludgeon of metric tonnage, but at the same time often retains a kind of grace—lurid, violent, dangerous, but nonetheless balanced, artful, and almost delicate. The best snapshots of the sound tend to occur in the first minute or so of each track, as it feels its way into what it wants to become, and suddenly bursts forward into that, like flowers blooming in stop-motion film. Obviously not everyone's cup of tea—after all, the wizards at Sub Pop have deemed it appropriate to leave it out of print all these years. It never caught on, lost in the shadows of the better known lords of the Seattle grunge flash. Although how something this big gets lost like that is beyond me to understand, let alone explain. Send email to Sub Pop. Demand the return of this album. (2010)

10cc, *The Original Soundtrack* (1975)
10cc is a strange beast that came lurching out of the swamps of '70s pop and art-rock, with some roots even in the '60s British Invasion. Perhaps too tuneful (and, frankly, commercial) to be considered prog, they nonetheless flit determinedly around the edges of it, showing off their smarts and their chops every chance they get, particularly on the eight-minute suite that opens the album, "Une Nuit a Paris," which Wikipedia tells me was a direct influence on both Queen's "Bohemian Rhapsody" and Andrew Lloyd Webber's *Phantom of the Opera* (don't forget the grain of salt). I am more often put in mind of a British comedy novelty act such as the Bonzo Dog Band or even Monty Python—there's a lot of broad humor larded through this, and as the title desperately wants to imply it probably wouldn't be hard fitting visuals to most of it either. How it came into my life I can't remember—I think a friend liked it, and I liked the hit "I'm Not in Love" (here in all its six-minute glory), and then I found it in a cutout bin. Something like that. I've never counted it a huge favorite but it's rife with melody and small-bore winning moments. "I'm Not in Love" happens to be the thing here that's not like the others, but it's a big beautiful mellotron boat and just fun

to experience floating by. "Une Nuit a Paris" gets on a *Ratatouille* / *Triplets of Belleville* Parisian underclass kind of thing long before those movies. "The Second Sitting for the Last Supper" and "Life Is a Minestrone" work jokes in sparkling pop and/or rockin' settings. After "I'm Not in Love" (which, you should know, you really owe it to yourself to have around, though you can probably still count on the radio to feed it to you on a regular basis), my favorite here has always been the album closer "The Film of My Love," a five-minute piece of bloated puffery that works like a piece of overly rich pastry, luscious, irresistible, monotonous, bursting with comic affect, high concept, a mocking love song that plays on the emotions even as it resorts to one movie pun after the next, "forever and ever and ever ... Over and over and over (over and over and over)." (2011)

The Texas Chain Saw Massacre **(Tobe Hooper, 1974)**
(Spoilers ahead if you can call them spoilers.) I had seen *The Texas Chain Saw Massacre* only once until recently. That was enough to convince me it was one of the most frightening and disturbing movies ever made. The decision to look at it again was hampered by gnawing unease and last-minute procrastination at the prospect. I realized the other movie that had given me this kind of problem was *Henry: Portrait of a Serial Killer,* and the link is clear. Neither particularly involves the supernatural, unworldly monsters, and/or abstract forces of evil. It's just human depravity, and that's enough—indeed, it's too much.

To be sure, *The Texas Chain Saw Massacre* is fiendishly conceived and full of exaggerations for effect large and small. Based loosely on the legends of Wisconsin serial killer and cannibal Ed Gein, it take a special glee in the everyday intricacies of the butchering industry as well as solemnly relating how Native Americans (apropos I forget) put to use every part of the whales and buffaloes they slayed. Accordingly, we see a lot of human bones, hair, and skin (and feathers, in a room where an unexplained live rooster squats in a cage hung from the ceiling) draped all over everything, including the killers themselves.

But the movie is remarkably free of blood and gore, though that may be offset in turn by larger-than-usual portions of screaming, which at one point toward the end seems to go on for quite some time.

It's free of blood and gore, but it never shrinks from making sure we understand what's going on. You don't have to see that much to understand what a sledgehammer to the skull means (especially with the sickening sound). *The Texas Chain Saw Massacre* is obviously a low-budget production but director and co-writer Tobe Hooper and cinematographer Daniel Pearl worked with what they had, putting the supersaturated color of the cheap film stock to work in methodical if lurid dimensions. Red and yellow pop, so red and yellow things are particularly unsettling. The images often have a clinical feel to them, as if studied through a lens. And these filmmakers are not afraid to let the screen go black when it suits them, worrying you to death at that point with the noises. The *Saw* franchise actually owes it quite a bit in terms of look and feel.

The range in tone goes beyond the visuals, keeping viewers continually off-balance. It lumbers with deadly pace. There's a lot of set-up in the beginning about grave robbers, corpses, slaughterhouse procedures, and one extremely unpleasant hitchhiker. But all of it is essential to what makes this so extraordinarily powerful. There are five teens and it seems to take forever to kill the first one. We have been so lulled by then it's as shocking as it is efficient. The next three go down fast, leaving only Sally Hardesty (Marilyn Burns), perhaps the original "final girl." In the last third the movie goes places I'm not sure have been matched anywhere yet, notably a dinner table scene where the demented family makes fun of the blubbering terrified Sally (and has more fun later when Grandpa can't keep his grip on a hammer). It is abjectly horrifying yet also weirdly funny but the laughter comes uncomfortably from inside of a void. The scene may be funny, but unlike the later ironic self-referential approaches of Sam Raimi, Wes Craven, and others, we're not really in on the joke.

They could be making fun of us next and it wouldn't be so funny then. There isn't much we could do about it.

Well, actually, there is one thing we could do, which is the thing Sally does: scream your head off and run if you can and don't ever stop screaming. Marilyn Burns, who died recently at 65, never did much in movies besides this and it's not hard to see why. Yet it is an iconic role and she owns it completely, working to good effect off the low-budget trappings, letting the story itself winnow away the others—an altogether distracting crew, including the raw vulnerability of Sally's disabled brother Franklin (Paul A. Partain), who travels in a wheelchair, and his haunting face. Finally it is just Sally and the fundamentals of life and death. And no one can argue she isn't one hell of a screamer.

I have some sense that people who do not watch horror movies on principle want an explanation from those of us who do—"enjoy" them is not exactly the right word, though obviously there can be elements of camp that provide a good old-fashioned entertainment to many (e.g., *The Bride of Frankenstein*). *The Texas Chain Saw Massacre* inevitably became a franchise and a camp supervillain emerged, one "Leatherface," the artist butcher of this film (Gunnar Hansen), who then became just another action figure with Jason Voorhees and Freddy Krueger. The reasons for watching are complex, a mixture of many different motivations, some so familiar now as to be hackneyed. Catharsis, for example, the exhilaration of surviving, which is also the kick with amusement park rides. Or testing limits—seeing how far "out there" you can go and still get back to a safe place (the implicit question: is it possible to go too far?). Then there's flinty realism—looking at the horror with a cold eye *because* it is "real." It represents reality, like it or not. This can be something of a passive-aggressive position, favoring things that are ugly by design simply because they are ugly (justified, again, because "real," which I think, enlarging some, would then apply to believers in regard to movies that are more overtly supernatural, wherein, for them, the "real" becomes Satan and evil). I suspect, most of all, that it's more like the proverbial 10% of the iceberg that's visible—a lot of horror movie business lurks out of sight in the unconscious, even among those who don't like horror movies. Maybe it all comes down to just my curiosity about how or why these movies have such a powerful effect. Aside from the violence, which looks like it hurts for sure (not to mention maims and kills, and I'm opposed to that), why does this mayhem frighten me, charge me with adrenaline, make it hard to breathe easy, worry me about the dark corners at night? It's only a movie, right? One thing's sure. Something keeps drawing me back. (2014)

Jim Thompson, *Pop. 1280* (1964)
In many ways *Pop. 1280* is the inevitable resolution to Jim Thompson's most celebrated and best-known novel, *The Killer Inside Me*—and in many ways it's much better. *Killer* is where Thompson hatched the idea of a sociopathic sheriff in a small Texas town who spouts endless clichés and homilies even as he lives the life of a depraved libertine. But I think *Pop. 1280* may be where he perfected it. Unlike *Killer*'s Lou Ford, who is vaguely troubled by his behavior and labels it "*the sickness*," sheriff Nick Corey of *Pop. 1280* more accepts it as a given of the human condition. Better him than anyone else, seems to be his credo, never doubting for a second that anyone else in his position would think the same. There's some tendency for Thompson to compress his cynicism into glib incident, for example in the whisper campaign Corey effortlessly launches against his opponent in an upcoming election, working obvious variations on Mark Twain's "The Man That Corrupted Hadleyburg." And much of the shocking cruelty of *Killer* is underplayed in *Pop. 1280* too, which is unfortunate. But nowhere is Thompson's worldview so curdled into such an expert latticework of foul human behavior. Sheriff Corey plays it straight always, outside of this narrative, while people just keep stepping up and voluntarily treating him

wrong because they think he's a nincompoop. And so, when he takes his various revenges, we are implicated, we are nearly always at least a little on his side, satisfied as we see him deal out comeuppances. Even as Nick Corey's veneer of self-serving rationalization is transparent, we believe enough in his justifications to minimize any moral concerns we might think to entertain as the action flashes past. Corey's own words to live by, which he repeats over and over, speak exactly to that: "I ain't sayin' you're wrong, but I cain't say you're right, either." *The Killer Inside Me* and *Pop. 1280* also represent a familiar dynamic in many careers of the great ones, and nearly all of them who lived long enough. First there is a moment of great discovery, raw innovation, and later there is a grand-statement consolidation of the gains. Inspiration drives the first, experience the latter. Think of *Highway 61 Revisited* and *"Love & Theft"*, think of *The Godfather* and *The Godfather: Part II*, think of *The Clash* and *Sandinista!* These two books by Jim Thompson, *The Killer Inside Me* and *Pop. 1280*, belong with them. (2014)

3:10 to Yuma (Delmer Daves, 1957 / James Mangold, 2007)

It's interesting to watch the two movie versions of the 1953 Elmore Leonard story, "Three-Ten to Yuma," made 50 years apart out of the same story—indeed, the same screenplay, as Halsted Welles (who died in 1990) gets first writing credit in both. Many of the same plot points and even scenes and lines of dialogue recur in both. Yet they are two rather different films. The 2007 remake is a remake, first, which makes it part of a metastasizing trend of the 2000s (and counting). It patches in state-of-the-art action scenes by expanding a good deal, and not unsuccessfully, the story's middle section. The 1957 original eschews a lot of the fancy set pieces of the remake, no doubt in line with budget considerations, instead focusing on the story much more as high-tension chamber piece with Rod Serling levels of ironical human foible.

Published originally in *Dime Western Magazine*, the story is a finely tuned instrument: a desperately impoverished rancher volunteers to

INDEX

join a militia delivering a very bad man to a train (the 3:10 to Yuma
of the title), which will forward the very bad man on to prison. But
the very bad man's gang, possessed of prodigious abilities, is determined to thwart this effort. The tension is established early and never
really lets up, even as the ending enters into bizarre and unbelievable realms with various narrative problems. For anyone interested
in treatments of Elmore Leonard stories, these two movies are an interesting pair, both coming from outside of the '80s and '90s bubble,
when Leonard may have been coasting a little on a superstar status
he had won. (I may need to see *Get Shorty* and *Out of Sight* again but I
remember them as bloated, self-satisfied, and underwhelming—the
opposite of what Leonard is good at.)

Both versions of *3:10 to Yuma* are worth seeing. If you only have
time for one—and I know how that goes, life is short after all—then
the 1957 version is your pick. For one thing, it doesn't put on Icarus
wings and attempt to soar on grand ideas of good and evil. It's leaner,
more focused, and more believable. Russell Crowe as bad man Ben
Wade is probably the better actor over Glenn Ford, but the role itself,
as written in the original, is more restrained—no super powers in
evidence, for example. That's an advantage for Glenn Ford, who may
be one-note but it is the right note here. Similarly, Van Heflin as Dan
Evans, the impoverished rancher joining the posse because he needs
the money, may not have the dazzle of Christian Bale but he has a
face and a manner out of the school of Robert Stack that works a
good deal better for the role as it is written and shot.

Just so, by hanging back a bit more than the remake and letting
Elmore Leonard's narrative take the lead, the nifty little 1957 production keeps its strongest points and details unassuming and blunt,
and then simply keeps them coming: Ben Wade whistling snatches
of the haunting theme at the most excruciating moments, a weirdly
complex minor key melody (sung by Frankie Laine produced like
Marty Robbins at start and finish) ... a nice realization of a funeral

march, with a boy leading it and slowly pounding a dead-sounding drum ... fun throwaway lines as when one of the posse philosophizes, "My own grandmother fought the Indians for 60 years, then choked to death on lemon pie" ... all that sustained tension written on Heflin's face ... even the soft strumming on an acoustic guitar that accompanies much of the action, working to create a forceful lulling tension.

Director Delmer Daves was a journeyman professional who rotated between westerns, war stories, noirs, and romances, most of them low-budget. His best-known pictures now are more often those he wrote—*The Petrified Forest* and *An Affair to Remember*, say—but his directing credits are not exactly unimpressive, including this, *Destination Tokyo, Dark Passage*, and *A Summer Place*. The professionalism is hard to miss, in fact, as *3:10 to Yuma* deals its elements swiftly and with confidence. The last third, set almost entirely in the hotel where everyone sweats out the wait for the train, is particularly good.

For his part, director James Mangold, who has also directed *Girl, Interrupted* and *Walk the Line*, is sharp on action sequences in the remake, such as an early elaborate sequence involving the takedown of a heavily fortified stagecoach. These sequences are often gripping and immediate—solid filmmaking. On the human interaction front, however, there is some tendency to overplay. Russell Crowe as Ben Wade is fine, but Mangold's version of the role leans decidedly in a Hannibal Lecter direction, which wears thin. Tick them off: Ben Wade is well spoken, erudite, irresistibly charming, capriciously generous, a talented sketch artist, and no one can defeat him with a gun. If he were a gourmet he could move to Italy immediately.

But even more than a narrative that makes sense, I appreciate a number of the incidentals in the 1957 original over the remake, with all its evident money. The 1957 version does the job with 30 minutes less running time. It maintains an evenhanded low-key atmosphere and never attempts to be flashy about anything, which ultimately makes the contrasts more convincing. Its low-budget look and feel calms us into a certain complacency, enabling it to make some of its strongest points more emphatically than anything in the flash and sizzle of the remake. But hey, flash and sizzle works too, so make it a double feature, baby. (2012)

The Tree of Life (**Terrence Malick, 2011**)
The Tree of Life is not a very old movie but it has already won an outsize following among critics and cineastes, whose open-throated clamor for it (encountered everywhere in the second half of 2011) helped enable it to enter at #6 on the list of 21st-century films at the website They Shoot Pictures, Don't They?, which is based on a wide-ranging survey of movie critic rankings. In fact, the biggest surprise for me about the update to that list which came earlier this year was that *The Tree of Life* did not push on even higher from there. I still think it could be the one to knock off *In the Mood for Love*, *Mulholland Dr.*, and/or *Yi Yi*, which have owned the 1-2-3 since I've been aware of the list.

But all that is horserace talk, and beside the point, of course. On many levels it's easy to see how contemporary critics could isolate *The Tree of Life* for high praise: it's written and directed by the redoubtable Terrence Malick, it's quite stunningly beautiful, and it traffics in a kind of gauzy, ineffable spirituality with Christian overlay that really seems to get people where they live, uplifting like a Sunday service.

I don't want to invoke the tired old "emperor's new clothes" story but I keep seeing telltale indications about *The Tree of Life*, which is only Malick's fifth of six films since 1973 (at least two of which, *Badlands* and *The Thin Red Line*, are personal favorites). In the theater where I saw it in downtown Olympia, Washington, a hand-printed sign taped to the door instructed that *The Tree of Life* is long and symbolic, with a story not necessarily intended for straightforward interpretation. "No refunds." I saw another sign like it in a Tacoma art-house when I was there to see something else. I have read many high-handed comments from critics and bloggers equating rejection of *The Tree of Life* with nothing less than rejection of cinema itself. As the signs imply, you are not looking at it right. It did not help that Roger Ebert gave it a very strong stamp of approval shortly before he died by putting it on his last submission to the *Sight & Sound* poll. Somehow, and perhaps yet temporarily, *The Tree of Life* became one of those things that does not fail. It can only be failed.

So I admit that, by and large, I must have failed it. The first time I saw it I loved the explosion of scientific photography in the first 30 or 40 minutes, was occasionally touched by the middle-American story of the Waco family, and wondered why Sean Penn was wandering around muttering to himself. More recently (watching it at home on TV) I thought the scientific photography was more of an empty conceit, was again occasionally moved by the Waco family, and still wondered what Sean Penn was doing. I just don't connect much with this movie. Roger Ebert saw all of his childhood written into it. I recognized evocative elements of my own from growing up, but I kept waiting for something that more or less mattered—on *this* plane—or some obvious point, or narrative momentum, or some reason to keep watching other than a sign in the lobby that says I can't get a refund.

At the risk of missing the forest for the trees, here are specific things I don't like: The incoherent voiceovers, usually whispered, which are constant. The Christianity compressed into it (and from the start, as the tired old false dichotomy of "the way of nature versus the way of grace" is one of the first things we hear about). Alexandre Desplat's suffocating new-age music and its thudding emotional cues. Jessica Chastain as Mrs. O'Brien waving at the cloud-scudded sky and telling her boys, "That's where God lives." The view of treetops from the ground looking up (also heavily featured in Malick's previous film *The New World*, along with tall grass). Sean Penn spinning around and/or the camera spinning around him. (In fact, the camera moves altogether too much for me in this movie, which has the effect of making it feel slippery and distracted.) The Oedipal strains are trite. The sound design is so overdone that a title card at the beginning of the DVD advises it should be played loud—and no, that's not in the rock 'n' roll sense. Playing it loud helps you catch all the muttering and bird calls.

It raises the question: Is *The Tree of Life* so good that it's bad? (2014)

T. Rex, "Ballrooms of Mars" (1972)

I know Marc Bolan almost surely qualifies as superstar to most, at least those of a certain age, but somehow I get the feeling he's been overlooked in the long decades since his death in 1977, by which point his star was certainly fading anyway. That's probably on me, coming late to the best of T. Rex, which to me are the matching pair of albums from the early '70s, *Electric Warrior* and *The Slider*. They are studies in cool bravado, tempered joy, and a smoldering hedonism restrained only by unknown laws of comportment, strictly enforced, all of it burnished to a fine buff. "Ballrooms of Mars" comes from *The Slider*, which I like a little better—but only because it's the one I've ended up playing the most frequently—and it's a nearly perfect example of the things that Bolan could do so well. I particularly like how everything about it is so deliberate, from the studied name-dropping (Bob Dylan, Alan Freed, John Lennon) to the science-fiction setting implied in its name to the various fashion inventories to the hoary old call to "Rock!" Everything is as cool as can be even as it manages to build itself up to a colossal head of steam. Indeed, Bolan makes the command to "Rock!" and sends the tune sprawling into nether regions of the solar system, tumbling and spinning slo-mo in a place absent all gravity. In the face of it, I really don't see how it's possible for anyone to do anything but exactly that—rock. (2011)

The Triplets of Belleville (**Sylvain Chomet, 2003**)
Even from the posters and trailers it's clear this picture is going to make it on charm and eccentricity, as animated features are peculiarly good at. But there's little to prepare one for how strange and ultimately satisfying on that level *The Triplets of Belleville* is. It's practically all visuals, music, and sounds, with virtually no dialogue whatsoever, and its plot points careen and linger seemingly at random. There's a lot going on for an 80-minute film but it's rarely confusing and never rushed. It is equal parts beautiful, funny, and weird beyond words.

It signals its essential positions in the opening sequence, a clip from a movie seen on TV, the kind of portmanteau picture of musical acts made more often in the '40s and '50s (with half a foot in a few of the Busby Berkeley musicals of the '30s)—*A Song Is Born* is one good example, *Orchestra Wives* is another, and so are some of the '50s rock 'n' roll pictures, such as *The Girl Can't Help It*—featuring performances by an array of well-known musical acts with a vague narrative dotted through. In the *Triplets* version it's the opportunity for a series of quick, economical, and amazing set pieces: a topless performance by Josephine Baker, a Fred Astaire routine in which his shoes turn carnivorous and devour him, Django Reinhardt working the frets with his bare foot so he can take a smoke break, and, of course, the Triplets themselves, performing their hit, which is ubiquitous, and ubiquitously well-known, all through this picture, "Belleville Rendez-Vous," a marvel of sleek syncopation, rhythm, and harmony.

Then the story proper, such as it is, begins. No need to get too deep into the plot; better to just experience it for yourself as it comes. It involves competitive bicyclists, gangsters, people who have made playing music a way of life, and the love of a mother for her son. It comes at you with a regular stream of quirky and intuitive gestures, which operate almost on the subconscious levels claimed by the original surrealists (such as Rene Magritte, who was also Belgian, as is director and screenwriter Sylvain Chomet). For example, there's an almost obsessive attention to vehicles: bicycles, of course, but also trains, ships, paddleboats, trucks, buses, and feet. There is a lazy old dog who barks at all of them and at night sleeps and dreams that he is on a train and the people he passes are barking at him. There are gangsters shaped like coffins, with sunken heads, giant squared-off shoulders towering over them; when they are in close proximity they lock together like Lego pieces.

There are so many nice touches, in fact, that it's tempting to simply make a pile of them with "and then," "and then," "and then." When a kidnapped bicyclist is taken onto an oceangoing liner and thence across the sea to Belleville (which appears to be New York), his mother and the faithful dog hire a paddleboat and follow. They stay with it even during storms at night on the high seas, with suitable choral accompaniment. A whale comes by and gives them a lift. The dog barks at it. The oceangoing liner, by the way, looks like a cruise ship riding on top of a giant narrow fin. Proportionality often skews crazy here. In the chase scene at the end, after an hour or more of a certain midcentury Parisian nightclub style of mannered sophistication, the music takes a decided turn toward the '70s blaxploitation style. Also cars explode. But it's all seamless.

The Triplets themselves, in the present time of the movie, are aged and impoverished but still perform with obvious zeal, not to mention their always surprising rhythmic skills and the general avant-garde bent of their jams. Their first "live" appearance here, perhaps halfway through, is ridiculous and sublime. The mother, still in search of her kidnapped son in Belleville, finds herself underneath a bridge at night with no place to go. She starts making music with the spokes of a bicycle wheel. And just like that the Triplets appear, out of the darkness, aged but slinky and twitchy, digging the groove laid down on the bicycle wheel. It's a magical, great moment.

Once they show up, the Triplets prove to have something of an Addams Family shtick, living bizarre and grotesque lives, catching frogs for food by using depth charges (which they seem to have in great supply), an umbrella, and a net. And make no mistake, they are crazy for frog. It's all they eat: boiled, barbecued, still alive, tadpoles popped like popcorn, or simply holding and licking them like ice cream cones. At night they stay up late watching reruns of *Benny Hill* together in bed, laughing at it uproariously and un-self-consciously.

The art is lovely and fastidious, tinged with sepia and its own syntax of exaggerated lines and indulgence, such as the muscle-bound legs of the bicyclists, that blocked shape of the gangsters, the various color palettes for dreamscapes or for Belleville. It's particularly good on cityscapes and often cuts to overhead shots from high in the air, where the traffic patterns are intricate and fascinating, as are the skylines and architecture.

It does not ever stop being weird or surprising—"surreal" is a popular word to apply to it, and Jacques Tati a primary referent. I don't know Tati's work well, though enough to discern the connection. It is often cold or even cruel, as in its treatment of the frogs, or Fred Astaire, an element that is there, I think, to maintain a reserved distance from some of its other factors that could be easily manipulated for the warm and treacly response, such as the mother's heroic efforts not only to rescue her son, but to support his dream in the first place of becoming a competitive bicyclist. In a picture full of nice touches, that formal restraint is one of the nicest.

Chomet's ability to balance a good many countervailing forces in a picture that runs fast to absurd extremes and to maintain an unmistakably sophisticated aesthetic may be the nicest of all. It's basically a silent comedy, but infinitely more deft at what it's doing than the recent *The Artist* (and I say that as one who enjoyed *The Artist*). Chomet's dedication at the end, "For my parents," somehow conveys the significance and extraordinary labor that must have gone into this for him. As do the eight years that would elapse before his next feature, *The Illusionist*, whose tie to Tati is more explicit, and incidentally more troubling, but whose artistry is at least the equal of this very remarkable feature. (2012)

Triumph of the Will (**Leni Riefenstahl, 1935**)
What appears at first to be mostly a lot of parade footage (expertly shot and framed) gradually turns into something chilling and extraordinary as it focuses on the closing ceremonies of the Nazi convention that it documents from 1934 in Nuremberg. Then it becomes almost unholy in a strange way, albeit likely dependent on my (our) historical vantage. If you and I were there, we might well have been bellowing "sieg heil" ourselves. That's just a matter of human psychology, but that's what makes it so chilling, especially when the light, glancing mentions of racial purity in the speeches start to come up. Is it OK to say it reminded me of the 2004 Republican convention? (2014)

Mark Twain, *Life on the Mississippi* (**1883**)
A friend and I once compared notes on 19th-century writers and found that we had opposed reactions to Charles Dickens and Mark Twain. For me, as much as I've tried, even the relatively shorter works of Dickens such as *A Tale of Two Cities* or *A Christmas Carol* are deadly turgid, ponderous, impenetrable, exhausting to try and crawl through. Whereas Twain, particularly in his nonfictional memoir and travel books, is as refreshing as a drink of water, for me one of those ideal kinds of reading matter for places like airplanes, dentist waiting rooms, and motel rooms late when sleep is impossible. *Life on the Mississippi* is a later volume of this type of Twain's work—*The Innocents Abroad* came first, then *Roughing It* (which I think is the best). It chronicles all things Mississippi River, including Twain's own career as a riverboat pilot when he was a young man. In fact, Samuel Clemens's pseudonym comes from riverboat parlance, which is explained here, though his reasons for adopting

"Mark Twain" is only obliquely covered. The book has a wonderfully discursive structure—much like the river itself, I suppose, or his excuse this time—rambling easily from factual history to legends and anecdotes, and dipping frequently into the intricacies of the piloting trade. (2010)

2001: A Space Odyssey (**Stanley Kubrick, 1968**)
In case you ever need it for a trivia contest, the first line of dialogue in this movie is, "Here you are, sir. Main level, please." And it occurs 25 minutes in. That's the primacy of the visual on which we are operating here, as baffling in its superlative totality as the overall effectiveness of this picture is itself. It's not easy to defend to bored, scoffing detractors—because it's not hard to find endless examples yourself of the monumentally silly, part of it a natural result of becoming dated. This movie should not work. The opening sequence, bombastically entitled "THE DAWN OF MAN," features what are obviously actors in ape suits. The typical inability of science fiction before 1990 (at least in film) to predict anything like the Internet or cell phones is once again apparent. The always popular video phone puts in an appearance but phone calls, even in outer space, are still made from phone booths, and there doesn't appear to be anything like voicemail. Fashions of the future are reminiscent of fashions the year the movie was made, 1968. The plot turns on the hackneyed-even-then computer gone amok scenario. A geometric figure is made out to be an agent of evolution—a black monolith, really? It appears to be a machine made by higher civilizations, maybe. The narrative is incoherent.

But somehow *2001* does work. Kubrick's clarity of vision and the alternately lush and harsh soundtrack carry the picture and, once you have been lulled into its slow-moving rhythms of spectacular sights and sounds, it remains as engrossing, penetrating, and mysterious, even watching today at home in the living room, as the day it debuted in ye olde Cinerama theatres of yon days.

Much of this, of course, reflects Kubrick's skills and talent and a number of shrewd choices. It's not actually a terribly long movie, clocking in at less than two and a half hours, which makes it shorter than, say, *Zodiac*. But all dressed up in its Cinerama frippery, opening with three minutes of a black screen and disquieting music before the first image is even seen (an MGM title card, as it happens), it feels deeply portentous and heavy. There's even an intermission—and the second half then resumes with another three minutes of black screen and the same disquieting music. The well-known light show, the most self-consciously "trippy" part of a determinedly trippy movie, takes up less than 15 minutes toward the end of the movie—and works, I think, above and beyond the pretty colors and the heady nerve of doing it at all, chiefly by reason of the visceral sensation the sequence provides of forward hurtling motion. It's easy to keep looking at such an abstraction because it's physically so pleasant to keep looking.

Dialogue is at a premium throughout—there's not much of it. Most is just mundane back and forth between scientists, reminiscent of the dialogue between scientists in '50s science fiction movies, or NASA space shots, wooden and self-consciously jocular. This may have been a deliberate choice by Kubrick to flatten the effect of events as they unfold, but at this point it also serves to remind how long this picture has been around now. At the time of its release, the classic '50s science fiction movies were little more than a decade in the past.

What really makes *2001*, of course, are the hard glittering surfaces of Kubrick's imagery, a brilliant and memorable concoction of model work, special effects, widescreen photography, and densely allusive symbology. Very few movies since have even tried to emulate it, as if it had waged a kind of scorched-earth campaign that most filmmakers heeded. The only movie I can think of that reminds me of it even a little is Duncan Jones's *Moon*, from 2009—which in retrospect seems fully marinated in it, though attempting to distract some from that by way of Sam Rockwell's bravura performance.

The sound design of *2001* is much celebrated for matching the clinical precisions of outer space images with the lush strains of 19th-century Strauss waltzes, which I never seem to get tired of. Making his film in the immediate aftermath of the first images seen of Earth from space, Kubrick obviously drew on the excitement those images had created, with relish, even abandon. But unspooling them to the majestic feel of those surprising, vaguely cheesy ballroom strains of another time, when space travel was barely even dreamed of, was a genius stroke. (And while I'm handing out over-the-top accolades let me also add I have no problem with characterizing the cut from the opening sequence to the rest of the film—the weaponized bone flung exultantly in the air to the spaceship in outer space—as the greatest cut in movie history yet.)

Not all of the sound is so ingratiatingly pleasant and soothing as the waltzes. There are many sequences, particularly once we get to the Jupiter mission proper, marked by harsh screeches and unpleasant warning tones of machines—my cats left the room, let me put it that way. And for a good deal of this film, across at least three separate sequences and occupying perhaps 30 minutes or more of screen time, the only sound that can be heard is breathing inside a space helmet, which works to color the events it accompanies with creeping feelings of dread and discomfort. It's also the one element here, that metallic scraping breathing sound, that seems to me to derive most directly from the LSD experience.

One last point I want to address is the general perception that Kubrick, for all his acuities, is by and large humorless, even pompous, and that it's nowhere more evident than here. But the scenes with the computer HAL after it has killed four of the five astronauts on the Jupiter mission and made an attempt on the fifth, who has

found a way back to the ship and set about "disconnecting" the computer, is very funny on a number of levels: the note of self-righteous
indignation HAL strikes first ("Just what do you think you're doing,
Dave? Dave, I really think I'm entitled to an answer to that question"),
then its unctuous pleading ("Look, Dave, I can see you're really upset
about this"). Even the HAL close-up that Kubrick resorts to, a tight
shot of an unblinking red light encased in bulbous glass, comes to
seem very funny juxtaposed with the voice of HAL (Douglas Rain).

Kubrick's masterpiece, arguably the greatest science fiction movie ever made and certainly one of the most ambitious ever attempted,
is altogether more entertaining than it would seem to have any right
to be, all things considered—the lugubrious, painfully slow pacing,
the story that never makes very much sense. But for me it only gets
better and better over time and multiple viewings, which is practically
a miracle. (2011)

Anne Tyler, *A Patchwork Planet* **(1998)**
I had a hard time getting a bead on this one by Anne Tyler. Its first-
person story of Barnaby Gaitlin, the poor little rich boy and black
sheep in a wealthy family of Baltimore philanthropists, has the usual
Tyler hallmarks: eccentric characters who bring the pathos, a jumble
of amiable incident, and moderately surprising twists. Gaitlin has rejected his wealthy family nearly as much as they have rejected him,
though all remain enmeshed. After some serious problems as a teen,
including a late graduation from high school and legal troubles involving burglary charges, he has spent his adult life working for Rent-
a-Back, which provides manual labor services to the elderly. Gaitlin
turns 30 as the novel begins. Divorced from a brief marriage, he has
a 9-year-old daughter who lives with her mother and stepfather in
Philadelphia. Gaitlin is a bit of a Holden Caulfield, reflexively label-
ing people and things phony and rejecting them. He lives in a basement he rents from a family, sharing their bathroom. The patriarchal
members of his family have a belief that angels visit them at portentous

points in their lives to deliver fateful messages. Gaitlin believes he may have found his angel in the person of Sophie, a woman he meets on a train ride between Baltimore and Philadelphia, when he sees do a good deed. Later, when they are involved, Gaitlin is no longer so sure. *A Patchwork Planet* notably has its oddities, perhaps none greater than Tyler's decision to tell the story first-person, related by Gaitlin. Over the duration of the novel he seemed to me less and less believable as a man, and indeed begins to come off like one of those Woody Allen characters—philosopher or TV comedy writer or documentary filmmaker—who only sounds like Woody Allen. Gaitlin sounds more and more like a typical garrulous, overfeeling Tyler character (usually a woman), with an overlay of pro forma male characteristics, such as a certain degree of handiness with tools. Some of Gaitlin's plaintive declarations and assertions started to remind me of Jack Handey Deep Thoughts, which brought things dangerously close to capsizing under their own weight at various points. Yet this is also one of Tyler's more tightly constructed and symmetrical plots as well and worth it for fans. (2011)

U

I like U, even if it is a bit of an underwhelming underachiever, 21st letter of the alphabet and last true vowel (we will be dealing with "sometimes" presently). It also boasts a peculiar and unique relationship with Q, which for reasons we don't exactly understand (or maybe we do? See Q) won't leave home without it. But compare the rest of the over-muscled vowels, whose rates of usage far outpace U's: E (#1), A (#3), O (#4), I (#5), U (#13). Underachiever! No fewer than eight of the worker-bee consonants outrank it. Yet U figures prominently in what could well be the two most used words in the English language: "uh" and "um." In its short form, represented in pronunciation guides by the schwa, it could be the most frequently used of all human sounds. In terms of its shape and form, for a long time it looked like the letter V, at least if stone chiselers are to be given any credence. We know that from all the "mvsevms" and "vniversities" we still see around. You also see U in relation to radioactivity, as the symbol for both uranium and the atomic mass unit. It's another letter whose fortunes changed with the coming of mass electronic communications— aided and abetted again by the rock star Prince, who was way out in front of that stuff. Truly, I do like the use of U for "you," not least for the symmetry it represents with the egotistical I. There is something pleasingly balanced about U and I. At the same time, unfortunately, it looks illiterate to me. I don't know if I'll ever get used to it that way. U may feel differently—U might get used to it. U also figures prominently in the negating process, whose many prefixes include "un" near the head of the line. I suspect "non" may now serve the more generic role, but I remember periods when indicating the opposite of almost anything was managed by hanging an "un" out front, viz., un-American, uncola, unhappy, untoward, unfunny. Those were better days for U but it's always been just a little bit of a laggard. Its top-open curve shape is a pleasing form but the question of the tail niggles at me. It destroys the simple beauty of the curve shape yet also seems wrong without it. Even the hand-printed version of the capital. Write it out for yourself. I bet you put a tail on it, didn't U? Coming off the right side on a downstroke. It's ungainly not least because now it just looks like a mistake, the lowercase figure but too big for its size, like an adolescent enduring a growth spurt. Like most letters, U is just full of tricks. Q is not the only place where it brings the W—"quick" and "quality," yes, sure, but also consider "anguish" and "suave" (and then compare "unique" and "guard," thank you Wikipedia). Funny fellow U are—or is, I should say, to be clear. Or unclear.

United 93 (Paul Greengrass, 2006)

There are no surprises or twist endings to this one, of course, though a narrative film along these lines, with its last shot of a farm field rushing toward the camera though a jet airliner's windshield, would likely feel jarring even if we could somehow forget the events we know so well. It might even seem like one of those feel-bad cheat endings popular in less hopeful times, such as in *Night of the Living Dead* and *Easy Rider*. But that's an impossible thought experiment. From the first image here of Arab Muslims in a motel room early in the morning praying and dressing, viewers pretty much know what they're in for, certainly the endpoint. It's thus tempting to turn away from this movie, but the fact is that it's good at what it does, working on a number of levels.

Its chief virtue is that it is not grinding away on some convenient politicized point—American heroes! In action! On a dark day!— nor wallowing in attempts to manipulate emotions, whether that would be rage against evildoers, compassion for the victims, or simply gazing across the abyss that separates us now permanently from such trusting, innocent times, even at 10 years still so close it feels as if you could get the do-over and just go back. *United 93* doesn't set out to do any of those things, yet it manages to accomplish them all, and more.

The strategy is simple. It takes on the trappings of a documentary, down to the now-so-popular handheld verite-style camera, and stays focused as much as possible on facts that can be verified, following the terrorists and the victims and the various authorities at their stations, civil and military, as the morning of September 11, 2001, unfolds in North America. It is concerned primarily with the flight of its title, United 93, which departed Newark, turned back somewhere over Ohio in a southeasterly direction, and eventually crashed in an empty field in Pennsylvania. No one survived. But it necessarily involves all the other events as the pattern of the day emerged.

At times it's excruciating, knowing what we know, to watch these people trying to figure it out. Air traffic controllers are simply puzzled when the airliner for flight American 11, which by that time they knew had been hijacked and they were tracking closely, disappeared from their instruments over lower Manhattan. Later, in the confusion, they have reason to believe it changed direction and they are once again tracking it. Other flights are believed to have been hijacked, then not, then yes again, then not. On some level, they know what is going on, whatever their mistaken instruments or perceptions are telling them. The early reports that it was a small plane that hit the first tower of the World Trade Center are belied by the gaping hole and billowing smoke air traffic controllers are shown looking at on live TV, so they know that too now, and they keep trying to

figure it out, keep arriving at the unbelievable conclusions and pushing them away again.

As happened on that day, hundreds of thousands or more were
watching in real time, including many of these authorities, when the
second airliner crashed into the second tower. Part of the shrewd design of this picture is that actual footage can be slipped in at the right
moment and you get a clear sense of what it had to feel like for those
authorities trying to manage air flights that day.

All this is quickly sketched in as the back-and-forth crosscutting
between these events and the slow boarding, preparations, inevitable
delays, and finally the takeoff of United 93 proceeds. One of the saddest moments of the picture is the way it lingers on a long shot of the
jet leaving the runway into the air.

Eventually the focus of the second half comes to rest on the events
of that flight, as the terrorists delay and quietly fuss among one another and finally put their plan into operation. Here is where Paul
Greengrass's strategies pay off, working the handheld camera and
swift cuts in the confined space as the violence erupts and eventually
the reality of what is happening dawns on the passengers and they
begin to plot what to do.

By all the evidence they were brave men and women, thrust into a
situation they never could have imagined and rising to the occasion.
The catalyzing moment appears to have been when they realized the
pilots had already been killed, and as they began to get word of what
was happening that day on the ground via the onboard telephones
and cell phones they used to call loved ones. The horror of it is plain.

Yet for all the heroism, what moves me most here, and continues
to move me most, are the calls they made to loved ones to say good-
bye. In the space of an hour or two they had already moved into

something like the era we have been living in for the past 10 years, and they knew it, and in these phone calls you can hear it. And you can also sense the futility they feel at trying to explain it, how much had changed in such a compressed time, when the people they were calling may not have even been aware yet of the disasters underway in New York City and Washington, D.C., may have just been out walking the dog or running errands and oblivious. It's wrenching to see them try, even knowing that the hour of their deaths had arrived. (2011)

V

V is for victory. Hold your two first fingers as if holding a cigar, with the back of the hand facing forward. Turn your hand the other way and that V is for peace, according to some hippies. V is very much of everything—including less popular, as, indeed, are all the letters we are about to encounter in the lowest tray of the alphabet as I learned it, V, W, X, Y, and Z. Among them, anyway, V rates pretty well—third after W and Y for frequency of use. But let's put that in perspective. W is #15 across the entire alphabet, well out of the top 10. Y is #18. And V is #21, just behind B and ahead of K. Lowly, yes, but such fine company right there. So what if V is infrequently used? It's a fun sound to make—the sound of the kazoo, essentially, with lower lip serving as vibrating surface across which the breath and vocal cords do their jimjams. V was well suited to the motor age, notably in its well known "vroom-vroom" application. It is a thoroughly modern letter somehow. A real V8. It had to be V for Vietnam. One nice thing about these lesser-used letters is the way little complexities can rush in to fill the gaps of a paucity of use. In online chat, lowercase, V has a busy life as "very," where it is prone to the inflationary impulse that follows such compression. I think four now are as many as I've seen in standardized use in front of an N (for "nice"): vvvvn. That's very, very, very, very sincere, ty. At that point the meaning begins to drain away from V, like the meaning from a word that you repeat too many times to yourself. You start to see the resemblance that it has to a checkmark, or mountain peaks side by side. You realize it can equally validly be expressed as a precise angle, say 35 degrees. It is, after all, also the mathematical greater-than and less-than symbols swung to balance impossibly on its tip. That's V all over for you—balancing impossibly on its tip. In the hard sciences, V really has a presence, almost celebrity status, with volumes, velocity, vectors, and such. In Roman numeral cloud cuckoo land, V is the number 5. With its connection to things visual, V is important in today's entertainment industry, as in TV, DVD, VHS, VCR, etc. As we noticed before with M and N, V and W are two letters sitting next to one another in the alphabet with a resemblance, as if they were put together that way purposefully. For that matter, U, which immediately precedes V, also has something of a family resemblance. However, V is the only one balancing impossibly on its tip (singular). If I ever see you online, you will have to admit that's a vvvvg trick.

Caetano Veloso, *A Foreign Sound* (2004)
It occurred to me for the first time recently, going back to this terrific cover songs album by Caetano Veloso, the great Brazilian singer and songwriter, that the title was plucked out of the compelling word salad of one of the bravest and most audacious covers here (of many), Bob Dylan's "It's Alright, Ma (I'm Only Bleeding)": "So don't fear if you hear / A foreign sound to your ear / It's alright, Ma," etc. At 22 tracks, this album is packed full, arms wide open, Walt Whitman style, *I-am-large—I-contain-multitudes*, with room for Fred Astaire, Cole Porter, Irving Berlin, Kurt Cobain, and Morris Alpert, which is the track order for the first five songs alone, so you know how fast it switches and which caps it reaches for: "The Carioca," "So in Love," "Always," "Come as You Are," and "Feelings." For every standard such as "Summertime" there's at least one mostly unexpected pick with an interesting history or twist: "Cry Me a River," which may or may not be associated with Barbra Streisand now but

Julie London owned it first, "Nature Boy," a Nat King Cole song later covered by Big Star, "(Nothing But) Flowers," late Talking Heads. So it goes. In many ways it's a perfect freak show of references. But Veloso proves over and over what an insinuating performer he can be. As suggested by the songs mentioned, there's extravagance in the choices, but after that it's strictly professional, with a variety of outfits assembled for the purposes of each song, some of which are just Veloso singing and playing guitar and others with big orchestras. At the same time, from all these disparate sessions, it feels like an organic whole, more than it perhaps has any right to. The bob and weave of the songs can be hypnotic, and there is much to be taken from close listening, and shuffle helps too—the best touches are also the finest, sneaking up on you, found in Veloso's phrasings and scans. (2013)

Velvet Underground, "I'm Waiting for the Man" (1967)
It was already the early '80s when I finally brought home a copy of this from the record store. One of those necessity purchases I had procrastinated, I guess—and I wish I had all those years back now so I could hear it that many more times. After the low-key and utterly pleasant overture of "Sunday Morning," this comes along to set the basic terms: a monotony of driving rhythm with pounding instruments stacked on top, packaged with a patented Story of Gritty Urban Reality (in this case scoring heroin out of Harlem). It's full of small wisdoms ("First thing you learn is that you always gotta wait") and sly humor ("Oh pardon me sir, it's furthest from my mind"), and it affords itself a good deal of untoward glee as it wallows in the indignities and ultimate highs of the adventure it describes. (2011)

Velvet Underground, "Sweet Jane" (1970)
It's practically impossible by definition to pick a favorite Velvet Underground album, but if forced I'm going with *Loaded*. There's a generous adolescence to it, looking forward to Mott-style glam, that

I love. It's an odd affect, particularly coming at the tail end of their ride. It doesn't hurt that it piles on upfront with one of the great rock anthems in "Sweet Jane," an allusive tale, supported by a nearly perfect array of acoustic guitar chords, about kids moving to the city and living their lives. In the right moment it is the thrill of a lifetime. I've talked before about how a person may aspire to master the phrasing of certain signature songs, enabling a kind of process of transubstantiation in order to actually become those beloved singers and songwriters (specifically, Everything But the Girl, Buddy Holly, and Prince), at least for the duration of the songs and one's ability to sing with them perfectly. I have long held strong suspicions that the same holds for Lou Reed and this one, but I have never managed (yet) to entirely duplicate the various asides and chortles and feints and dodges of his deceptive singing in the verses, not for lack of trying. It's a pleasure every time to hear, particularly when it gets down to the nitty-gritty, folksinger Lou Reed style. As loud as you can now: "And there's even some evil mothers / Well, they're gonna tell you that everything is just dirt / Y'know, that women never really faint / And that villains always blink their eyes / And that, y'know, children are the only ones who blush / And that life is just to die." P.S. Never mind the later metal versions of this, as on *Rock n Roll Animal*. I insist it's the *Loaded* version you want. (2012)

Velvet Underground, *Velvet Underground Live* **(1969)**
Every time the Velvet Underground released an album they seemed to reinvent themselves and present an entirely new face. Some of this was surely due to personnel changes, but I don't think it was particularly evidence of an identity crisis. They stayed busy reinvigorating the music to its roots. They wrote the songs. They looked into various abysses. They played it arty, loud, and soft. They played it with the movies playing on them. With this, they removed any doubt about their legacy as a live act (only reinforced decades later with the release of the Quine tapes). This was not the Monkees or the Archies. This was a *band*: 2 guitars bass drums. And they rocked fine. (2007)

Verve, "The Drugs Don't Work" (1997)

Another drug song obviously, but one I find tender and beautiful. I always took it to be about someone whose antidepressant regime has begun to fail, whether it was the singer or his significant other was never entirely clear, but maybe that was always too trendy or easy. Look into it a bit and you learn that singer/songwriter Richard Ashcroft had drug problems of his own when he wrote it; also a dying father on drugs with side effects. "The Drugs Don't Work" comes from the album *Urban Hymns* and was a #1 hit in the UK. Stateside, only "Bitter Sweet Symphony" cracked the top 40, along the way earning a frivolous lawsuit from the Rolling Stones, which the Stones won (and you still wonder about the crossroads). I like the Verve album pretty well even though it tends to clot a bit, the sawing sadness of it only clarifying less or more on various songs but never changing much across its length. "Bitter Sweet" works it pretty well, so does "Sonnet," but it comes into sharpest focus for me here. (2011)

Videodrome **(David Cronenberg, 1983)**

I've seen *Videodrome* in the theater, but the first time I saw it and the greatest impressions it has made on me have tended to come from semi-degraded VHS tape versions. Back in the day, one friend always seemed to know how to put his hands on them early—bootlegs in the first place, of course. Seeing a DVD version now, you quickly note how the look and feel is slanted in exactly that direction. For much of the movie, in fact, we are either watching "television," or we are watching people watching televisions. One thing it gets surprisingly right still is the sense of intimate connection that develops between people and televisions—or monitors, perhaps I should say, or screens.

In many ways indeed *Videodrome* appears prescient now, certainly in terms of today's Internet culture, which is at least as bewitching and entrancing as anything on the TV in *Videodrome*. It also correctly imagined the casual acceptance of pornography we see nowadays. "Got any porno?" says Nicki Brand (Deborah Harry), picking through the videotapes of Max Renn (James Woods), back at his place at the end of their first date. No embarrassment, no self-consciousness. But *Videodrome* is way more than a science fiction film that happened to get a few guesses right about the future—and quite a bit more ambitious than that too.

Videodrome wants to get right down into the muck of identity, fracturing it every which way and reassembling again in the context of media saturation. In our hero Max Renn, a principal at the wonderfully named Civic TV, a sleazy fringe cable-TV channel in Toronto in near-future 1983, we see identity literally mediated, refracted into a hundred shards and fragments, before it is fused again and then exploded to smithereens. *Videodrome* is the exploding head of *Scanners* done at the psychological level.

The basic science fiction conceit is that an electronic signal can be carried on video transmissions that induces brain tumors in viewers. The signal is most effective with brain states caused by passive viewing of violence. Once the tumor has grown it causes hallucinations, which make its victims easy prey of others. All this is set in motion when Renn's able assistant Harlan (Peter Dvorsky)—a sign on the door of Harlan's office reads "Home of the buccaneers, pirates of the high frequencies"—shows Renn fragments of mysterious "Videodrome" broadcasts he has downloaded and unscrambled from satellite feeds. They are simple scenes ("incredibly realistic," Renn says of them) showing torture, beatings, and humiliations of victims in a room with stone walls.

Never mind that *Videodrome* devolves in the end to a right-wing plot to purge society of immoralists. That's part of the comedy, a rich vein of which that runs along all through. When Max Renn first shows a tape of the Videodrome show to Nicki, for example, she says, "I wonder how you get to be a contestant on this show." "I don't know," Max replies. "Nobody ever seems to come back next week." Renn's introduction by Nicki Brand to sadomasochism is equally rich with comic possibilities. There's a cigarette burn scene here I recall the movie being notorious for that puts me in mind now of the ear scene in *Reservoir Dogs*, or indeed the head in *Scanners*—a bit too far on those, perhaps.

The sharpest point of *Videodrome* to me is how it's so carefully predicated on the brain state caused by passively watching violence. Renn is fascinated by the Videodrome show. He can't take his eyes off it, and we're not necessarily looking away either. It is an insidious element that churns away inside. Cronenberg is ingenious about the way he sets up and stages and shoots scenes of the Videodrome show, which we see only for the briefest moments at a time, before Cronenberg cuts away again, or the show is otherwise cut off. It's just long enough to make it seem alluring and compelling, not long enough to entirely horrify and alienate. Thus we are comically enlisted in the depravity unfolding in front of us. If the premise of this movie were true, everyone watching it would have a brain tumor. Speaking for myself, I would have six.

In many ways *Videodrome* operates much in the standard low-budget B-movie style, using character actors for texture and highlighting. Professor Brian O'Blivion (Jack Creley), the leader of a cult who appears only as a talking head on television sets, is a bald homunculus with a pencil mustache. "The television screen has become the retina of the mind's eye," he says in sonorous tones. Masha (Lynne Gorman) is a hard-bitten television producer and industry insider, a lusty old chickenhawk with a Russian accent. Barry Convex, the mastermind who uses an eyeglass manufacturing corporation as a front, is like nothing so much as the life insurance salesman who stayed too late.

Most of the budget evidently went to the special effects, which are always pretty good, and keep up even as the story begins to take on operatic excess ("I am the video word made flesh," etc.). What better excuse, after all, than hallucinations caused by a brain tumor caused by the mindset of passively watching violence on TV? Even as it looks forward to the virtual reality helmet of the '90s (prescient again) *Videodrome* goes back even further, to iconographies suggested by our old friend Dr. Sigmund Freud, for much of its most compelling imagery, such as the peculiar new orifice that may or may not appear in Max's abdomen, and the things people may or may not put into it.

Videodrome is harrowing, riveting, and droll, in no particular order, continually overtopping itself in a calibrated series of events that compromise anyone who watches simply by watching. I don't know how you can ask for any more than that in a movie. (2013)

**Heinrich von Kleist, *The Marquise of O—and Other Stories*
(1806-1811)**
Heinrich von Kleist was a somewhat morbid German writer who did most of his work during the period of the Napoleonic wars, before committing suicide (with his girlfriend) in his mid-30s in 1811. He is one of those writers of the relatively distant past, two centuries now in this case, who somehow seem strikingly modern—"cinematic" is a term I have seen applied to von Kleist more than once. Interestingly, the movie treatment of *The Marquise of O—* (which I have not seen) was directed by Eric Rohmer, a filmmaker regarded with suspicion in some quarters as being overly literary. The Penguin collection of von Kleist stories, translated by David Luke and Nigel Reeves in the '70s—I have it on good authority that a Martin Greenberg translation is to be preferred, but couldn't find it—is indeed some kind of revelation. Modern, cinematic, yes, all true enough. But even more than that, von Kleist is a stone master of intricate plotting. The complications are legion in *The Marquis of O—*, a mixed-up story of sexual intrigue, honor, and class, and yet presented so lucidly that one races to finish. There are few cheats, and the tales remain sturdy and symmetrical

as clockwork. On the surface these stories would appear to be anything but, with long convoluted sentences and paragraphs that may sprawl for pages, confronting one with virtual walls of type. But never mind that. Just start reading. You won't stop. *The Marquise of O*— vies with another novella, *Michael Kohlhaas,* as von Kleist's most famous. They are both fine. In *Michael Kohlhaas* an honorable horse-trader seeks justice in a relatively minor civil matter, only to see it explode into international catastrophe. This one is truly cinematic, playing much like a Sergio Leone picture. Contrast these novellas with "The Beggarwoman of Lacorno," a short short ghost story of merely three pages, brilliantly done: scary, uncanny, and with its pieces moved expertly even in the tight confines of the space. None of the rest of the stories in this collection were up to those three for me—"The Earthquake in Chile" came closest—but once started with this guy you don't tend to want to stop anyway. He's that good. (2013)

Kurt Vonnegut, *Slaughterhouse-Five* (1969)
I read this book back in the day, though I'm pretty sure only the once, when I was so entirely in thrall to Vonnegut, toward the end of high school. I don't think I appreciated the enormity at the center of it, the February 1945 fire-bombing of Dresden, the way he intended. By the numbers (135,000 dead and the images he gives us of the destruction, comparing the Dresden landscape to the moon), it was worse than the March 1945 fire-bombing of Tokyo (81,000 dead), which was worse than August 1945 Hiroshima A-bomb attack (71,000 dead). Dresden was very bad, and 25 years after the fact Vonnegut is still gnawing away at it here, even as it gnaws at him. He is still shattered by it. This is reflected in part by the strange way that his short novel proceeds, with its Tralfamadorian aliens that kidnap the protagonist, its use of "so it goes" to punctuate every death (including any mention of the thousands in Dresden as well as various life-forms), and the mystifying use of time travel, the coming "unstuck" in time that our hero Billy Pilgrim experiences.

It's something more than intense memory, but not by much. Then there is the calculated and self-conscious way that Vonnegut injects himself. It's a novel, but there's Vonnegut using Chapter One the way others might use a preface or foreword, where he talks about how he begins the novel, which then actually starts with Chapter Two. Just weird, but also somehow sign of a soul in extremity. It was easier this time to set aside Vonnegut's various tricks and focus on what he tells us about Dresden and to imagine what it must have been like to experience it and understand the horror. It's no wonder he spent the rest of his life opposed to war. It also raises questions about our conduct in and prosecution of the "good war." Both Dresden and Tokyo (and of course Nagasaki, and there's a case for Hiroshima too) appear to stand as acts of a kind of state-sponsored rage, a real type of terrorism, justified or not, nevertheless coming from impulses that sensible people have always known must be set aside for the sake of civilization and humanity and other quaint ideas. It's cause for despair that these atrocities have mostly been covered up by history—which, I know, the victors get to write, and all that. But that's the despair that haunts this strange little novel. (2011)

W

S ome things you should know about W: Every other letter in the English alphabet is satisfied with a single syllable as its name—sometimes a single mouth noise, as with E. That is only in the spirit after all of what a letter is. What does W do? Helps itself to not one but *two* extra syllables. How does it accomplish this? By looking at the letter U (of all things), puffing up its widdle chest, and saying, "I'm twice that." W is embroiled in practically every scandal of the alphabet there is. For subtlety, it participates in an odd round robin of oppositional pairings: L and R, left and right, R and W, right and wrong, W and L, wins and losses. Too subtle for you? All right. Why don't we saw away awhile on the silent letter. There it is, where it belongs, as the first letter in the word "wrong." Talk about meta. Wikipedia says words such as "wreak, wrap, wreck, and wrench" originally had the W pronounced by sly dog Angle-Saxons. It still is apparently in some Scottish dialects, woe to we all. I don't see a word in Wikipedia, by the way, about W as consonant and "sometimes" vowel. But I recall hearing that my younger siblings were taught W that way. In the wilds of the Internet I found a paragraph at dictionary.com concerning the issue. A couple of archaic Welsh words—"cwm," "crwth"—would indeed appear to be using the W exactly as a vowel, but who uses those words? By the time the short article was on "low" and "bow" it was clear someone somewhere at some point wanted to make a distinction about the direction in which the lips are traveling as they glide in and out of pursed position for W. Coming in, it appears, somehow makes it a vowel. The dictionary. com article concludes that L, M, N, and R may also be considered "sometimes" vowels in this regard, offering as examples "bottle," "bottom," "button," and "butter." So there you have it: A, E, I, O, U, and sometimes L, M, N, R, W, and Y. What a world, what a world. But then I remembered the knowing way someone actually inserted W into the word "vowel" itself, and I was all right again. It's all wrong, but that's the way we do things around here. As for its utility, well, W is ranked #15 for frequency of use, just behind M, just ahead of F (a motherfucker). I'd like to propose changing the pronunciation of W to "I'm twice that," which you'll note is also three syllables, preserving its dignity. Well, it may scan a little differently, for you poets and singers, and might take some work in places. But some applications already work quite well: George I'm-twice-that Bush, for example. Walla Walla!

Was (Not Was), *What Up, Dog?* **(1988)**
I have a soft spot for the Was brothers and am fond of their admittedly spotty releases. I think of them as the Steely Dan of another era, all studio sheen and deceptively laidback, perfectly professional funk shtick. Maybe it's the oddly mimicked "real" name of Don Fagenson. But what I like best are the choice pop gems and the way they could turn them out over and over. They surprise me a lot. This album produced their biggest hits in "Walk the Dinosaur" and "Spy in the House of Love" but I don't think they're the best things here by a ways. I count at least four winners way in front of them, suffused by a wonderfully wistful light-in-the-midnight-window sadness: "Somewhere in America There's a Street Named After My Dad," "Love Can Be Bad Luck" (co-written with Marshall Crenshaw), "Anything Can Happen," and "Anytime Lisa." "Dad I'm in Jail" is for the laughs, but it hurts too. I also love the way "Out Come the Freaks" makes a cameo on most of their albums. (2007)

Weakerthans, "One Great City!" (2003)

Just because I made a big deal out of the song "Nightime" by Big Star, and just because I'm about to do something like that for this great song by the Weakerthans (from Winnipeg, Manitoba, Canada), that doesn't automatically mean I love songs just because they use the word "hate" with such conviction. But it doesn't hurt. And it doesn't hurt that I think I know something of where chief songwriter, singer, and guitarist John K. Samson might be coming from. For at least the three minutes this lasts the focus of his loathing, and a very pure version of it too, is the city of Winnipeg. Some places are cold—they're cold even when they are warm for others, and some places feel like they are always cold. Samson runs down some good details in the verses—mostly he puts the sentiment in the mouths of others, a clerk at a Dollar Store counting loonies, a commuter stuck in traffic. But in the end it seems to be coming more or less from Samson: "... our Golden Business Boy will watch the North End die, and sing 'I love this town,' then let his arcing wrecking ball proclaim, 'I hate Winnipeg'"—taking dead aim at a Manitoban symbol with scorn and derision. On the other hand, it's 10 years later and Samson is still living in Winnipeg and by all indications reasonably happy—married, solo career, etc. So we all grow up, I guess that's another lesson here, and a good thing. But we pass through times, through moods, through sour days or hours, when we feel like this song too. It's almost exhilarating to hear it expressed so purely. (2013)

Tony Joe White, "Polk Salad Annie" (July 26, 1969, #8)

Practically a novelty in the summer of '69, with a dirty Elvis aura all its own, this song resonates with me in a number of different ways. First—what a great song, snaky and muscular, with horns, electric guitar, blues licks, a wah-wah break at the end, distinctive singing, and trashy narrative ("Mama workin' on the chain gang" ... "Her daddy claimed he had a bad back"). Fun to sing with once you get it down: "*Polk*-uh [beat] [beat] [beat] salad" Or: "The gator's got your granny. Chomp. Chomp chomp." Or: "Sock a little polk salad to me, know I need a mean messa." This was Tony Joe White's big moment and his only chart hit, along with "Rainy Night in Georgia," the Brook Benton hit which he wrote. I don't know of any album of White's that has even drawn comment, and he now seems long gone. Still, if all he will ever take to his grave is this and "Rainy Night," he chipped in his share, and there's no denying it. It may not budge him from his obscurity, though remember, "Polk Salad Annie," now a novelty more than ever, and Benton's gorgeous "Rainy Night" still hold down well-deserved corners of oldies station playlists. (2003)

The White Ribbon (Michael Haneke, 2009)

It's not so surprising that veteran director and writer Michael Haneke has erected a scene and setting for *The White Ribbon* that is rich with allusion and evocative suggestion. That's pretty much business as usual for him, hefting oversize significance out of the everyday with a deceptive lack of effort, as seen in such earlier pictures as the original *Funny Games*, *The Piano Teacher*, or especially *Cache*. What's surprising here is where he appears inclined to take it, spinning a story that is equal parts *Village of the Damned* and the whole of Ingmar Bergman's catalog, a stark, spooky, demon-seed tale, never settling into anything certain, forcing us instead to take the pieces and attempt to put them together ourselves.

In a small farming village in Germany shortly before World War I, something is terribly wrong. The doctor suffers an accident when the horse he is riding takes a fall as the result of tripping on a wire strung between two posts of a gate. A worker's wife dies in accident; her death leads to her family's ruin. The baron's son is kidnapped and brutally caned and left hanging upside down with his pants at his ankles. A barn burns to the ground. These events are oppressively sinister, individually and taken together. They seem slightly more than accidents, but no one has any idea who to blame. The fragile emotional ecosystem of the village, with its various classes and inter-relations, begins to rot under suspicion.

Much has been made by others of the fact that a group of adolescent children, with their haunted and distinct faces, are most naturally suspected for the crimes and are also of an age to make them the eventual political base for the German Nazi movement in some 15 or 20 years' time. These critics have read into this film some kind of treatment of the German version (or inversion) of America's "Greatest Generation," somehow uniquely given to the characteristics that would serve the Nazis so well. I don't see it that way, not inclined myself to the belief that whole generations tilt uniquely in specific moral directions.

The near-maddening vagueness of much of the picture leaves it open to an array of readings even as Haneke, for his part, remains resolutely agnostic about explanations. From its ambiguous beginning to its ambiguous ending, the sequence of events is mostly witnessed and all related from the point of view of the young village schoolteacher (played by Christian Friedel, with Ernst Jacobi supplying the voiceover narration), remembering the incidents in old age—his courtship with the young nanny (Leonie Benesch) is one of the few bright moments here. Perhaps it's just speculations of an old man. Yet we become acquainted intimately with the many small ways the villagers mistreat one another. Even as events proceed and become more gruesome it becomes more and more difficult to find anyone who is truly innocent. Some scenes, even so, such as those between the normally rigid and controlling pastor and his youngest son when they discuss caring for birds (the pastor's is named Peepsie), are at pains to show that no one is entirely guilty either.

Society is self-consciously represented in miniature, as in an allegory. The wealthy baron stands in for a feudalism very much still alive here. The doctor is the rational man of science, although also unfortunately despicable. The pastor, for the church, rules his flock and especially his family with the old-school iron hand, authoritarian to his core yet capable of love. The numerous and anonymous laborers, mired in their lives, try continually to make the best of their lot. The haunted children are innocents but they are doomed. I think Haneke does tip his hand in the direction of the gaunt gang of adolescents as responsible for the transgressions. But it doesn't actually clarify much. The next question, obviously, would be, "Why?" (other than nascent fascism). Adolescent hijinks? There Haneke is even more confounding. As usual, he poses questions with no answers. Even a casual viewing uncovers any number of glaring plot holes, but I suspect they are exactly as he intends.

The result is a splendid, unnerving mess of natural filmmaking. Shot in color and later transformed into black and white, there is an unsettling muddiness to it that only makes it denser in impact. Long sections tell the story by the simple expedient of visuals, with events unfolding in front of us that are perfectly plain but stubborn about explaining anything. And still the narrative momentum is unceasing, like the current felt swimming in a river. There's very little music (what there is is mostly homely in-scene Germanic classical and/or church fare), which only adds to the severe air.

Haneke's explorations of the inexplicable cruelties and psychological tensions between people in uncomfortable union with one another—let's call it "society" for the sake of argument—have never been more sharply focused, I think. It is almost as if he enjoys playing with us the way a cruel child (one of these cruel children, perhaps) will play with a helpless animal—abstracted and rarefied, to be sure, with distance and disconnection built into the mix, but finding ways to return to images and ideas intended not so much to jolt as to nick, rendering one unsure and tentative about assumptions and realities.

In the end, almost against my better judgment, I see in *The White Ribbon* something like an old-fashioned allegory for the 20th century. There's little chance it's a coincidence that the events here occur in the 12 to 18 months leading up to and shortly after the beginning of World War I—in fact, the assassination of Archduke Ferdinand in Sarajevo is noted in passing by the upper-class characters as a news event of some worrying moment. Haneke focuses on the rich emotional tapestry of a small and inconsequential village, populating it with a startlingly broad world of motivations and behavior, shocking as he feels the impulse, until finally what we're left looking at is something we already know all too well, the various unexplained features and weirdnesses of 20th-century life—paranoia, totalitarianism, brutal random violence, class conflict, and all-out war. (2012)

Who, *Tommy* (1969)
Probably the first album I lusted after and eventually acquired on the basis of reading a rock critic, the beginning of a lifelong habit for better or worse—in this case it was Nik Cohn and *Rock from the Beginning*. I admit at first I found the vaunted "rock opera" a bit disappointing—when hasn't *that* happened as a result of reading of a rock critic? But over the years *Tommy* has held up surprisingly well for me. Often under the charge of furiously strummed acoustic guitar and sweet harmonies, with Keith Moon's spastic and majestic drumming submerged in the mix, it's not nearly the noisy proto-metal head-banger you might expect from the hoopla, endless live versions, and abominable Ken Russell treatment. Poised just before the band raised the curtain on recorded versions of exactly that, with the vastly more assaultive *Live at Leeds*, this sounds like a folk exercise in this day and age, and it is their transition point from the goofy Kinks wannabe pop fare of *Sell Out* and the like. And its moment is a lovely one. Calling it an "opera" in any kind of way at all is a basic misnomer, of course, in spite of its "Overture" (5:21) and "Underture" (10:09). But so what? And if I rarely take a

listen to it any longer, doing without for years and even decades at a stretch, that only underlines the surprise and pleasure over how good it still sounds when I do. (2010)

Who the #$&% Is Jackson Pollock? (**Harry Moses, 2006**)

More mysteries of abstract expressionism (see also *My Kid Could Paint That*). This mystery starts one day in the 1990s, in southern California east of Los Angeles, when Teri Horton, an Ozarks native who escaped to the Golden Land and a life of long haul trucking, decides to buy a gift for a friend in need of cheering up. An inveterate prowler of the goods to be found in rummage sales (and even dumpsters behind upscale malls), Horton finds a giant canvas in a thrift store covered with paint. The price is $8. Horton talks it down to $5. "It was ugly," she says in this documentary. "If you wanna call it artwork." It wasn't exactly what her friend needed either, so Horton attempted to unload it at her next yard sale, where she was approached by a local high school teacher who told her it might be a Jackson Pollock. At which point the action in this documentary, such as it is—starting with the title—gets underway in earnest. When Horton finds out that Pollock's paintings command prices starting at $50 million, she sets about authenticating her canvas, and the door is opened, for her and for us in this wonderful little picture, into the strange world of art connoisseurs, with its frauds, deceits, and pretensions.

Very quickly the film establishes that the canvas probably is authentic by examining the work of a forensic scientist, brought in by Horton, who finds a fingerprint on it that matches a fingerprint found in Pollock's studio, as well as on two other Pollocks that have impeccable provenance (we also find out more than we might have ever expected to know about such concepts as "provenance"). Consistencies among unique trace elements of the paint are also discovered. Comically and exasperatingly, this means very little to the connoisseurs, who as a class may be represented best here by a fatuous clown named Thomas Hoving, who died in 2009 and here proclaims that he is, ipso facto, expert on everything he sees because he has lived and worked most of his life in New York art circles. (This movie is incidentally very good at explicating the elements of simmering long-term resentments held against elitists on the coasts.)

From there it's on to the slimy inner workings of that New York art world when Horton hires a man previously imprisoned for fraud to represent her interests; he subsequently attempts to sideline her. There's also a detour involving John Myatt, previously convicted for art forgery, who says that he would never even try to forge a Pollock, because, counterintuitively, it would be too difficult. As terrific as this story is it's marred some by how unlikable Horton can be. You want to be on her side, if anyone's, but she's as infected by greed as anyone here. During the course of the filming she was offered $2 million for the painting, "no questions asked," and during post-production, by another party, $9 million. Either one would be a nice profit on a $5 investment, of course, but she turned down both offers. Latest word I can find is that she has had it for sale in a Toronto art gallery since 2008, with an asking price of $50 million, but it hasn't moved. Still, I defy anyone to see this and not find themselves at least temporarily obsessed with the various shades of truth of everything it looks at—the problems of authentication, the intrinsic values of abstract expressionism, the greed and pretentiousness of the art industry, and the deep fractures of class divisions. (2010)

Carl Wilson, *Celine Dion's Let's Talk About Love* **(2007)**
I like the original subtitle for Carl Wilson's book about Celine Dion and Wilson's revulsion for her: "A Journey to the End of Taste," because in many ways that's how I felt reading it. The fact that the book started life as an entry in the 33 series of monographs on individual albums (in this case, ostensibly, Dion's *Let's Talk About*

Love, from 1997) only makes a weird and wonderful book even weirder. He dislikes Celine Dion at least as much as I do and most of the people I discuss issues of taste with too. That I now feel warmly toward her as a person after reading Wilson's book is further weirdness. Wilson finds a dozen ways to shame himself and the rest of us for our loathing: the unaffected sincerity of Dion's fans ... her own humble origins ... the sources of immigrant culture, pride, and adaptation lurking in music otherwise casually dismissed as "schmaltz" (including a nicely researched capsule of its long tangled history in North American music) ... and an affecting anecdote about Elliott Smith's encounter with her at the Oscars ceremony in 1998 and Smith's subsequent lifelong defense of Dion as a person. I even found a way in to appreciating Dion more on a personal level, reading Wilson's account of her origins in rural Quebec from a family of 14 children, recalling my North Dakota extended family (with a grand total of 16 siblings in my mother's family, 11 of whom made it to adulthood) and their affection (which I have inherited to some degree) for Lawrence Welk and the Lennon Sisters. Yet nothing makes a dent in the abhorrence for Celine Dion's music, for me or for Wilson either. Wilson's formal position of directly addressing this hatred as a matter of taste is absurd on one level; he knows it and he knows we have to know it too. But as he pushes on with the thought experiment he uncovers a new way of looking at the issue, new to me anyway, when he gets into sociological studies demonstrating that taste is likely in large part a social construction, a subconscious choice about material satisfaction and perceived gain. A ringing explication of what until now I have only muttered to myself and others incoherently about as "junior high bullshit"—which it seems more obvious than ever to me now is exactly what most matters of taste turn on. Wilson even gets into it explicitly by brand name: "cool." Wilson's book (and its original subtitle), along with Daniel Levitin's look at the neuroscience of music, *This Is Your Brain on Music,* are leading me to view the good old question, "What have you been listening to lately?" in what feels like all new ways. In a world where all taste is equal, there may be no taste at all, replaced only by interpersonal connection and alliances, which are affirmed by the music (and other connecting points) in a feedback loop, or "virtuous cycle." The more you like your friends the more you like the music you share—and more importantly, the sharing. That's all it is. This is at once terrifying and exhilarating to anyone with a stake in the critical enterprise, which I think is finally the great big kick of Wilson's book. Really, it's one not to be missed. (2015)

Kai Winding, "More" (July 27, 1963, #8)
Just try to forget that you ever decided to look at *Mondo Cane*. But you can't. You never will. (2010)

The Wizard of Oz **(Victor Fleming / George Cukor /**
Mervyn LeRoy / King Vidor, 1939)
There are things I trace back directly to my early exposure to those annual television airings of *The Wizard of Oz* hosted by Danny Kaye, which usually occurred around Easter time, if I recall correctly. A fascination with tornado footage (better than ever nowadays via the storm-chaser shows). An appreciation for long roads that stretch to the horizon—my idle meeting-time doodles are full of them. How many shots of long roads and horizons, only partially blocked by the backs of our heroes, are in this? You'd be surprised.

More than anything, I think this is one place where my taste for horror movies started, because that's what basically happens here. It's a bit like that joke about going to the fights and a hockey game breaks out. Right in the middle of a colorful, goofy MGM musical, there's a witch who scares the hell out of any sensible 9-year-old expecting carefree, happy-go-lucky, parent-approved saccharine. Or anyway that's the way it happened to me. *Mary Poppins* this is not. Getting through it was a rite of endurance for a lot of years, a battle with my own adrenaline, and I didn't always win. But I survived, and that's the paradoxical pleasure of horror reduced to its fine point.

I know I am a wimp nonpareil on these matters, but I'm not the only one who started to feel queasy at the first sign of those grumpy talking apple trees throwing fruit. The full might and malevolence of the green-toned witch is on display at one point, with hordes of flying monkeys that darken the skies. The woods are terrifying. Dorothy is chased to ground and unceremoniously hauled away, and her dog too. One of the characters is literally torn limb from limb. "That's you all over," says another, gathering up the pieces. But the comic relief didn't help when I was a kid.

As with *It's a Wonderful Life* and *Blue Velvet* I keep coming back to this for the dynamics, the tensions that threaten to tear it apart, and the ability it has to hold itself together and remain entertaining every step of the yellow brick way. It's one of the best and most original dream movies, not least for its famous switch from the sepia tones of Kansas to the blazing technicolor of Oz and back, but also for the way it incorporates all its characters into both of its halves, with that kind of insane dream logic not often done well. And, yes, I do go for the cheese whole. Judy Garland: "If I ever go looking for my heart's desire again, I won't look any further than my own backyard. Because if it isn't there, I never really lost it to begin with." Somebody get me a hanky. (2011)

X

X marks the spot. Or should that be "Marx"? The first thing to understand about X, more or less, is that it's just a decoration, most of its letter functions handled quite nicely by K and S together. Or Z, in the case of Xavier who is taking xylophone lessons. But what a decoration, two bold slashes defining at their intersection the infinity of a single point. X is not often used in words, outranking only Q and Z for frequency, but what are words when the very shape of X makes it almost notorious? It is how illiterates sign their names when witnesses are available (literate themselves, one hopes, else the last will and testament begin to resemble the diagram of a football play). It's where the loot is buried on treasure maps. Triple it up and it's the hottest sex you never had. In cartoons it appears as eyeballs to indicate drunkenness or general confusion. Christians were all over the X back in their underground days, seeing it as a symbol of the cross, with "Xmas" a term of respect and convenience, and not Exhibit 999 in Fox News tales of War on Christmas. The red circle and slash has become more the marker of "get the fuck away from this," but X can work in a pinch. In late night infomercials, for example, scenes of muss and fuss are often demolished by a flashing X. It's utilitarian as hell, but speaking of hell, there's also some aura of the forbidden, even evil, about X. Yes, the porn associations, but they came later.

I suspect it's what's behind all the objections to "Xmas"—the re-
duction of our lord and savior to the eyeballs of a drunken repro-
bate, the representation of an infinite singularity of nothingness.
If ABC is all that is good and holy and respectable, XYZ is NOT.
That makes the counterpart of the fine and upstanding letter A,
which is the George Washington of the alphabet, none other than
X, the thief, hiding in the cellar of the alphabet, stealing sounds
that aren't even used that much anyway. It's just hanging around
down there. For what purpose? What does it want? It is terrifying
me. Aiee, I must flee! X somehow induces this panic terror of the
unknown. X is always the mysterious factor. X is what death looks
like, we somehow suspect. So you have to respect that. It chips in to
the negation prefix streams of "un-" and "non-" and "dis-" with one
of the most powerful, in "ex-," which of course also comes with all
its own tender painful connotations. In retrospect, I'm not sure the
rock band X was ever up to the great and terrible burden of the letter, but give them credit for trying. The cover of *Under the Big Black
Sun* has always looked to me like something X itself might have
designed—the letter, I mean, not the band. That's the thing about
X. It's the only letter that actually might be sentient itself. Think
about that the next time you're playing tic-tac-toe.

Y

Y has a lot to yell about, I'd be lying if I told you any different. Yes, it has a personality crisis, but who doesn't? The fact is it's *both* a consonant and a vowel, though who thought this was a good idea is unclear. It is a consonant in words such as "yellow," "yuck," and "yes," where it approximates the J sound but without the tongue involved. Because of its association with yes, perhaps, it's taken as a generally upbeat noise to make, as in "yay," "yahoo," and "yippee." Interestingly, in "yay" (an "informal word"), we happen to see both functions of Y, though it is here more on the order of another blasted silent letter, inflecting the "a" to make it long. A better example is "xylophone," where it represents the long I. We don't know why, but I have to admit "why" is a much better-looking word than "whi" or "whei." Aiyiyi. Even doing this freakish double duty, Y still only manages to make #18 on the ranked list of most frequently used letters, just behind G, just ahead of P. Apparently somebody somewhere calculated it and determined that Y is more often a consonant and only "sometimes" a vowel. Or perhaps that is because its uniqueness is found in its consonant function, whereas the vowel only tends to mimic variations on E, I, and whatever it is doing in words like "joy" and "decoy." Y stands for some of the things we most treasure: yes, youth, and yesterday—even better, make that yesteryear. Also "you"—even though U certainly also has fair claim to the, er, "objectified other." The consonant Y opens naturally into loud vocal eruption from the diaphragm, heading up words such as "yell," "yelp," "yowl," "yodel," and "yargh"—not all sounds of pain, I assure you. Chronic alphabetizers know already that Y is the last sad little bump in the alphabet. Not many things begin with X or Z and Y usually matches or outdoes them in an index. Still, T and W would probably have to be counted as the last alphabetical urban outposts of any size. But Y always stubbornly makes a dent. This reminds me. Have you seen the movie *Yi Yi*? It's really good. The word "yawn" is associated with Y's consonant function. Maybe you're yawning now, because that's how yawns work, the more you see or hear the word (or the yawning itself) the more you want to yawn. Y obviously pairs with N. Do I have to explain that? Y / N (circle one). Y also has a profound relation (marked by decorative crossbars) to yen, the Japanese currency. I'd like to make a joke about Yugoslavia but nothing about Yugoslavia is funny. In German, by the way, J is assigned Y's consonant function, and the mouth noise is again associated with the assenting: yes and ja (or, for you Germans, *yes und ja*). That's Y all over for you! You can't always get what you want. But if you try sometimes, a vowel.

Yi Yi (**Edward Yang, 2000**)
Don't act surprised, but I'm having a hard time translating "yi yi" based on hasty Internet searches. Good old Wikipedia tells me that "yi" means "one" and "yi yi" means "'one one,' in the sense of 'each one,'" whatever that means. It goes on to mention that the Chinese characters for it (一一), when vertically aligned, mean "two" (which at least helps explain the off-point British adaptation of the title, *A One and a Two*). Thus, the best I can make out is that it may be an idiom describing an aspirational level of spiritual integration, a oneness. At least, that happens to be the state that virtually every person occupying this vast picture of small family drama (not to mention you and me) yearns for every minute of their waking lives.

In fact, with these insights, I find it helpful now to remember the old joke about the Buddhist monk placing his order at a hot-dog stand: "Make me one with everything." Set in modern Taipei, Taiwan, a city of some 3 million, it's that profound human yearning as much as anything—I mean for spiritual integration, not hot dogs—that drives the emotional complexity of this deeply meditated story. It's about an extended middle-class family coping with death and life and meaning in a modernized Western society. It's charming, provoking, sad, and lovely by turns, with the deceptively placid feel of a Lifetime movie whenever the music starts to play (I say that as someone who appreciates Lifetime movies, but don't worry, the music doesn't play that often). It's nearly three hours, with a host of complicated characters and interrelations, but it goes fast, as you simply enter into this life, engrossed somehow even when it is so uneventful.

Or, no, that's not right. It's not uneventful. There is plenty going on here—a matriarch on her deathbed, fractured marriages, bruised relationships, lost children of all ages. But it's so good at approximating the flow of everyday life, with climactic events that are rarely grasped fully in their moments, but only later. The lack of such dramatic contrasts is good in terms of the literary realism, the Western style into which *Yi Yi* fits most naturally, with dramatic situations emerging organically. But it can be a little confusing to sort out too.

It is so rich with detail it is like a feast, a smorgasbord. You never have to wait long for the next dish to arrive. Take the character of Yang-Yang (Jonathan Chang), the eight-year-old son who first and most obviously delivers an undeniable cute factor of impressive reach and shelf life. He is adorable, a familiar figure in all the promotional material for the movie. In manner, he plays it something like a pint-size Buster Keaton (taking after his father NJ in that regard, who is played by Nien-Jen Wu, a regular in director Edward Yang's pictures)—stoic and stone-faced, teased to terrific comic effect by the girls in his school. An early scene at a wedding, with Yang-Yang and the girls posing for a photo and the girls secretly teasing him to amuse themselves, is a remarkable set piece.

But Yang-Yang, for all his massive imposition of cute, is also the one to raise the most profound and interesting issues, which somehow manage both to fathom the largest themes of the picture and also to sound like any 8-year-old asking a lot of questions: "Daddy, I can't see what you see and you can't see what I see," he says at one point. "How can I know what you see?" NJ tells him, "That's why we need a camera." And he always has more questions: "Daddy, can we only know half the truth? I can only see what's in front, not what's behind. So I can only know half of the truth, right?"

This observation was still echoing in my head the next time I saw the powerful scene where Yang-Yang's mother Min-Min (Elaine Jin, also a Yang trouper) is speaking to NJ, her husband, about her mother, who lies comatose in the apartment. Min-Min speaks with her back to a mirror, so we see her from the front and back at once—yet even so, one of her profiles is obscured. Thus, in Yang-Yang's formulation, we still can't know the whole truth about Min-Min even as we see her front and back in one of the most nakedly confessional moments in the whole film.

It's an amazing scene, opening up in numerous ways to a variety of bottomless emotional places, and a total marvel of economy, such that after it passes you don't even know exactly what hit you (the picture is packed full of such turns). Min-Min is confronting and trying to understand and accept her mother's imminent death, speaking to NJ in their bedroom, who simply listens in his gentle brooding way. Then the neighbors in the next-door apartment begin to have a loud, vicious fight. NJ closes the shades and turns down the lights. In the darkness from the window we can see the headlights of traffic on a freeway. All at once we can hear the traffic, and Min-Min's wracking weeping, and the couple squabbling and saying horrible things to each other.

As a social realist story, the characters and their stories are pushed well into the foreground, but *Yi Yi* is also beautifully composed. Many scenes are shot a great distance away from the characters, to the point where it's almost hard to pick them out sometimes, even as we distinctly hear them speaking, as if to emphasize how easily these particularities blend into scenes full of other people and life and motion. Another recurring strategy is to shoot through the glare of great slabs of reflecting plate-glass, as in the tall windows of modern office buildings. This also obscures the characters, who become ghostlike even as their dialogue remains sharp and crisp, the frame resolving to shapes and colors flashing against surfaces, reflections of people, traffic, logos, office interiors, abstracted and mushed into a modern miasma. This is done often, but also subtly, not constant but rather continual.

It's a sprawling modern domestic landscape that we experience here, and it feels as if it could as easily be Chicago or Cape Town or Tehran, with an immediacy that gets you the first time, and has even more to tell as repayment for looking again. It's a total keeper. (2012)

Yo La Tengo, *Fakebook* (1990)
Yo La Tengo works an interesting, even bold idea, staking out their roots in an album of 11-5 covers vs. originals, doing so in remarkably straightforward fashion. And relatively early in their career—some five years, but this is the Cal Ripken of indie/alt bands. Guns N' Roses did it basically as their parting shot of an era, and garagey bands such as the Cramps, Chesterfield Kings, and others have done a version of it. But they are different. From beginning to end here, of course, it's name-check, name-check, name-check. What else would you expect? Daniel Johnston, NRBQ, the Flamin' Groovies, the Kinks, Cat Stevens, even The Scene Is Now for crying out loud. The atmosphere is suitably hushed throughout. Melody after melody after melody is achingly beautiful. It's a terrific album. (2007)

Neil Young & Crazy Horse, "Powderfinger" (1979)
Neil Young is obviously some sort of student of American culture, and hailing originally from Canada has always, I suppose, he has been at a good vantage to observe it. But it still amazes me that he can reach so far back into primal American experience and just pull something out like this. It's a Civil War story, away from the fields of battle, about an anonymous young Southern man killed in an ambush. There's not much to it: the attacking boat appears on the river, the kid foolishly tries to defend against it even in the absence of elder male family members. He can't, and he dies. The moment of his death is recorded: "Raised my rifle to my eye / Never stopped to wonder why. / Then I saw black / And my face splashed in the sky." It's a particular moment I have somehow found myself pitching headfirst into, so stark and matter of fact and profoundly universal. It's amazing—the whole thing is. I can't think of many other moments in all of rock that get to such depths with such economy and so little bombast. Some years ago, Phil Dellio compiled an exhaustive list of Neil Young covers, identifying six for this song, by the Beat Farmers, Chris Burroughs, the Cowboy Junkies, Tonia Sellers & Laura Hagen, Uncle Tupelo, and Yung Wu. "Not sure why," he writes, "but this is one case where any voice other than Neil's seems to automatically diminish the song." Young offered an early version of it to Lynyrd Skynyrd in the mid-'70s, perhaps some kind of response in their mutual "Southern man" quasi-contretemps (or whatever it was). I wish we could have heard what they'd done with it, but their faces splashed in the sky first. (2011)

Neil Young, *Trans* (1982)
If it weren't for *Arc* this would probably have to count as the weirdest Neil Young album ever. His first for Geffen, it marks an auspicious kick-start to a relationship that eventually soured to the point where the label filed suit against him, claiming he was willfully creating "unrepresentative Neil Young albums." Interesting theory. Back on Earth, I count this among my favorite Neil Young albums—if not on the short list, certainly in the top 10 of his sizable catalog. He's no

electronics wiz, let alone proto-techno artist in any sense of the term, as has been pointed out ad infinitum elsewhere—even such basics as fancy beats are missing in action here. In fact, I think I hear a drumkit. The exotics of it really boil down to just vocoders and keyboards. And, oh yeah, it's a bunch of Neil Young songs too, which is something, writing songs, that he's always been pretty well known for. Now that we are decades beyond the mentality that overshadowed this at the time ("disco sucks and so does new wave, probably"), much of the daringness of it is lost, as are the various transgressions against Neil Young fan dogma, which I just like to think means we can make the appropriate assessments now. Or try looking at is this way: if you are a Neil Young rockist and dislike the folkie exercises, or vice versa, there's probably no point checking into this one. You probably never have. If, on the other hand, you like *both* the rock stuff and the folkie stuff, then you probably already know this is pretty good. It's also possible that I am insane. (2010)

Neil Young, *Weld* (1991)
Yeah yeah, the tour was basically a reprisal of the Neil Young / Crazy Horse *Rust Never Sleeps* tour, down to the oversized amplifier stage design. Twelve years later is a long time to be doing the same thing, but when you consider the careening of Neil Young's career between, the times at hand in 1990 and 1991 and the war of the moment, and the brilliant addition of a cover of "Blowin' in the Wind" to the repertoire—I mean, it was like they were literally *blowin' in the wind* as they performed the song. Oh, that was giant fans they were using? Anyway, what really works here is the unabashed appreciation for the sonics of rock 'n' roll as it emerges from the crucible. In fact, I think it was because the exuberant, prolonged turns toward feedback of those shows sounded so good that a 35-minute selection of them was compiled for a throwaway disk, called *Arc*, included in original releases of this set. Didn't quite work isolated that way, but somebody's heart was in the right place. (2007)

Z

A nd in the end, the letter Z: last *and* least in the English language. The buzzing business of Z is common in speaking. It represents a unique sound, made more often by S (and occasionally X, as previously discussed), in many pluralizing usages (such as "usages"). Note that Z does get pride of place in the word "pluralize," or actually more like the suffix "-ize," which takes passive nouns and punches you in the face with them: visualize, fossilize, modernize. Heady stuff, Z! Yet there it languishes at the back of all the letters in all ways. In cartoons, it is tripled up (or more) to indicate sleeping, some might say snoring—some might say boredom. In recent times people have begun to talk about needing their Zs, meaning sleep or naps. It's only appropriate, as the last thing. At the end of the day, sleep is what happens. Like most of the lesser-used letters—J, Q, and such—Z has a bit of a forlorn buffoonish aspect. One is tempted to make fun of its mouth noise as something to be classified with whistles, cork-popping, and whoopee cushions. Maybe that's some association with the word "kazoo." But Z also has its cozy, lazy elements—I'm only speaking "zee" truth, as the French say. Speaking of the French, in the UK they call the letter "zed," which sounds more to me like an out-of-town relative in for a surprise visit. It's so wrong I don't even know what to do with it. I'll just leave it at that. Don't forget, in spite of its lastness and leastness, Z is still often found where the action is. Consider zero, which is probably the single most interesting number if we were going to rank them (other than numerically—and no, I'm not going to write about all the numbers, that would take too long). Z stands for zebra, which most children learn early—again, a highly insignificant fact to know at all, let alone introduce into the developing human brain. At some point in recent years Z has come to stand for zombies too, which only makes sense in this crowded and overheating world. Teach that to your children. The letter Z and its insignificance reduce us to questions like, "Hey, did you ever see *Zardoz*?" Yes, I did, and it was about as memorable as the letter Z. Perhaps I'm engaging in blaming the victim. Which raises the question: is Z really a victim, if it is *both* the least used letter*and* the last letter in the alphabet? Isn't it actually more like a case for once in its miserable life that the English alphabet behaves rationally? Kudos, I say. Kudos. Zebras in zoos for the children, zombies in the countryside for the rest of us, the inimitable zero, and what? We know we are reaching the end now because soon all will be zzz. By the way, I still think we should kick Q out of the alphabet. I say again, 25 is a much better number than 26. Good night, everyone.

www.ingramcontent.com/pod-product-compliance
Lightning Source LLC
Chambersburg PA
CBHW072109270326
41931CB00010B/1498

*9 7 8 0 6 9 2 6 2 9 5 8 1 *